CHARLES HAPPELL was

a journalist for twent

politics in the 1980s, he turned to sports writing and moved
overseas, working in London and then for the Reuters news
agency in Milan. He joined *The Age* newspaper in 1993, and
became the Sports Editor in 2002. He lives in Melbourne with
his wife, Paula, and their children, Thomas and Gretel.

THE
BONE MAN
OF KOKODA

*The extraordinary story of Kokichi Nishimura
and the Kokoda Track*

CHARLES HAPPELL

PAN
Pan Macmillan Australia

First published 2008 in Macmillan by Pan Macmillan Australia Pty Limited
The Pan edition published 2009 by Pan Macmillan Australia Pty Limited
1 Market Street, Sydney

National Library of Australia
Cataloguing-in-Publication data:

Happell, Charles.

The bone man of Kokoda : the extraordinary story of
Kokichi Nishimura and the Kokoda Track / Charles Happell.

978 0 330 42484 4 (pbk.)

Nishimura, Kokichi.
Japan. Rikugun. Hohei Rentai, Dai 144.
Soldiers – Japan – Biography.
World War, 1939–1945 – Campaigns – Papua New Guinea.
World War, 1939–1945 – Participation, Japanese.
Kokoda Trail (Papua New Guinea) – History.

940.5426516

Cartographic art by Laurie Whiddon, Map Illustrations
Typeset in 13/15.5 pt Granjon by Midland Typesetters, Australia
Printed in Australia by McPherson's Printing Group

For Paula, with love

Contents

INTRODUCTION

I STUMBLED – ALMOST LITERALLY – on the story of Kokichi Nishimura while walking the Kokoda Track in April 2006. As we passed through the village of Efogi, one of the Papuan porters in our group pointed out a stone monument on the edge of the village, which bore Japanese characters on its headstone. The person who built that, he said, was a former Japanese soldier who came back to New Guinea after the war to look for the remains of his comrades; he had lived in the country for more than twenty years. The story bore further investigation. I made a mental note of the soldier's name and resolved to research him when I returned to Melbourne. And that was the start of a project at times laborious and painstaking, but always fascinating, that almost two years on has culminated in this book.

The research has involved two trips to Tokyo to interview Nishimura, a further flight to Kochi City to attend his regiment's annual reunion, and perhaps fifty telephone interviews with him, his friends and family. The exercise, like an Olympic Games dive featuring backward double-somersault with half-twist, carried a high degree of difficulty. While Nishimura was as alert and lively as any 88-year-old had a right to be, he spoke virtually no English and had no email.

The simple matter of clarifying a point with him meant writing out a question in English, sending it to a translator in Melbourne, then faxing that translation to Nishimura (and hoping he was at home). He would search his records and be ready with an answer when the interpreter called days later. The answer would then be translated into English. The whole process would take a week, or more.

In Nishimura, I met a man deeply scarred by his war experiences. They seemed to consume his every thought. At times he became prickly, especially when it came to discussing his estranged wife and children, but generally he couldn't have been more agreeable. He was only too happy to assist with the book, perhaps seeing it as a fitting way to honour his dead comrades. He was a formidable subject but, in the end, I came to understand and like him. Although he had obvious reasons not to feel any fondness towards his enemy, Nishimura had a strong regard for Australians and especially admired their soldiers' courage in battle.

In piecing together his life story, what has been revealed is an epic tale featuring loyalty, determination and courage on a scale that is difficult to comprehend. And, of course, a sense of duty that knew no bounds.

Charles Happell
Melbourne
December 2007

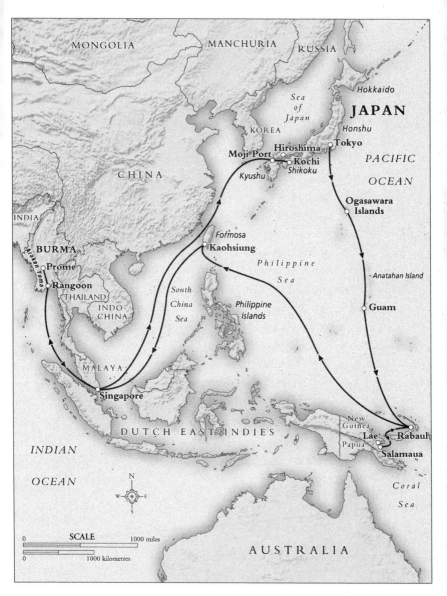

Nishimura and the 144th Infantry Regiment in the Pacific Ocean, 1941–45

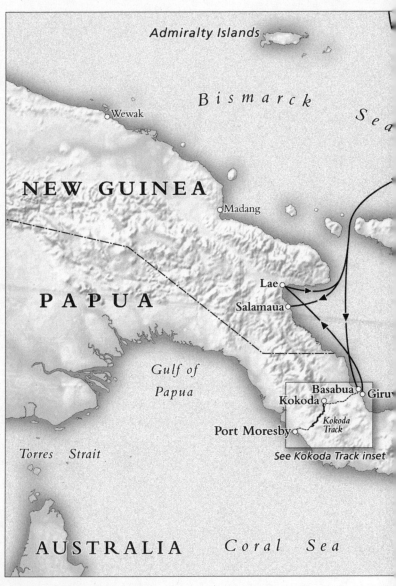

Nishimura in Papua New Guinea and along the Kokoda Track, 1942–43

PACIFIC OCEAN

From Guam

To Kaohsiung

New Ireland

Rabaul

Tol Plantation

New Britain

Bougainville

Solomon Sea

The Kokoda Track

Kumusi

Gona
Basabua
Giruwa
Buna

Mumuni
Popondetta

Kokoda
Oivi
Awala
Deniki
Isurava
Waju (Baribe)
Kaile

Owen Stanley Range

River

Kagi
Myola
Menari
Efogi
Ioribaiwa
Nauro
Ilolo
Owers' Corner

Port Moresby

Kochi Warrior

CHAPTER 1

Skull

THE SKULL SAT IN a box beside him on the passenger seat, its grim, greying visage washed clean by the Solomon Sea and picked bare by the Giruwa sand crabs.

When the shovel had first jarred in his hands, Nishimura thought he'd struck a turtle shell. But then he had got down on his knees and begun to brush away the grit, and the hollow stare and hideous grin were gradually revealed.

What excited Nishimura about his find was not so much the skull itself – heaven knows, he'd dug up enough of them over the past twenty years – but the four gold teeth set in its ivory casing. Bones were one thing to identify, femurs and tibias and clavicles all tended to look much the same after they had been buried fifty years, but a skull with four gold teeth intact? How many 22-year-old soldiers sent to war in the South Seas would have boasted that sort of dentistry?

It was this thought that gave Nishimura hope as he set off from his home in Tokyo's sprawling northern suburbs on the road towards Hiroshima. He had a good feeling about the trip ahead.

It was late 1999, the eleventh year of the Heisei Era. The old soldier wasn't as sprightly as he used to be but, for seventy-nine, he wasn't in bad shape either. His uncommonly prominent cheekbones, combined with the gradual loss of most of his teeth, gave his sunken cheeks an ascetic's look. There was not a gram of fat on his wiry frame, and he tipped the scales at little more than fifty kilograms. He could still vault up his stairs at home, and not so long ago would have done the eleven-hour drive to Hiroshima in one stretch. Now, however, he'd have to break it up with an overnight stop, when he'd pull over and sleep in the back of his Honda Accord station wagon.

Ever since the Pacific war, and the final dreadful weeks of the New Guinea campaign, Nishimura had shied away from extravagance. He felt more comfortable living a spartan life. Why fork out thousands of yen on a fine restaurant when you could boil a handful of rice at home? Why sign a cheque for a tradesman when, with a bit of sweat and improvisation, you could fix the problem yourself? And why spend money to sleep in a *ryokan* or inn when there was a perfectly good space in the back of the car? He didn't like to think of himself as stingy, just a man of simple tastes.

Nishimura sped south-west along the Tomei Expressway towards Nagoya; as he passed through Shizuoka prefecture he could see to his right the snow-capped peak of Mount Fuji standing in vivid relief against a blue sky. As always, the iconic scene got him thinking about his regimental commander, Colonel Masao Kusunose, who, after the war ended, had waited each day at Asakura railway station in Kochi until the last casket carrying remains of his troops arrived back from New Guinea. Then Kusunose came here, in mid-winter, to the woods at the foot of Mount Fuji, and starved himself to death, the same way that so many of his men had died.

The Tomei Expressway hugged the Pacific Coast as it passed through Hamamatsu, where Honda, Yamaha and Suzuki were based, and then stretched on all the way to Nagoya. There, Nishimura stopped for lunch; nothing extravagant, of course, just some dry biscuits, tinned fish and a cup of water.

As he drove on, entering the Meishin Expressway near Nagoya Airport, which would take him to Osaka and then Kobe, Nishimura could hear the skull bouncing around next to him in the cardboard box that he had reinforced with plywood. On the dashboard he had rigged up a basic global navigation system, one of the first in Japan, and he glanced at it from time to time to check his progress, but the sound coming from the box sent his mind drifting elsewhere.

To New Guinea and the shallow graves that lined the Kokoda Track. To his family in Tokyo and the life he'd left behind. To Popondetta and his jungle odyssey.

Dusk began to descend as Nishimura reached the outskirts of Kobe, so he looked for an off-ramp. There was a time when he could detect the slightest movement of leaves in the New Guinea jungle, but his eyes were not as strong as they used to be, and he found driving at night among the glare of car headlights increasingly difficult. He pulled over in a lay-by and readied his bed, pushing the back seats down flat, and spreading out a thin mattress, sheet and blankets. It was hard on his back, but for Nishimura it would do just fine. It beat sleeping on the jungle floor and having to flick leeches off your legs in the morning, or spending the night in a foxhole ankle-deep in fetid water.

FOR ALMOST TWENTY YEARS now, Nishimura had made it his personal mission to retrieve the lost remains of the dead Japanese soldiers of the Kokoda Track and return them to their families in Japan. His own family and friends in Tokyo found his project difficult to comprehend. They were puzzled why he would forsake the comforts of home for such a primitive and uncomfortable life in New Guinea.

Some of them looked at him strangely, perhaps wondering if the relentless equatorial heat had fried his brain. But Nishimura had given his word to his dying comrades that he would return for them, so it was his duty to fulfil that pledge. He felt it was a privilege and honour to be carrying out his project.

He understood that the virtues of honour, duty, integrity and loyalty no longer mattered to Japanese society in the way they had in his youth, sixty years ago. Now, they were slightly quaint notions. But if only the youth of Japan knew what had been sacrificed so that they could go gallivanting around Ginza and Roppongi with iPods in their ears, mobile phones in their hands, and hairstyles that looked like upended bowls of soba noodles.

So here he was, steaming along the Chugoku Expressway on the last leg of his journey to Hiroshima, a city recognised the world over as the place where World War II had come to a searing and apocalyptic end.

Hiroshima prefecture today is home to more than three million people, spread across 8500 square kilometres. Nishimura had plenty of supplies – biscuits, rice, fruit, tinned fish and water – and enough money to buy petrol for the thousands of kilometres he'd surely cover. He was prepared for the possibility of a long and arduous search for the family of the soldier with four gold teeth.

Narrowing down the possibilities had not been easy. More

than 13,000 Japanese troops had died in eastern New Guinea in the six months between July 1942 and late January 1943, at the rate of 500 a week.

But Nishimura set to work with the zeal that had become his trademark. Researching war records, he discovered that a unit from the 41st Infantry Regiment, recruited largely from Fukuyama City in Hiroshima prefecture, had defended that section of Giruwa Beach where he had discovered the skull. In a severely weakened state, the unit had been pushed back to the beach by Allied forces counter-attacking from the south, and there they made their last stand.

Nishimura tracked down and contacted the widow of Colonel Kiyomi Yazawa, who had commanded the 41st Regiment, and she was able to provide him with a full list of the men from her husband's regiment who fought and died in New Guinea. The soldiers belonged to the Takenaka Unit, which was made up of the remnants of the 41st Regiment's decimated 2nd and 11th companies and named in honour of one of its officers.

By cross-referencing the dates of their deaths with those two key months either side of Christmas 1942, Nishimura eventually came up with the names of seventy men who had been killed at south-west Giruwa between 19 November and 12 January. They had died there beneath the palm trees, within shouting distance of each other, and only a week or two away from evacuation.

Encouraged by the progress of his search, Nishimura next contacted the veterans association of the 41st Regiment. Could they give him the addresses of the relatives of the seventy young soldiers? If they couldn't find immediate family, perhaps they could trace cousins or nieces or nephews who lived in the region. It transpired that most of the relatives were spread out around Hiroshima prefecture, although some were dotted through the neighbouring Shimane, Yamaguchi and Okayama prefectures.

Armed with the list of the seventy families and their addresses, Nishimura mapped out a rough route that would enable him to visit them all. It would involve travelling up and down the Toyota district, motoring through the Aki district, traversing the Yamagata district and, finally, if necessary, searching high and low through the Jinseki and Sera districts.

The prefecture, which is mountainous and includes many small islands on an inland sea, was not the easiest place to conduct such a search. Sometimes, Nishimura was able to visit three or four families in a day; in more remote rural areas or on the islands, it might be just one. As he went along, travelling through the countryside, passing through villages and traversing village streets, Nishimura ticked off each family he visited. Whenever he stopped at an address on his list, he kept the skull in the car, hidden away in the box. His questions about New Guinea were often enough to get people suspicious and offside; no point in alarming them further, he decided, by producing a skull.

Whenever he knocked on a door, his inquiry was the same: Pardon my intrusion. I am Kokichi Nishimura of Tokyo, a veteran of the New Guinea campaign, and I wonder if you lost a relative in New Guinea during the war, a relative who had some gold teeth?

When they said no, he bowed and said: I'm sorry, that's my mistake, I apologise for bothering you.

Some treated him like a tramp, a no-good vagrant who was delving into a part of their history they wanted to forget. Others were more welcoming, inviting him in for a cup of green tea or a bowl of noodles, and asking him about his mission. Some begged him to find the remains of their long-lost relatives. Four families told him they had lost sons or brothers who had one or two gold teeth so, thinking he may have stumbled upon the right family at last, Nishimura rushed out to the car and produced the skull for identification. But no, they said. Sorry, but we know no one who had four gold teeth like that.

Crossing off the names as he went, sleeping in his car all the while, Nishimura put a line through twenty names, then forty and then sixty. By the seventh week of his search, down to the last ten families on the list, he was starting to feel a rising tide of desperation as he wound his way through the north-east part of Hiroshima prefecture and into Shobara City.

Built on a wide terrace of the Saijo River, Shobara is surrounded by rice fields and the Chugoku Mountains. But it's a new city, built in the early 1950s, and sits uncomfortably close to the Chugoku Expressway, robbing it of any traditional rural charm.

Still, its planners were prescient enough to create a massive park, the Bihoku National Hillside Park, a short drive from the city. Here, among 340 hectares of rolling hills, Nishimura, tired, bedraggled and nearly drained of hope, occasionally came to rest his sore bones and to watch children play soccer, throw Frisbees and paddle canoes on the lake.

He could see his dream of fifty-six years, of reuniting his comrades left behind in New Guinea with their families, disappearing into the thin Chugoku mountain air.

But early one evening, outside a village in the valley, he drove alongside a river and then peeled off up a driveway that led to a lovely old traditional-style house. The estate looked like it belonged to a well-to-do family. It was set in the middle of a massive cypress and cedar tree plantation, and the nearest farmhouse was more than a kilometre away.

This was family number 68 on his list, and his fiftieth night away from home. Nishimura cleared his throat and knocked on the front door. The man who answered was tall and dignified, and looked even older than Nishimura. Well practised by now, Nishimura started his spiel about New Guinea and the skull. The man's eyes brightened. Yes, he said, I lost a younger brother in New Guinea, and he had four gold teeth. Nishimura hurried to the car and got his exhibit out of its box with a growing sense of elation.

The man took the skull and cradled it in his hands. He gazed at it while Nishimura waited nervously alongside him. The macabre offering obviously connected the distinguished-looking old man with another time and long-repressed memories. Tears began to well in his eyes and he tried to speak, but his voice was choked with emotion. Nothing came out except heaving sobs and a low, sad moan.

CHAPTER 2

Childhood

NISHIMURA WAS NINE WHEN his father died. The boy remembered little of his parent's final weeks, but never forgot the date that he disappeared forever: 16 April 1929. The doctors described his father's condition as 'gnawing hunger'. Emaciated and weak, constantly hungry, Nishimura senior could not put on weight or regain his strength, no matter how much he gorged himself. After almost twelve months of this unhappy existence, he finally passed away.

His death was a double blow, for his family was left not just grief-stricken but very nearly destitute as well. The medical expenses and grocery bills accrued over a year forced Nishimura's mother to sell the plot of land they owned and the house they had recently built on it. His maternal grandmother was able to soften the blow by letting them stay in a small house she owned in Kochi City. Still, Nishimura's childhood was notable for its austerity.

He had been in grade three when his father first fell ill and the medical bills began to pile up. Nishimura's mother thought it might be a good idea if he delivered newspapers to help bring in some income. Every morning a bus came with a load of newspapers, and Nishimura took some on his bicycle for delivery. After a while, he became friends with the bus driver, who sometimes sat him behind the wheel and taught him how to drive on his regular route between Nagahama and Nishibun.

When there were passengers on his bus, Nishimura would help to check the tickets; when there was none, he was allowed to drive. In climbing up into the driver's seat, the nine-year-old Nishimura first began to show his maverick streak, a tendency towards the unconventional that would come to mark his later life.

Because his father had been an engine-room operator on merchant ships and was away at sea for months at a time, Nishimura was not used to having him around the house much anyway. He was only in grade four when his father died, and while they had never really been close, the death left a profound void in the boy's life.

Nishimura became withdrawn, self-contained and self-reliant, traits that while hardly ideal in a young child, would stand him in good stead in adulthood. He caught insects and went fishing, usually by himself. He rowed a small boat on Urado Bay. He picked sweetcorn and ate it after school. A few years later, he bought an air rifle. He didn't much care for sport, certainly not team sports anyway.

The family rarely went on holidays, and his big treat was being taken on a picnic up on the hill behind their house in suburban Nagahama. Then, the mothers from the neighbourhood would pack up lunch boxes and bring their children out for a day in the sunshine, spreading out blankets in a field full of flowering azaleas. It was a simple outing, but one Nishimura would often recall with pleasure in later years.

Otherwise, his holidaying was confined to school trips at Kochi's Nagahama Elementary Primary School. In grade one, the class went to Katsurahama Beach, a place Nishimura would revisit later in life on a vastly different mission. In grade two, they went to the Chikurin-ji Temple and Godaisan Mountain; and in grade three, to the Ryuga-do Cave where Nishimura was entranced by the cave's luminous green interior.

He was a very capable student without being brilliant, his grades hovering between High Distinction (*Ko*) or Distinction (*Otsu*). After his father's death, Nishimura began to immerse himself in his textbooks, often completing a year's worth of exercises within the first month of the school year. When he found the problems too difficult, he'd take them to his mother. If she couldn't help, he'd walk across to the local temple and ask the monks for assistance, especially in reading the complex Kanji characters that he was discovering for the first time.

The house given to the family by his mother's mother was auspiciously located, right in front of Setsukei-ji Temple, the thirty-third of eighty-eight temples built on Shikoku in the eighth century by a monk named Kobo-Daishi. The island was considered holy ground by many Japanese, and each year thousands of devotees made the traditional six-week pilgrimage, walking a 1700-kilometre circuit to visit each of the temples.

In befriending the monks at the temple and devoting hours each day with their help to finishing every last one of his textbook exercises, Nishimura first displayed signs of the obsessive, almost fanatical, behaviour that would later characterise his approach to any task he tackled.

At home, though, the lack of money was beginning to bite. Nishimura's mother had her hands full with four children, the youngest aged just three. There was barely enough to feed the family. As the eldest son, it was incumbent on Nishimura to start earning a wage.

NOT LONG AFTER HE turned eleven, Nishimura was taken out of primary school by his mother and, with his younger brother and two sisters, brought to Tokyo where they lived in the Ota district in the city's south-west. His older sister, Ayako, soon began working as a 'bus girl', or conductor.

Nishimura worked during the day in a factory and studied at evening class at a special technical school, Keihin Kogakuin, learning architectonics and technical drawing. For the first two years in the factory, he was a trainee, earning 65 sen per hour (when 100 sen was the equivalent of 1 yen). A tram ticket cost 7 sen (5 sen in the morning peak hour), the same price as a packet of cigarettes or admittance to a public bath.

At night, Nishimura applied himself diligently to class, never missing a lesson despite his tiredness, and soon developed an outstanding talent for technical drawing. He understood that hard work and application were the only ways to escape the poverty he had grown up with, so he attacked his studies with single-minded intensity.

Despite the relentless regime of work and study which made any of the fun normally enjoyed by boys his age nearly impossible, Nishimura lived this punishing routine for four years. When he matriculated, he took up a job as a fitter and machinist at an iron-making foundry. It was 1935 and he was barely fifteen.

But such was the quality of his marks at Keihin Kogakuin, and the reputation he was building as a technical draftsman, that soon various people approached him for help. A professor from the Tokyo Institute of Technology came to him asking for lessons and advice. The former manager of the Japanese Navy factory at Sasebo also sought him out for help with technical matters. Then, when full-scale war with China erupted in mid-1937, Nishimura became a consultant to the Japanese Railways, working as an adviser to the Nagareyama Dentetsu Line in Chiba prefecture. At seventeen, he found himself in big demand.

Nishimura's thoughts were not overly concerned with the war. He figured he'd be passed over for conscription when he turned twenty, and earmarked for some big engineering project in Tokyo. Not that he'd ever consider shirking his duty if he was called up. If they wanted Nishimura to fight, he'd fight.

The adversity he grew up with, and from which he was trying to escape, helped make him immune to many of the privations he would later endure as Japan's war spread throughout the Pacific. He had lost his father, and was supporting his mother and three siblings, even though he was of an age when most boys were still at school. He never drank or smoked, and couldn't understand people who did. His childhood and adolescence were notable for their frugality, hard work and self-reliance.

In his efforts to improve himself and the lot of his family, he was largely unaided, unallied and undaunted.

Therefore soldiering, with all its attendant hardships, was a job that came easily to Nishimura. You could almost say he was born to it.

CHAPTER 3

The soldier

KOCHI CITY IS SET in lush green hills at the mouth of the Niyodo River on Shikoku's south coast, which faces the Pacific Ocean. It's a pleasant city, with lively weekend markets that stretch along its streets for more than a kilometre from a gabled seventeenth-century castle, and an array of restaurants that cook the local delicacy, whale meat, in a dozen different ways.

But behind its peaceful appearance lies a bellicose history. The men of Kochi are descended from the fabled warriors of Tosa province, as the area was known in feudal times, and the city has traditionally produced some of Japan's fiercest fighters. The famed courage of the Kochi soldier had even been given a name, *Tosa-jin Kishitsu*. In the nineteenth century, Kochi warriors helped depose the Shogunate and restore the Emperor's power. Japan's most famous samurai warrior, Sakamoto Ryoma, was one of the Tosans who played a key role in bringing about the Meiji Restoration and was assassinated for his trouble at the age of thirty-three.

In no great coincidence, it was to the sons of Kochi that the nation's military chiefs turned in 1940 when they decided to form the Nankai Shitai, or South Seas Detachment, an elite unit that was the rough Japanese equivalent of the US Marines.

When Nishimura was growing up, every Japanese male faced the prospect of military service, and had to undergo a medical examination once he turned twenty. So in 1940, Nishimura, who was still living in Tokyo, travelled by train to his home town, and lined up with hundreds of other young men for the medical. The group was divided into five ranks: Very Healthy and Strong, High Distinction, Distinction, Average and Pass. No one failed, but a soldier who merely passed was not exempt completely from military duty; he would be called upon only in an emergency. Nishimura was rated *Ko* (High Distinction).

He received his conscription papers the following year, and joined conscripts from other Kochi families – sons of rice farmers, merchant seamen, public servants and tradesmen – in forming up at the nearby village of Asakura to begin training.

Now, Nishimura would happily keep fighting for as long as the army wanted him to. But what he was thinking to himself – though not daring to say out loud, in case he was misunderstood – was this: *why have I been conscripted to fight when surely I am of more use to the Emperor and the war effort by continuing my work in Tokyo? Many young men could become soldiers with the right training, but how many had the skills to draw, invent weapons, dream up new technology, and solve engineering problems?*

Nishimura did not want to be seen as arrogant, or as shirking his duty, so he never mentioned these thoughts to anyone. But what a misguided policy, he thought, to be sending the best and brightest to the battlefield when clearly they could be of much greater help to their country by exercising their brains back in Japan.

THE IMPERIAL JAPANESE ARMY tended to recruit its battalions from the same town or district, in much the same way as the British Army had drawn together units known as the Liverpool Pals, the Tyneside Irish and the Glasgow Tramways Battalion in the Great War. The Japanese military leadership believed this approach engendered a team spirit based on familiarity, while acting as a deterrent against desertion. Soldiers were always aware that their comrades knew their families back home and that the loss of face resulting from anything less than total commitment to the Emperor would have been overwhelming.

The Nankai Shitai had a special status within the army: it was the only force to come under the direct control of Imperial Headquarters in Tokyo, rather than answering to an army division.

The 144th Regiment, to which Nishimura was assigned, formed the nucleus of the Shitai's infantry. Its 3500 troops would become specialists at coastal invasion and beach-landings. Indeed, they would practise their landings at Katsurahama Beach, the same stretch of coastline outside Kochi that Nishimura and his grade one classmates had visited during a school excursion sixteen years earlier.

The Kochi combat troops teamed up with a collection of specially chosen units – engineers, mountain gun artillery, signals, medical, veterinary, and water supply and disease prevention – and then were joined by the 41st Infantry and 15th Independent Engineer Regiments. Together they formed the South Seas Detachment, under the command of Major-General Tomitaro Horii, a formidable figure in spite of his diminutive stature.

Nearly six months after his induction, on 22 September 1941, the 21-year-old Nishimura set off to war. Now, he was Corporal Kokichi Nishimura, grenade launcher, of the 4th Squad of the 3rd Platoon of the 5th Company of the 2nd Battalion of the 144th Infantry Regiment. As a corporal, he earned a monthly wage of 7.5 yen. The work he had left behind at the Tokyo foundry paid a monthly salary of 550 yen.

Along with Nishimura in the 144th Regiment were several other young men from the Kochi region whom he would soon befriend. Mitsuo Itahara, the same age as Nishimura, joined the regiment at the same time. He hailed from Tosa City, and was the younger brother of the Tosa mayor. Yoshimi Kubo, seven years older, was a graduate of Takushoku University, and had an impish sense of humour. Fluent in English, he had to leave a good job with the Imperial Oil Company to join the army. Satoshi Watanabe was honest in the extreme, dependable, patient and trustworthy, traits that Nishimura valued highly. And Kanichi Ishiyama, another Kochi man, never lost his cool and could be relied upon even in the trickiest situations. He was small, even for a Japanese, and had unusually pale skin, but his somewhat delicate appearance belied his resolute nature.

In photographs taken shortly before he left for war, Nishimura stood proudly in his army uniform behind his mother, their high cheekbones betraying the family connection. There was no hint of a smile on his face, just a look of grim determination. And with good reason.

For the conscripts' training had been brutal. Recruits were kicked, punched and punished on the slightest whim of their officers. Reveille was at 6 am, when the young soldiers were taken outside for 'warming up' exercises which sometimes consisted of rubbing down their naked bodies with a brush or towel. Manoeuvres were frequently conducted in the snow; some went all night and into the next day.

If Nishimura or his comrades spoke a word out of place or took a step out of line, they were heavily beaten. Soon enough, any rebellious notions or thoughts of insubordination – even any attempts at practical jokes – were abandoned. They were trained to do exactly as they were told, no questions asked, no explanations given.

Nishimura felt like he had been turned into a kind of zombie in army uniform, one capable of running twelve kilometres in an hour in his boots and gaiters, devoid of any emotion except the will to fight. When he was given an order, he carried it out without complaint or question.

He remembered later being so desensitised that he neither felt scared of fighting nor feared dying. Such was the level of indoctrination that the Emperor became a kind of living god: if soldiers were ordered to die for him, they died.

As brutal as this training was, Nishimura believed it helped toughen up young soldiers and taught them to ignore trifling discomforts such as sleeping on the ground or marching in the rain. Relentless beatings and punishments were the best education for raw recruits, he felt, because they forged stronger discipline.

However, it was Nishimura's good fortune that one of the instructors at Asakura, Yoshiyuki Morimoto, was more humane than most. Second-Lieutenant Morimoto was the personification of hard but fair, a young officer who was able to temper rigid Japanese Army discipline with a smidgin of humanity. He took charge of Nishimura's unit, and Nishimura was assigned as his batman, or personal attendant. That meant doing an officer's washing, preparing his dinner, carrying his bags and so on. Some officers made life hell for their batman, taking advantage of their lowly station, but Morimoto was far too reasonable for that.

One day when the unit was conducting a military exercise

within the regimental camp, Nishimura lost one of the parts of his grenade launcher – a smallish, one-man weapon that fired grenades roughly the size of normal hand grenades. He was aghast. The soldiers were taught that their weapons were issued by the Emperor, and it was seen as a terrible mistake to lose or damage them. For half an hour the fifty novice soldiers of the 5th Company searched the grass on their hands and knees, without success.

Nishimura feared the worst: this was a crime that meant a beating so bad his face would be disfigured. But Morimoto stood up and said to his troops: 'I will take entire responsibility for this. Now dismiss!' It was an act of kindness Nishimura never forgot.

Another day, when they were resting between military exercises at Asakura, Morimoto handed his aluminium lunch box to Nishimura, and asked him if he could carve Morimoto's name into it. Morimoto was aware that his batman had worked in a foundry, and had a gift with his hands. Neither of them could know it then, but many years later, this small episode would come to have a powerful significance for Nishimura.

After a relentless regimen of intensive training and indoctrination, the 144th Regiment set sail on 22 September for the Ogasawara Islands, an archipelago of thirty subtropical islands a thousand kilometres due south of Tokyo. Here they completed final training and, with anger building in Japan over perceived unjust treatment by the United States, awaited the seemingly inevitable call to arms.

Then on 4 December, Nishimura and his mates gathered at Hahajima port to embark on the troopship *Yokohama-maru*, bound for the South Seas. The regiment's first ports of call would be the American-controlled island of Guam, and Rabaul in New Britain; then, if everything went to plan, New Guinea, further south.

Soon after they set sail, the troops were ordered to fall in on deck by Lieutenant Tokushige Kihara, commander of the 5th Company. In a booming voice, Kihara told his men that war was imminent, and that everyone on board should prepare accordingly. 'The Japanese Government is still working towards diplomatic solutions with the United States to avoid war. However, if this doesn't bear fruit, we will declare war against the United States, Great Britain and the Netherlands on 8 December,' Kihara said. Nishimura, who wanted to remember what his commander had said, later recorded his words in his private diary.

'Our 144th Infantry Regiment will separate from the 55th Division and participate in joint operations with the navy, as the South Seas Force is under the direct control of the Imperial Headquarters in Tokyo. The South Seas Force is instructed to occupy Guam in a joint action with the main body of the Fourth Fleet under the command of Vice-Admiral Narumi Inoue. As we arrive in Guam the day after the declaration of war, naturally we must expect fierce resistance from Americans. This operation will be deemed successful if more than one third of our force survives the hostile landing. Each of you, make appropriate preparation for the occasion so that you don't leave any regrets.'

Shaken into action, Nishimura quickly wrote a letter to his family. He couldn't tell them where his company was or where it was heading. The military censors would allow only 'southern lands' as a generic description of their position. He told his mother and the rest of his family how proud he was to be serving his Emperor and his country, and that he hoped to bring his family honour by dying a valiant death in the service of his nation.

Nishimura was born on 8 December. The date is well known to many Japanese for, early on that day in 1941 (Japanese time), the Japanese Air Force attacked the US Navy at Pearl Harbor, jolting America out of its neutrality and signalling the start of the greater Pacific war. So, Nishimura was not only born in the warrior city of Kochi, but also shared a birthday with one of the bleakest episodes in Japan's history. All the portents were there: Nishimura was born to a life of conflict.

At 7.53 am on 7 December (Hawaiian time) – or 3.23 am on 8 December where the *Yokohama-Maru* was sailing, some way to the west in the Philippine Sea – the attack on Pearl Harbor began. Japan was now irredeemably involved in the war.

When Nishimura awoke to the news that morning, it was his twenty-second birthday.

ABOUT FORTY-FOUR HOURS later, near midnight on 9 December, lookouts on the nine Japanese troopships escorted by the Fourth Fleet first caught sight of Guam. But as they entered Talofofo Bay, a strong wind sprang up, producing a two-metre swell. The fleet anchored three kilometres from shore and smaller boats were used to ferry soldiers to the beach, one nearly sinking in the heaving seas. The first party landed just before dawn, and when all the troops were safely landed, the Japanese began marching inland.

Kihara's warning about the red-hot reception they could expect proved unfounded. The Nankai Shitai found they had almost unfettered access to the island.

At the foot of Mount Chachao, a soldier in the advance party brought back three American troops carrying water bottles but little in the way of weaponry. One had a small dog with him. Private Kubo, Nishimura's good friend who spoke English well, was summoned to interpret the dialogue between the interrogators, Kihara and platoon commander Kiyomichi Inoue, and the three Americans. It was a farcical scene, which Nishimura later recorded in his diary.

Clearly, news of the Pearl Harbor attack forty-eight hours earlier, and of subsequent air raids on Guam's capital, Agana, had somehow eluded the Americans on their day off. Given that Talofofo was in the south-east of the island, and Agana was on the central-west coast, the scenario was not implausible.

Kihara (through Kubo): Are you American soldiers?

Americans: Yes.

Kihara: What are you doing here?

Americans: We are off-duty today and having a look around this area. Who are you guys and why are you here? What are you doing here, and why did you have to capture us?

Kihara: We are the Japanese Army. We have declared war against the US and we came here to occupy Guam.

Americans: You must be joking. There is no way Japan would start a war against the US. If anybody comes here to attack us, it would be the Germans or the Spanish.

Kihara: You are wrong. We are definitely Japanese soldiers and you are our enemy. You are now our prisoners of war.

Americans: Don't be silly. Stop that foolish joke and let us go. Or is this some sort of field practice?

Kihara: No, this is neither a joke nor field practice. This is war.

Americans: Let's stop this drill now and let us go. By the way, we ran out of cigarettes. You guys haven't got any spare, have you?

It was all Nishimura could do to stop from laughing. Some of his comrades were not so restrained. This was not what Nishimura had expected at all from his first engagement with the enemy, nor what he'd been trained for. The trio reacted in the way that bushwalkers might after meeting other adventurers on a remote track. Nishimura was confused: how could you feel any hostility towards these easy-going, smiling Americans? Still, they were taken as prisoners.

It transpired most of the US military and citizens on Guam had been evacuated before the Japanese arrived.

To Nishimura and his comrades, the island proved an unlikely paradise. Brief tropical showers arrived at much the same time each day, and there was no sign of the twin scourges of mosquito and malaria. Nishimura and Kubo often visited the home of a village chief who lived near their billet and insisted on preparing a home-made brew of coconut liquor for Kubo every time he turned up. Nishimura, who had never let alcohol pass his lips, remained abstinent despite the temptation of the chief's sweet-smelling brew. On 13 January 1942, the day before the regiment departed from Guam, the chief gave Kubo a one-dollar pocket watch as a farewell gift. Touched by the gesture, Kubo promised he would come back after the war to visit his new friend, and they embraced before parting.

Guided by the battleship *Tsugaru*, the South Seas Detachment began its journey again on 14 January. After six days spent steaming south, the fleet crossed the equator. When this was announced to the troops, an enormous cheer went up; it was the first time the Imperial Japanese Army had been south of the equator since its formation in 1867. That night, a lavish feast was served and eaten without any of the formalities that usually accompanied mess time.

WHEN THEY LANDED ON New Britain, Nishimura and his comrades in the 144th Regiment encountered the Australian military for the first time. After running their barges ashore on the night of 22 January, they soon met fierce resistance from a small Australian force. But the 1400 or so Australians were hopelessly outnumbered by the 13,000 Japanese invaders, and their defence was soon quelled. Facing annihilation, elements of the Australian garrison escaped along the north and south coasts of the island.

At dawn the following day, Nishimura was called aside by platoon leader, Second Lieutenant Inoue. He took away Nishimura's rifle and gave him a sabre and pistol instead, saying he wanted the young corporal to lead the march into Rabaul, the main town on the eastern end of the island. 'You will lead our platoon with these,' said Inoue. 'There are no Japanese or scouts in front of you. Whenever you sense someone else's presence, pull the trigger without uttering a word.'

Uncomplainingly, Nishimura responded that he would be honoured to perform this duty. Deep down, though, he felt his time had come; it would be impossible to survive such a mission. He started walking through the eerily quiet streets of Rabaul, thinking death was waiting around the corner, crouched in the next doorway.

Squad leader Tanaka and his men were right behind him, though, which gave Nishimura some comfort. The town appeared deserted; word of the Japanese advance clearly had sent the locals fleeing into the jungle. With Nishimura leading the way, and Tanaka close behind, the 3rd Platoon moved slowly through the streets and side alleys, checking the houses as they went. When the entire town had been searched without incident, and it became apparent the danger had passed, Nishimura sat down, shaking, and breathed a silent sigh of relief.

But the reprieve was short-lived. On 26 January orders were given for the 5th Company to pursue the Australians who had fled, and to mop up enemy resistance. Japanese troops landed five barges on the shores of Henry Reid Bay, near the Tol and

Waitavalo plantations, and rounded up prisoners in the surrounding jungle. Some prisoners lay down their weapons and surrendered; finally, about one thousand Australians were captured.

Many surviving veterans of the 144th Regiment later claimed to remember little of the events that followed, but what is known is this: on 4 February, 157 Australians were shot or bayoneted to death in cold blood, an atrocity that became known as the Tol Plantation Massacre. The Japanese unit responsible for the murders was the 3rd Battalion, commanded by Colonel Masao Kusunose, the same Kusunose who would later starve himself to death at the foot of Mount Fuji after being summoned to a war crimes tribunal at the end of the war.

Nishimura's 2nd Battalion was on a day's expedition from Rabaul and had been given the job of rounding up Australians who'd escaped into the jungle. They were on the north coast of New Britain. The 3rd Battalion was maybe fifty kilometres away, south of Rabaul, on the south-east coast of the island. Kusunose's outfit had been told to load Australian prisoners on a landing boat bound for Rabaul, but it was not large enough to take them all. This was when Kusunose made the decision to execute the POWs, an act later characterised by the Allies as one of the most monstrous war crimes of the Pacific conflict.

Nishimura knew nothing of the barbarity that had taken place until his unit returned to Rabaul later that night.

The incident sat unhappily alongside some of Nishimura's own experiences with Australian POWs in New Britain. One day before the Japanese landing at Rabaul, a Japanese reconnaissance plane crashed into a mountain in low cloud and both pilots were killed. The Australians dug a grave and gave them a proper burial. When the Japanese command subsequently learned of this civilised act, a directive was issued strictly forbidding the abuse of Australian prisoners. They were to be treated well.

Each platoon in Nishimura's 5th Company took turn in shifts to oversee the POW camp in Rabaul. It was Nishimura's job to supervise two Australian prisoners to assist in the cleaning and overhauling of weapons. He came to know the men well. Each morning, the prisoners, carrying buckets of water, met Nishimura in his yard, where together they worked for an hour or two maintaining the guns. Then, according to Nishimura, they all sat around and talked. His friend Kubo sometimes translated the conversations. Otherwise, Nishimura would communicate by writing and drawing pictures.

At 4 pm, the Australian pair returned to camp. When they left, Nishimura sometimes gave them cans of food to take back to their friends. If not, he'd deliberately cook too much rice for his dinner and give the leftovers to the Australians to carry back in their buckets.

One of the prisoners had been a sewerage worker before the war. He showed Nishimura a picture of his wife in a swim-suit. Both men gave Nishimura their names and addresses in Melbourne, and they all pledged to get in touch after the war. But Nishimura lost the piece of paper when his troopship was torpedoed and sunk by an American submarine near Taiwan late in 1943. It was one of his great regrets after the war that he was not able to contact the men or their families.

At his commander's instruction, Nishimura suggested to the Australian POWs that they write letters to their families and girlfriends back home. He explained that a navy bomber would drop the letters in bags over the airfield in Port Moresby. The two prisoners convinced the other Australians that the Japanese offer was genuine. After the first letter drop, the Japanese got the Australians to write another letter three days later. Again a navy bomber rained down bags of letters on the Moresby airfield, amid Australian anti-aircraft gunfire. Nishimura believed the gesture was genuine – so that POWs could make contact with their families in Australia – but he could not be sure the letters were not censored before being tipped into the giant postal sacks.

After overrunning New Britain, the 144th Regiment had three weeks before setting off on the final leg of their South Seas campaign to New Guinea. The commander of the 2nd Platoon, Lieutenant Mori, was a passionate sumo follower and decided to make the most of this time. He ordered the construction of a sumo ring in front of the platoon's billet. Here, he let the men from 5th Company practise their sumo skills, an ideal way for soldiers to release pent-up aggression. Nishimura often practised with Lance Corporal Teiji Yamazaki who, despite being the oldest soldier in the platoon, was a strong and agile wrestler.

Another of Nishimura's good friends, a Private Kono, had been a professional sumo wrestler before the war. He was a pupil of the Grand Champion Tama-Nishiki of the Nisho-no-Seki stable, and had once ranked as *Jyuryo*, a leading junior wrestler.

One day, another sumo wrestler by the name of Tama-no-umi, who also held the rank of *Jyuryo*, visited Nishimura's platoon from the navy. He wanted to pay his respects to Private Kono, who had been his senior at the Nisho-no-Seki stable. He kindly offered practice sessions with any of the members of the Sumo Club game enough to take him on. First, he wrestled with Private Kono. Tama-no-umi prevailed, then asked for any other volunteers.

Nishimura put up his hand. And in the dusty, makeshift ring outside his platoon's billet, he fought one of Japan's best young sumo wrestlers until the seasoned professional eventually forced him from the ring. Nishimura said his love of sumo was a blessing, for it gave him the mental and physical strength to survive the myriad crises he faced during the war. The practice session with Tama-no-umi became one of his most treasured memories from his time away.

But the Japanese revelry in New Britain would soon end. And while Nishimura's sumo practice was a pleasant diversion from the relentless army drills, it was no preparation for the real fighting that lay ahead on the Kokoda Track.

CHAPTER 4

New Guinea

Duty is weightier than a mountain while death is lighter than a feather.

From the Imperial Rescript to Soldiers and Sailors, originally issued by Emperor Meiji in 1882, and given to every member of the South Seas Detachment before their departure for war in 1941.

RABAUL SECURED AND GARRISONED, the 13,500-strong Nankai Shitai now set its sights on New Guinea. With thousands of troops left behind to safeguard New Britain, the 2nd Battalion boarded two transport vessels headed for the only land mass that remained between the Imperial Japanese Army and Australia. Given the ease with which they'd completed the first stage of their Pacific campaign, Nishimura and his friends had no reason to believe New Guinea would be any more of a challenge.

They anchored offshore at Salamaua, south of Lae, on 7 March 1942 and, in a characteristic operation, landed at night. Just before 1 am on 8 March, Nishimura's battalion stepped on to Salamaua Beach, the first members of the Japanese Army to reach New Guinea.

As they moved cautiously inland under the cover of darkness, Nishimura saw an airfield in front of them, and an Australian plane, its exhaust fumes casting an iridescent red trail in the sky, took off over their heads. As the troops approached the airfield, they crawled on their hands and knees, unable to see the ground around them. Nishimura felt a cord or string pulling at his body. Was it some sort of fuse? He fumbled for the string and gently pulled it towards him. At the other end was a smooth, heavy-ish ball, about forty centimetres in diameter. Nishimura thought: Holy hell, this really must be a bomb.

A soldier crawled up behind him and Nishimura asked who it was. 'Private Watanabe,' came the answer: it was his Kochi friend Satoshi Watanabe who had moved alongside him in the dark. Nishimura asked him to keep guard over the mysterious object while he went to report it to the squad leader. But Watanabe said to Nishimura: Hang on a second, come here and smell this thing you think is a bomb. He was giggling. Nishimura put his nose to the ball, then started laughing, too. It was a watermelon. He turned to his comrade and said: Hey, Watanabe, how about taking a rest from the operation and eating the melon with me? So, within seed-spitting distance of an enemy airfield, Corporal Nishimura and Private Watanabe sat down in the long grass and ate an entire watermelon in the middle of the night. It was to be one of the many incongruous moments in Nishimura's war.

As dawn broke, Nishimura was performing sentry duty at a junction of three roads near Salamaua Peninsula, when a large formation of bombers appeared on the horizon and flew towards them from the sea. Nishimura immediately reported this to his squad head, Corporal Hitomi Tanaka. Tanaka appeared unconcerned. He said he thought they must be Japanese aircraft visiting, since the date was Army Memorial Day.

No sooner had he spoken than the planes began dive-bombing their position. Nishimura sheltered under a palm tree and watched as the planes strafed their ships and inflicted terrible damage. The casualties included the *Yokohama-maru*, the troopship that had been Nishimura's home for the past four months. She sounded a weak whistle as she gently disappeared beneath the waves: a meek end for such an imposing vessel. Down with her went most of the clothes, photographs, letters and personal belongings of Nishimura and his comrades.

The sinking of the *Yokohama-maru* forced the Japanese back to Rabaul aboard a troopship left unscathed by the air raid, the *China-maru*.

Nishimura and the 5th Company should have returned in early May for another crack at Port Moresby, but the Battle of the Coral Sea put paid to their second seaborne attempt on the New Guinea capital. Then, in the first week of June, an even bigger defeat at the Battle of Midway resulted in the loss of four aircraft carriers and 250 planes, leaving the Japanese carrier fleet almost crippled. The Japanese command abandoned plans to take Port Moresby from the sea. For the first time, an overland invasion was considered.

Whoever it was that made the final decision to cross the Owen Stanley Range from the north could not have possessed even a vague working knowledge of the terrain. The Japanese could scarcely have chosen a more dismal place in which to wage war.

Towering saw-toothed mountains covered by mountain forest and rainforest rose vertically out of the flat, malarial coastland that was covered in matted jungle, reeking sago swamps, and broad patches of knife-edged kunai grass two metres high.

The annual rainfall in some parts of New Guinea was as high as 6000 to 7000 millimetres; during the rainy season, daily falls of 150 to 200 millimetres were not uncommon. The heat and humidity in the coastal areas were almost unbearable, yet high in the Owen Stanleys there was biting cold at altitudes over 1500 metres. Turbulent rivers such as the Kumusi flowed from the mountains, and in the wet season they became a torrent.

Along the lower reaches of the streams, the fringes of the forest became interwoven from ground to treetop level with vines and creepers to form an almost solid mat of vegetation. Troops had to hack and slash away with machetes to make any progress. The vegetation in the mountains was almost as luxuriant. Leeches abounded everywhere; and the trees were often so overgrown with creepers and moss that the sunlight scarcely filtered through to the muddy tracks below.

There was one hundred kilometres or so of trekking through coastal scrub to reach Kokoda, which marked the start of the Track, then the Track itself pitched up and down over the Owen Stanleys for a further ninety-six kilometres. Many of the Japanese troops were issued with barely eighteen days' rations in their packs, enough food for a hiking party encountering no obstacles, but hardly enough for an army engaged in continual combat. Their military command had written an ambitious timetable for them that relied on unimpeded progress and a compliant enemy – neither of which the Japanese got. It was a tropical nightmare, an undertaking that could almost be filed under the heading: mission impossible.

Advance troops from the Nankai Shitai landed on New Guinea's northern beaches on 21 July. One soldier from the advance party assumed, as many of his superiors did, that there was a road over the Owen Stanleys, so he brought his own bicycle with him. But the Track was narrow and muddy, often with a steep grade. After crossing the Kumusi River with the bike on his shoulders, he threw it away.

Nishimura and his mates from the 5th Company were

aboard the *Kotoku-maru* and came ashore at Basabua Beach on 29 July. Immediately, they began marching west towards Kokoda village, at the head of the Track, encountering few obstacles and arriving there five days later. Here they waited for almost three weeks for the main force of the Nankai Shitai to arrive, while living off rations at camp headquarters.

By now, through months of close living and shared experiences, the members of Nishimura's platoon had developed a strong comradeship; they knew that the wellbeing of the unit depended on each and every one of them. The mutual reliance helped form a bond among the platoon; as inheritors of the *Tosa-jin Kishitsu* mantle, they had a reputation to uphold.

Nishimura had been assigned a private, Zenzaburo Ushimado, as the first loader of his grenade launcher. Another son of Kochi, Ushimado had endured a painful childhood. Orphaned as a young child, he had been brought up by relatives who bullied him mercilessly. This caused him to be bitter and spiteful, and something of a loner.

He was a difficult person to like, but Nishimura felt sorry for him. Because he was Nishimura's first loader, the pair had to work together in the battlefield, side by side. By dint of circumstance, they were inseparable.

Nishimura forced himself to put aside any feelings of ill-will and to dwell instead upon his offsider's good points. Ushimado was an excellent singer and, when he was in a good mood, would break into song, completing the performance with hand gestures and a winning Hollywood smile. At these rare times, he looked a different person. He especially loved to perform *Tosa Ondo*, a local folk song from the Tosa region.

Kubo, the former oil executive, was Nishimura's second grenade loader. Given his lofty managerial position before the war, and the excellent English he spoke, his job and rank in the army must have been something of a comedown. But that was the army, where conscripts were thrown in together, regardless of the status they held in their previous civilian life.

Nishimura and his company were told nothing of the terrain they were about to enter, nor about the battle plans; they knew only that Port Moresby was their objective, and that they were to advance as far as possible each day. One Japanese officer told them that the American commander, General Douglas MacArthur, had evacuated from the Philippines and was in Port Moresby. That provided a great spur for the men, who wanted to capture the big-talking American and his corncob pipe.

They thought that if their supplies of ammunition and food held up, they'd definitely get to Port Moresby. That's what Major General Horii had drummed into them all along: as long as we have the necessary supplies, we will reach our goal. Military defeat was never countenanced. The general is said to have ridden a white charger over part of the Owen Stanley Range, in the manner of other senior Japanese officers who liked to ride at the head of their troops. The horse's remains were reportedly later found in a creek halfway along the Track.

The Japanese troops did not know their exact position on the Track, nor the names of the villages they walked through. For Nishimura and his comrades, it was just an anonymous jungle, with kilometres of broad jungle canopy overhead and a path underfoot that rose and fell at extreme angles and was rarely flat.

They knew nothing of the Australian Army, or of its numbers, strength and firepower. They were not told how many of the enemy there might be in the jungle, or their approximate locations. There was no information about how well-equipped the Australian troops might be, let alone the type of guns or artillery they would be using.

The only time the Japanese knew the enemy was nearby was

when the bullets started to fly. The Australian troops, by contrast, were relatively well informed about their position and the enemy's strength.

Occasionally, there were the natives to contend with as well. The indigenous people living in the tribal villages along the Track could become aggressive, especially the Orokaivans, a much-feared warrior tribe who not many years earlier had been head-hunters. But, generally, the villagers weren't ill-disposed towards the Japanese at the start of the campaign. They were a peaceful people, and many of them had been visited by Christian missionaries; some had become Seventh Day Adventists. They lived happily off the land, raising pigs and growing fruit and vegetables. It was only when they were forced into service as carriers, and their peaceful way of life was irredeemably shattered, that the Papuans became hostile towards the invaders.

Nishimura, as one of three grenadiers in his platoon, did not carry a rifle or bullets. His pack weighed almost thirty kilograms at the start of the march, comprising a change of clothes and tent (five kilograms), purse, sewing kit, writing materials, medicine pouch and cleaning kits for his weapons (three kilograms), ammunition and grenade launcher (ten kilograms), and food and provisions for at least sixteen days (twelve kilograms).

Some of the Japanese weaponry dated from the Russo-Japanese war forty years earlier and could be very unreliable. But the Japanese had in their favour two important pieces of heavy artillery: wheel-mounted mountain artillery and the Juki heavy machine-gun, both of which inflicted major damage on the Allied forces. Because the Track was so difficult to climb, the wheel-mounted artillery, which weighed more than 500 kilograms, had to be dismantled and the parts carried over the range by dozens of soldiers.

The gun barrel alone weighed ninety-four kilograms and required at least three soldiers to carry it up the mountain track. Nishimura was one of a group of soldiers handed this thankless task, three of them at a time lugging the lump of iron for dozens of kilometres, up precipitous slopes and over five ridges the highest, Mount Bellamy, at 2190 metres.

With efficiency and dedication, the troops took the myriad parts of the disassembled gun from their packs, and painstakingly reassembled it high in the mountains. Later, as they pounded Australian positions with its shells, keeping the enemy on the retreat, Nishimura felt the agony had been worthwhile.

Under cover of night on 24 August 1942, Nishimura's 2nd Battalion finally set out for Port Moresby, carrying rations in their packs for sixteen to twenty days. They passed through Deniki and crossed Eora Creek in fierce rain before mounting a steep slope before dawn. It was a long and arduous path that taxed the strength – and patience – of all. The climb continued through until the midday meal, which they ate while clinging to the steep slope.

At 4 pm, as the terrain flattened out a little, the company was instructed to set up camp for the night. As Nishimura's platoon gathered together to receive instructions from their commander, one of their number, Lance Corporal Mitsuo Okamoto, moaned that he would rather die than put up with this hardship any more. A moment later, the platoon heard a rifle crack from the valley below and suddenly Okamoto collapsed to the ground, groaning.

Lieutenant Inoue told Okamoto to stop his nonsense and get up, but there was no response. A soldier walked across, turned over his slumped comrade and realised he'd been shot through the stomach. Even though his eyes were wide open, Okamoto had been killed instantly. He was the first member of Nishimura's 56-man platoon to be killed in action.

Scouts were sent out to discover where the Australians were hiding, and soon found themselves engaged in a fierce battle near Kaile which resulted in six further casualties: Sergeant Iazuyoshi Nishimura (no relation to Kokichi), Corporal Masao Tsuno, Lance Corporal Kageyoshi Ikeda, Lance Corporal Yoku Fujita, Private Kasumi Miyazaki and Private Namitaro Higashikawa, all killed.

If he hadn't comprehended it fully before, Nishimura was now beginning to understand the realities of war. He understood how one day you could be sharing a joke over lunch with a comrade, and that afternoon be staring at his bloody, lifeless form lying on the jungle floor.

ABOUT THIS TIME IN late August, the main Japanese force of about 5000 troops swarmed south and soon engaged Australia's 2/14th Infantry Battalion in the bloody battle of Isurava. They outnumbered the Australians at least five to one.

Further up the Track at Myola, Nishimura's unit, which had been spared the carnage at Isurava by being sent on a parallel track to the east, was engaged in two further battles on 29 and 30 August. These skirmishes accounted for the deaths of another seven members of his platoon, taking the total fatalities to fourteen. A quarter of his unit had been killed within a week of setting out. Nishimura didn't need to be a mathematician to work out that, at that rate, his chances of seeing out the end of the year were slim.

An incident during the first battle at Myola left a lasting impression on Nishimura. His friend Watanabe, with whom he had shared the watermelon, had contracted a bad case of malaria and was suffering a high fever. He repeatedly refused Nishimura's advice to see the doctor. After ten days, Nishimura could no longer bear to see his comrade in this debilitated state, so he approached Lieutenant Inoue and told him that Watanabe was very ill and needed help. Inoue ordered the private to rest in the medical unit.

The following day, 30 August, Australian soldiers appeared in front of the hospital, on the flank of Nishimura's platoon's position. The medical staff, alarmed by the proximity of the enemy, began to fire off their guns in a panic. The platoon had to duck for cover as a hail of bullets tore into the foliage around them. Yet they couldn't respond with fire, because they realised the shooting was being done by their own troops. Lieutenant Inoue was struck and wounded near the right temple, by a bullet that penetrated his helmet and grazed his head.

Surrounded by the Australian forces thirty metres to the front, the other Japanese platoon from 5th Company on the right, and the majority of the 2nd Battalion behind them, Nishimura's group was pinned down. He tried shouting at the medical staff to stop, screaming the passwords *yama* (mountain) and *kawa* (river), and yelling: We are an ally! This is the 5th Company! Don't shoot.

Still, bullets continued to fly for hours from the direction of the medical centre. Late in the day, a message was successfully conveyed to the medics and the shooting stopped.

Watanabe, who was thought to be out of harm's way in the hospital, was hit in the chest by a shell splinter from the Australian pursuit artillery and killed. Nishimura was mortified. If only he hadn't interfered in Watanabe's business, uninvited, his friend would still be alive. He felt responsible for Watanabe's death, even though he told himself over and over that his motives had been pure and he had only had Watanabe's wellbeing at heart.

Nishimura was wracked with regret. He recalled the happy times he had spent with his smiling, good-natured comrade. In Rabaul, Watanabe had been assigned the job of collecting fruit from local farmers and orchards. After Nishimura had led the march into Rabaul, he and Watanabe had broken down the front door of a house which appeared to have been used by Australians working there. He asked Watanabe to help find two boxes which could be used to support either end of the door and thereby build a makeshift bed. Watanabe soon came across two boxes that were perfect for the job but unusually heavy.

A day or two later, local people approached Nishimura and asked him if they could take back the contents of the boxes. Suspicious, Nishimura looked inside and found finger-sized packets that contained a dark, gummy substance. The villagers offered baskets of fruit in exchange for the packets. Nishimura could see no value in the boxes but plenty of value in fresh fruit, so happily made the trade. Only later did he discover the reason for the villagers' enthusiasm in reclaiming the boxes: he had been sleeping on more than fifty kilograms of opium.

Watanabe had been Inoue's batman, so Nishimura immediately volunteered to replace him, even though it was a menial job usually assigned to a private.

He took on this extra work while still operating his grenade launcher during combat. Now he had to carry Inoue's rations for fifteen days, as well as his own. So Nishimura's pack that then might have weighed more than twenty kilograms, given that they had already been walking for a week, suddenly became much heavier, perhaps even in excess of thirty kilograms. As Nishimura himself weighed not much more than seventy kilograms at the time, the load he had to bear was almost intolerable.

The Australians were conducting what they termed a fighting retreat. This is how the fighting went for those first few weeks: the Japanese, with superior numbers and greater experience on their side, pursuing an opponent that was numerically inferior but had the advantage of being able to pick the best places along the Track to strike back.

In this way, the Australians offered stubborn resistance, embedding themselves in strategic positions and then picking off the enemy's advance guard. Then they would fall back along the Track, past another line of Australian troops ready to do the same job. And on and on it went, this fighting retreat which inflicted such enormous damage on the Japanese, whose tactics, by comparison, seemed one-dimensional.

Once, Nishimura's unit had some happy news when it came upon an Australian supply store. In their haste to evacuate the position, the Australians left behind tobacco, blankets, dried egg powder, biscuits and other food. Making camp, the Japanese ate their fill and replenished their supplies before heading off again in pursuit of the enemy.

The Japanese strategy was this: once forward scouts had engaged the enemy on the Track, they would try to pin the Australians down with frontal attacks and mortar shelling. Meanwhile, they would be feeling for the flanks, with a view to cutting off enemy forces from the rear in a sort of pincer movement. They were to harass the enemy with ceaseless fighting. Finally, after exhausting the Australians, they were supposed to complete the offensive thrust.

Soon, the Australians recognised their modus operandi and sent sentries out on either side of the Track to head off the flanking movement. This held up the Japanese even more. Superior numbers and an indomitable spirit were great assets, but Major General Horii was on a strict timetable and any delays now would mean the gradual debilitation of his force from starvation and disease.

Nishimura's heavy grenade launcher was proving pretty ineffective for jungle fighting. The grenades would explode on impact but, given the density of the tree canopy, that often meant it would blow away the branches, vines and jungle foliage above their heads rather than the enemy further down the Track.

When they were pinned down for any length of time and had to prepare a defensive position quickly, the Japanese would dig trenches, sometimes in an elaborate network. Unlike the rectangular Australian trenches for two men, which are still visible along the Kokoda Track today, the Japanese version tended to be circular one-man pits. Often covered by logs and branches, they were usually difficult to detect until it was too late. The Australians called them foxholes.

On 6 September, while closing in on the Australian force, Nishimura's unit crossed a creek and mounted a steep hill near Kagi. Near the peak, they saw Australian planes closing in overhead, dive-bombing from low altitude and strafing the column of troops. One after another, they attacked, pinning the Japanese to the jungle floor.

During a break in the barrage, Nishimura and his mates climbed to the peak and ran across grasslands towards the jungle, but the planes returned when they were halfway across the plain and attacked again. So open was the terrain here that the Australians were using it as a drop zone for supplies; their pilots would have had no trouble in spotting the Japanese company cringing below them.

Nishimura tried to camouflage himself by plucking out clumps of grass and sprinkling them on himself. It did little to conceal him. Another round of shellfire burst around him and the grass nearby caught fire. With one eye on the enemy planes, Nishimura tried to put out the fire which crept closer to him. Somehow he patted down the flames in between evading the air attacks. Then the planes disappeared.

Down in the Efogi valley behind Nishimura's company, the rest of the Japanese force suffered terrible casualties in the attack. Thereafter, they called the place Hell Valley.

Yet, by the time they arrived at Efogi the following day, Nishimura's 3rd Platoon still comprised forty-two men; it had managed to get through the week since Myola without suffering any more casualties.

The Japanese soldiers were urged on relentlessly by their superiors. When there was a break in the battle, there was no emotion among the troops, no exultation or despair, just men sitting trance-like, trying to rest their bones and gather their thoughts. The platoon members checked each other's health at night, and made sure they were in reasonable physical shape, but that was about the extent of their interaction. There was little joking or horse play. That had been left behind in Guam and the makeshift sumo ring in Rabaul.

Despite the exhaustion and growing mortality rates, the mood among the men was buoyant. They felt confident that the goal of taking Port Moresby was achievable. After all, the Japanese had been in New Guinea for little more than a month and had advanced two-thirds of the way from the north coast to the south, where Moresby lay. Provided supplies held up, and the casualty rates levelled off, everything pointed to a successful operation.

Then they reached the killing field of Efogi.

CHAPTER 5

Brigade Hill

FROM THE TOP OF Brigade Hill, near the village of Efogi, there are spectacular views towards Port Moresby in the distant south, Mount Victoria in the north, and into the lush valleys that unfold east and west. Under a dense canopy of tropical vegetation, the track along Mission Ridge up to Brigade Hill drops away alarmingly on each side, and walkers require a level of concentration just to negotiate the pathway without toppling off into the jungle. At the top of the ridge, the oval-shaped clearing provides one of the most beautiful panoramas on the Kokoda Track.

Australian trekkers these days visit Brigade Hill not just for the vista, but because it was the site of an horrific battle in September 1942 when, outnumbered six to one, a thousand or so Australian troops confronted and temporarily halted the Japanese Army streaming south.

The battle was notable for an audacious Japanese offensive that threw the Australian forces into chaos and led to terrible casualties on both sides.

The last thing a soldier occupying a commanding position on Brigade Hill would expect is an attack up the sides of these precipitous slopes, but that was what was in store for the Australians from Maroubra Force camped there on 8 September.

After an eleven-hour trek through thick forest flanking the base of Mission Ridge, about ninety Japanese soldiers carrying a Juki machine-gun somehow negotiated the 45-degree incline. They burst from the jungle shortly before dawn, set up their machine gun on the summit, and attacked the Australians from the south.

The Australian Army suddenly found itself sandwiched between the machine-gun on the summit and thousands of Japanese troops who were advancing along the Track from Efogi. The men of Maroubra Force faced being killed in a pincer movement, or plunging headlong into the jungle to continue their fight there.

To make matters worse, the surprise attack cut the troops off from their brigade headquarters, and the Australian command was forced to beat a retreat along the Track, back towards the village of Menari.

Nishimura participated in the offensive and, after the war, he wrote an account of the battle, based not only on his memory but on records that he brought home hidden under his shirt. At the end of the war, every Japanese soldier was ordered to destroy or burn any paperwork, records of battles, maps and instructions that might be in their possession, but Nishimura – anxious that the truth be told in honour of his dead comrades – defied the directive. He also scribbled notes when he could on his letter-writing paper and kept them hidden in his belly-band, even though he knew the punishment would be severe if he was caught with this unauthorised diary.

In his account, he called this engagement the Battle of Efogi, although history records it as the Battle of Brigade Hill. On the morning of 8 September, Nishimura's company started its advance, the men feeling their way with hands and feet in the dark, walking sideways like crabs while clinging to the side of the slippery slope about fifteen metres below the Track on Mission Ridge. The 3rd Platoon was closest to the Australian position, on the east side of the Track, in an area the Australians were almost certain to use for their withdrawal. The platoon commander, Lieutenant Inoue, was with Nishimura, his head still swathed in bandages after the friendly fire incident nine days before.

Of the four squads comprising the platoon, it was Nishimura's that took up the most dangerous position of all, where they would engage the enemy first. He and eight other members of the 4th Squad occupied foxholes in a small area the shape of a crescent, almost within arm's length of each other.

None of the soldiers knew exactly where they were; as usual, their commanders had not informed them of their precise location. But by the side of the Track, they saw a huge tree, with a trunk more than three metres in diameter, so they referred to the fight as the Battle of Ippongi, which meant 'one tree'.

The first skirmish began just before dawn. Having set up their machine-gun on Brigade Hill, the Japanese attacked the rear guard of the Australian 2/16th Battalion to the north and Brigade headquarters to the south. Bedlam ensued.

Nishimura's platoon was on high alert now, realising the Australians would soon be heading their way as they fled from the Track. Before the second phase of the battle began, at 7.10 am, Nishimura had to dig two trenches, one for himself, one for Inoue. The trenches needed to be deep enough to conceal a crouching soldier, a metre or more down into the red earth, a taxing job that left Nishimura exhausted and sweating profusely.

As the Australians attacked their position, and Nishimura's platoon returned fire, the air resounded with machine-gun fire and grenade explosions. Nishimura recalled the enemy's fire coming in a steady stream like, he said, water pouring from a shower. Amid the din, Lance Corporal Harukazu Oka, another of Kochi's warriors, said to Nishimura in a thick Tosa dialect: 'They keep appearing one after another, like *Daruma Otoshi* [a popular Japanese children's game], however many times we shoot and however many we kill. There's just no end to them.' Nishimura thought it was brave of Oka to joke in the heat of battle.

Oka was nicknamed Karl, after the German shepherd he had kept when he was involved in training army dogs. When friends in the platoon called him Karl he'd bark back at them, and a running joke developed. He was a talkative, happy personality, an ideal man to keep up the platoon's morale. Then suddenly, he fell silent. Looking back to see what had happened to his friend, Nishimura gazed upon the grisly sight of Oka's decapitated body lying nearby, his head effectively blown away by grenade shrapnel.

Oka and another soldier, Yoshiharu Inoue, a lance corporal from Tosa City in Kochi, who also died in the second attack, would be awarded posthumous promotions. In the meantime, Nishimura's platoon was down to forty men.

The headquarters of the 144th Regiment sent down a message to platoon leader Inoue: prepare for an intense assault from the enemy, who will soon be streaming your way. Then, at 8 am, somebody in the platoon shouted: 'They're coming!'

An avalanche of Australians poured out of the jungle towards the Japanese position, firing their machine-guns from the hip and spraying bullets everywhere. The entrenched

Japanese had no shortage of targets but, given the density of the foliage, had visibility of little more than ten metres. The battle was fierce, and the Japanese troops called out to each other in the mayhem, offering encouragement.

Lance Corporal Teiji Yamazaki, the oldest soldier in the platoon, with whom Nishimura had often wrestled at Rabaul, was next to die, his head blown off by a hand grenade. Then Lance Corporal Kazuaki Obata was also killed by a grenade. Obata had helped Nishimura back in the days of his military training. When Nishimura's army boots were stolen, Obata, a veteran, who slept next to Nishimura in the billet, gave Nishimura his own pair because, he said, he had a spare pair.

It turned out that Obata's new boots belonged to the staff sergeant, who belted Obata in the face with them, the force of the blow knocking him to the ground. Nishimura was about to step forward to explain that it was he who should be punished when Obata stopped him in his tracks with a stern look. The staff sergeant continued to beat Obata severely, while Nishimura looked on helplessly, feeling an acute sense of guilt.

Obata had protected him because he knew that Nishimura, as a new recruit, would have been more severely punished and his chances of immediate promotion to first-class private severely reduced. 'How could I ever forget about Obata, who was so kind to me?' Nishimura wrote in his account of the battle.

There were many more casualties to come. Nishimura's first grenade loader, Private Zenzaburo Ushimado, was shot through the right shoulder, the bullet passing down to his waist, as he leant out of a trench to fire his gun. He was killed instantly. While Ushimado had never become a close friend, he and Nishimura had been forced to spend a great deal of time together in training and battle, and Nishimura felt an acute sense of loss. Now the folk song that Ushimado used to sing over and over would become stuck in Nishimura's head, haunting him from the grave.

At 10.05 am, Corporal Kazuaki Ike, who was leading the 3rd Squad, was hit in the chest by a bullet, and died. Fifteen minutes later, Corporal Hitomi Tanaka, the leader of Nishimura's 4th Squad, was fatally wounded in the head. Although he had been one year younger than Nishimura, Tanaka was a strict disciplinarian, a great soldier, and generally considered the finest squad leader in the 5th Company.

It was he who stayed right on Nishimura's shoulder, only half a dozen steps behind, when the young corporal was given the thankless task of leading his company, alone, into Rabaul. And Tanaka had always been supportive of Nishimura during his training, realising the potential he had and pushing him forward for jobs above his rank. Now, ironically, in Tanaka's absence, Nishimura was promoted to the position of temporary squad leader.

In the third wave of battle against the Australians, a further twenty-five troops from the 3rd Platoon – almost half the original unit – were killed. Nishimura was now left with just fourteen comrades. But there was no complaining or cowardice. Their training had served them well. Nishimura wrote in his diary: 'All remaining soldiers accepted their fate and we tried to defend the current position to the best of our ability.'

Apprehensive about the next Australian offensive, Nishimura and his men dug new trenches. None of them had eaten since before dawn, and it was now after 2 pm. Then the fourth wave of the attack began. The enemy opened fire at close range; before long a swarm of Australians were all over the Japanese positions, and hand-to-hand fighting broke out.

Nishimura crouched in a trench alongside Lieutenant Inoue. The platoon commander had exhausted the magazine on his gun, and asked Nishimura to hand over another rifle. Just as Inoue leaned forward on his elbows and prepared to take a shot out of the trench, he was hit by a barrage of enemy bullets and killed instantly.

Stunned, Nishimura looked at his fallen comrade and platoon leader, momentarily unable to move. Then, pulling himself together, he tried to retrieve the rifle from Inoue's grip, but couldn't prise it loose. He jumped back into the trench empty-handed, panic spreading through his body and clouding his thinking.

Now he had to find a way to recover his commander's body. With the fighting continuing all around him, Nishimura crawled out of the trench, watching the enemy all the while, and grabbed Inoue's right ankle. As Nishimura slowly dragged him back to safety, Inoue's legs started to spread apart and he became snagged on the root of a bush.

In desperation, Nishimura abandoned caution and crawled further out into no-man's land. He took hold of Inoue's right wrist, which was stretched out above his head. Then he stood up and raced back to the trench, dragging his commander's body behind him.

In this fourth attack, seven of Nishimura's comrades died, so the platoon was left with just seven fit men. Everyone in the senior ranks had been killed, and it was left to Nishimura to lead the remnants of the platoon. He immediately dispatched his friend and second grenade loader, Private Kubo, to 5th Company headquarters, to report the dire situation and ask what to do with Lieutenant Inoue's body.

Kubo arrived back shortly with Yoshiaki Yamamoto, a lance corporal in the medical unit. Nishimura and Yamamoto examined Inoue's body and took off his clothes. They found four bullet wounds: one in the head, two in the torso and one in the arm. Yamamoto carefully cleaned the wounds, applied new bandages to them, and then dressed Inoue. Nishimura could not believe the bravery of the medic who did all this while kneeling, in grave danger of being picked off by the enemy.

Yamamoto left, after entrusting Inoue's body to Nishimura. Without realising it, Nishimura bowed to him. For all his boldness, the medic had been calm and polite while carrying out his duties. To Nishimura, he embodied the virtues of the noble warrior; perhaps it was soldiers such as Yamamoto who should be regarded as the true heroes of the war.

Nishimura set about trying to bury his commander, a difficult job given the enemy activity and the needs of his depleted unit. Trying to stay as low as he could in the makeshift trench, Nishimura began digging a shallow grave for Inoue. Yet he knew the enemy would have been able to see him and wondered why they didn't shoot him then and there. It was only after the war that Nishimura learnt that Australian soldiers often refrained from attacking unarmed enemy soldiers known to be engaged in recovering or burying an officer's body.

AT 4.15 PM, THE AUSTRALIANS launched another attack – the fifth of the day. It lasted about an hour, with bullets splattering into the mud only centimetres above Nishimura's head. He silently gave thanks to Inoue: if it were not for his commander's death he wouldn't have dug such a deep hole, and would surely be dead himself by now.

After a lull in the shooting, Nishimura put his head over the parapet and could see not one soldier who had escaped injury or death. In the trench to his left, Private Kubo had been shot in the shoulder and waist, and was crying for help.

Nishimura leant out of his trench towards his friend, but, at that moment, he saw an Australian soldier rushing towards him. Before he could get to his feet, Nishimura felt the Australian put a machine-gun to his helmet and fire.

He should have been killed instantly. But the barrel of the gun somehow glanced off Nishimura's helmet and three bullets ripped into his right shoulder instead. His helmet was broken during the incident and left dangling from his neck.

Seeing the Australian run back into the jungle, Nishimura gave chase and caught him after fifteen or twenty metres. Nishimura's wounded arm was useless, but he withdrew his sword with his left arm and thrust it at the Australian's chest; it hit a rib and stopped. The Australian grabbed the sword's blade with his bare hands and kicked Nishimura in the stomach. The Japanese fell on his back and the sword went flying.

Noticing his enemy's face up close, Nishimura was struck by how young the Australian was. He was considerably taller and heavier than Nishimura but looked as fresh-faced as a teenager. For a moment, he thought: Why am I fighting this boy whom I don't even know? But in the next instant he realised he would be killed himself if he didn't get to his feet and tackle the Australian.

Nishimura launched himself again at the bigger man. Somehow, in the ensuing struggle, he regained his sword from the ground and this time drove it into the Australian's stomach. The soldier pierced the air with a wail that sounded like an air-raid siren as he fell down, and slipped into unconsciousness. It was a chilling scream that Nishimura never forgot.

Feeling dizzy and weak, Nishimura too collapsed. He did not have the strength even to sit up. As he lay there, he watched the Australian, who had fallen onto a small bush metres away. Every time the Australian looked like trying to heave himself to his feet, Nishimura also tried to sit up and brace himself for another fight to the death. Soon, though, as darkness descended on them, Nishimura was overcome by fatigue and fell asleep on the ground.

Next morning, he looked across. His opponent was spread-eagled on the jungle floor: death had finally come to him in the night.

Nishimura was never one to feel pity, certainly not towards enemy soldiers, but as he looked at the dead Australian he could not help but think: By the good grace of some divine force, I am here alive and he is there, dead. Where is the good sense in being involved in a war that metes out justice in this totally arbitrary way? Why did I have to kill this young man who has a family just as I have?

Given that Nishimura's platoon had been almost obliterated, there was no one with whom to share these thoughts.

He discovered a short time later that another of his friends, Itahara, had died while trying to protect Nishimura from enemy fire as he leant out of his trench and began to help Kubo. Itahara stood up and began firing at the Australians with little thought for his own safety, and a bullet pierced him through the torso, killing him almost instantly.

Nishimura, whose own wounds were now extremely painful, fell into a sort of reverie, in which he recalled happier days with Itahara. They had joined the army on the same day as recruits and developed a strong camaraderie. Together, they withstood the battering from senior officers during their training. If they tried to defend themselves, they were only beaten harder.

Together, he and Itahara had encouraged and looked after each other, and were able to withstand their ordeal. The furnace of army training had forged an unbreakable friendship.

Unlike Watanabe and Kubo, Itahara was a serious young man who had little time for frivolity and jokes. He and Nishimura were separated after their training because Itahara was a light machine-gunner and Nishimura a grenadier. But they often met up in one of the study rooms at Asakura after evening roll call and studied together, Itahara because he wanted to be a non-commissioned officer; Nishimura because he wanted to get a better understanding of the Imperial Japanese Army's military structure and history.

But now Itahara, too, was gone, killed as he tried to protect his friend.

Four Japanese soldiers had died in this fifth attack, and now there were just three of his platoon left – Nishimura, Kubo and Lance Corporal Masao Nakahira. All of them were badly wounded.

Nishimura collected the dying Kubo from his trench and, after a creeping search, came across Nakahira, who had been wailing in pain all night. The three of them waited together for contact from army headquarters.

Kubo had been with Nishimura through thick and thin, and they had shared some good times. Nishimura could never forget the look of joy on his friend's face when, only months earlier when they had just arrived in Guam, Kubo received a letter from his wife and found that she had safely delivered their first baby. She had been six months' pregnant when her husband left Japan for the South Seas. In the letter, she included a photograph of the child. What made Kubo even happier was his wife's decision to give the baby the name he had chosen.

Now he was dying, too, having been shot twice in the shoulder and once in the hip. And at 10.25 am, muttering 'Help me, help me' until the very end, Kubo passed away. He would never fulfil his promise to the village chief in Guam to visit after the war. He would never practise his English again and never again play a practical joke on Nishimura. Nor would he ever get to see his first-born.

Nishimura turned to consoling Nakahira as best as he could.

He could hear groaning in the distance but did not have the strength to investigate. He spent the night tending his comrade and listening to the deathly moans of other platoon members in the jungle.

The new day dawned, the third without food or water. Nishimura was on the verge of collapse; his eyes would not focus, his eyelids felt peculiarly heavy and his wounds strangely numb. So this is what dying feels like, he thought. He couldn't tell whether it was morning or afternoon. He had been sleeping in the hollowed-out stump of a tree. Then he heard a voice ask: 'Hey, Nishimura, are you all right?'

He strained his eyes to see where the voice had come from, and recognised the face of Captain Naoma Fujisaki, a machine-gunner from another company whom he barely knew. Fujisaki had been given the nickname of Onigawara, or Devil Face, that much Nishimura knew, but he was totally confused as to how the captain of a different unit recognised such a low-ranking soldier as himself.

Unable to get up, Nishimura reported the battle situation since 8 September and asked Fujisaki to rescue any wounded soldiers, a task the captain undertook with dispatch, ordering his subordinates to conduct a thorough search of the area and collect the injured.

After a two-hour search, they found Private Toshimasu Okayama and Private Hisami Iyota, both badly wounded but still alive. They prepared four stretchers for Okayama, Iyota, Nishimura and Nakahira. Fujisaki approached Nishimura before he was taken away to the field hospital and asked which platoon had been involved in the battle. Nishimura said the 3rd Platoon of the 5th Company. 'There were more than five hundred dead enemy bodies left in this area. You have done a good job,' Fujisaki said.

History would show this figure to have been inflated – the

actual number of Australians dead was closer to one hundred – but the littering of bodies around the Track was testament to the viciousness of the fighting, some of the bloodiest in the Pacific War.

NISHIMURA'S SHOULDER BARELY HURT when he was first shot, but the pain grew steadily worse over the following days. When the doctor in the field hospital began to move his arm up and down to gauge his range of movement, Nishimura nearly yelled the roof off the makeshift building.

Lying in bed one day, he could feel a small lump on his back and asked the doctor to have a look at it. The doctor soon discovered a second bullet just under the skin and with a flick of his scalpel, removed it into a metal tray. The medic told Nishimura he could now see two entry wounds and two exit wounds. So the prognosis was good: he should be fine in no time. There was no sign of another entry wound, which meant that a third bullet that had lodged deep inside him near his lungs would remain undetected for almost forty years.

The medics believed that after a few days' rest and rehabilitation, he would be fit enough to rejoin the fray. As Nishimura lay recuperating in his hospital bed, Okayama, Iyota and Nakahira, one by one, all passed away.

At the beginning of the Kokoda campaign, there had been fifty-six Kochi warriors. Now, fifteen days later, fifty-five of them had been killed by the Australian Army in skirmishes and battles along the Track, with only the wiry, durable and inestimably lucky Nishimura surviving the annihilation.

Brigade Hill was a key battle, not just in terms of Japan's plans to capture Port Moresby but in shaping the rest of Nishimura's life. For 8 September 1942, the day forty-one members of his platoon were wiped out or critically wounded, became a date that defined his destiny.

The engagement dented the morale of both sides. Back in Port Moresby, the Australian commander, Lieutenant-General Sydney Rowell, cursed the conflict, saying 8 September was the blackest day he had endured since the New Guinea campaign had started.

The battle, which had raged for three days, delayed but did not halt the Japanese march south. While Nishimura lay, barely alive, in the hollow of a tree stump the Japanese captured Menari, after the smoke from an Australian cooking fire was spotted. Having clearly established the enemy position, the Japanese rained down artillery and mortar shells on the Australians while they were eating. Once again caught by surprise, the Australians fled from their position further south.

The next village along the Track, Mawai, was taken by the Japanese on 11 September.

And then they streamed towards Ioribaiwa where the Australians had dug themselves in and were prepared for a long and bloody battle. The Japanese were only forty-five kilometres from Port Moresby now, far too close for comfort for any of the Australian soldiers on the ground in New Guinea, let alone the Allied commanders, General Thomas Blamey and General Douglas MacArthur, back in Brisbane.

A fierce battle lasted four days, in which the Japanese were fired on from ridges and the high ground, and hand grenades were hurled at them by the hundred. Eventually, though, after a severe pounding from the Japanese mountain guns and artillery, the Australian resistance was broken and the ridge fell at 4 pm on 16 September. Now the Japanese were within a day's unimpeded walk of their goal.

As the Japanese troops up the Track ahead of Nishimura looked from Ioribaiwa ridge across to the lights of Port

Moresby in the distance, a company clerk by the name of Nakahashi, from the 55th Mountain Artillery, wrote of the soldiers' joy at seeing for the first time a city that was beginning to take on mythical proportions in their heads. Port Moresby really did exist and it was just over there, on the horizon:

> Gazing out from the summit in a southerly direction, there was not even one mountain to obstruct our range of vision. A dense, overgrown sea of forest, rising and falling like ripples on the water and, far off one was able to see – as the sun's rays came through a break in the clouds, a glitter and a sparkle – without doubt it was the sea! Over there was Moresby, the object of our invasion, which had become like an obsession.
>
> Officers and men alike embraced one another, overcome by emotion. During the battles so far, the South Seas Force had, to date, suffered one thousand dead and wounded. The line of captured positions more than atones for their blood, even if they will never be able to gaze upon this splendid spectacle.

But, while the soldiers could almost smell victory, the scene was quite different in Major General Horii's tent, as he pored over battle plans by candlelight. He knew by now his worst fears had been realised; his troops were starving and the supply lines from Rabaul could not match the Nankai Shitai's ambitious timetable. Horii, who had set out with more than 10,000 fighting troops, had lost nearly half of his men – many more than Nakahashi had estimated – in the three-week slog over the mountains and the daily rice ration was severely limited. Something had to give.

For Nishimura and the Imperial Japanese Army, this was to be the end of the road.

CHAPTER 6

Retreat

THERE WAS NO WORD in the Japanese lexicon for 'retreat'. It simply didn't exist. When an army representing the Emperor and fighting beneath the Rising Sun standard went into action, it did so in one gear: forward. Never had there been an occasion for Japanese officers to issue an order to withdraw.

So when Major-General Horii, on 25 September 1942, reluctantly carried out the orders from his commanders in Rabaul and announced to his shocked troops that they were to retreat, it translated as something different: We're changing marching direction or we're advancing to the rear.

Among the 5000 or so men of the Nankai Shitai still alive, there was frustration and dismay. Some of the troops pointed their mountain battery at Port Moresby, set it at maximum distance, and fired several rounds as a farewell salvo. 'This at least gave an uplift to our downcast spirits and to those of our dead comrades,' the company clerk, Nakahashi, noted in his diary.

The decision was completely unexpected, and brought about an overflowing feeling of emotion which could not be suppressed, he reflected later. 'It was compounded by feelings of anger, sorrow and frustration,' wrote Nakahashi. 'The purpose, the dreams and the desires of the officers and soldiers of the South Seas Force had vanished in an instant.'

Nishimura was especially horrified at the order to retreat. Having made so many sacrifices, witnessed such carnage and lost so many friends, he felt incensed. The men could see the lights of Port Moresby from Ioribaiwa Ridge. Yet, within striking distance of their goal, they had been told to pull back. For Nishimura and the rest of the Kochi warriors, these orders ran counter to everything they had been taught in training.

Yet the situation on the ground was more grim than the troops could ever have known. While Australian forces had delayed the Japanese advance with a clever fighting retreat, American and Australian aircraft had inflicted serious damage on their troops and supply lines. The Japanese had exceeded the limits of their logistical support. By now daily rations had been reduced to two cups, or roughly 300 grams, of rice which was barely enough to keep office-bound men sustained, let alone soldiers engaged in action, or on the march, for twelve and fourteen hours a day.

The soldiers were not just starving; they were also wracked by disease such as malaria and dysentery. And the Japanese defence of Guadalcanal in the Solomon Islands was in desperate trouble as the Americans landed barge-loads of troops ashore. The Japanese occupying force there needed to be reinforced with troops from New Guinea.

Even if Horii had been allowed to press on to Port Moresby, against a heavily fortified and entrenched enemy it would have surely proved a fruitless and suicidal move.

So at 5 pm on 26 September, the Imperial Japanese Army abandoned its position at Ioribaiwa and began to retrace its hard-won steps all the way back across the Owen Stanleys.

Nishimura had been carried to Ioribaiwa on a stretcher, his bullet wounds cleaned and dressed but his right shoulder still causing him a lot of pain. He had travelled there with Captain Fujisaki, the man who had rescued him from the tree stump at Efogi on 14 September. He had expected to be fit enough to join the Nankai Shitai's final thrust into Port Moresby. But there would now be no triumphant final thrust, just a miserable retreat.

By now, fortunately, Nishimura was well enough to walk, and this certainly saved his life. His shoulder and right arm had not yet regained much movement. But what would count against him in the coming weeks and months was not his injuries, but something far more serious: as the lone survivor of his platoon, he became an outcast in his own army.

Down the Track the Japanese straggled, past Nauro village, Menari and back through Efogi and Myola once more, Nishimura seeing and making a mental note of Japanese gravesites as he went. No units had been officially assigned to burial duties; the work had simply been done by available men during breaks in the fighting. So the graves all looked different. Some were marked with stones, others with simple stakes. Occasionally, white sapling markers indicated burials; at one mass grave site at Brigade Hill, a single wooden stake was adorned with Japanese characters.

While Nishimura was off his stretcher and marching with his colleagues, his right arm in a sling, those more incapacitated were suffering a double torment. Not only did they have to bear the agony of their wounds, but they could see the strain they were placing on the stretcher-bearers, who were often in a terrible state themselves.

The thought of being such a burden to their comrades was too much for some. Nakahashi's account records the wounded crying out: 'Please leave us here. Let us die.' But the group continued to struggle on until, eventually, the officers were left with no choice; if they carried on this way then the stretcher-bearers would die as well as the wounded. A sacrifice would have to be made. 'The matter was settled. Before long, rifle shots reverberated throughout the jungle,' Nakahashi wrote in his diary.

Walking at the tail end of the column, Nishimura could see clearly the deplorable state to which the 144th Regiment was reduced. He had to look twice at some men to convince himself they were the same soldiers who set out with him from Ogasawara Islands a year earlier. They walked slowly, oh so slowly, some of them in bare feet after their boots had worn out, putting one foot in front of another, and trying not to think about the pain of their wounds, the aching joints from their illnesses, and the weakness brought on by their hunger. 'It seemed as though we had been transported to hell,' wrote Nakahashi in his diary. 'Who could ever have imagined the Japanese Army being in such a shape? Certainly not their families and especially their mothers.'

Malaria, dengue fever, scrub typhus, and bacillary and amoebic dysentery were endemic. Malaria brought high fever, drenching sweats and uncontrollable chill tremors. Dengue fever, another mosquito-borne disease, afflicted sufferers with throbbing joint pain. The much-feared scrub typhus could kill a man in a few hours. And most soldiers had some form of bowel disorder, ranging from mild diarrhoea to fully-fledged dysentery, which reduced its victims to a squirting, trouserless mess.

Lesser ailments – such as jungle rot, dhobie itch, athlete's foot, and ringworm – were almost as prevalent. Beriberi, which often accompanies malnutrition, was rife, inducing fatigue, poor reflexes, memory loss and irritability. Night blindness, a result of vitamin A deficiency, and the age-old problem of scurvy, meant the Japanese Army was stumbling along in a debilitated, almost hallucinogenic, daze.

The regiment, emaciated and exhausted, set up camp at Waju – or the village known to the Japanese as Baribe – on 3 November. It had taken more than a month of walking to cover the ninety or so kilometres from Ioribaiwa to Waju. The 2nd and 3rd Battalions were based here, as was the regimental headquarters. The Japanese had just enough time to dig themselves in before the advancing Australians came upon the position, and those nearby at the villages of Oivi and Gorari, two days later.

One of the bloodiest skirmishes since the start of the Japanese retreat then ensued. The Australians decided on a wide, encircling sweep – which developed into a textbook pincer movement – that resulted in heavy fighting over four days from 9 November, and the deaths of at least 600 Japanese soldiers. Here, much of the remainder of the 144th Regiment was wiped out. The survivors buried them close to where they had fallen.

On 11 November, Nishimura was ordered to evacuate Baribe amid the fighting, and to head east towards the beach. But this was where his troubles really began. Nishimura was assigned to the 2nd Platoon of the 5th Company, but, in that dire situation where food was scarce and every grain of rice needed to survive, his new unit abandoned Nishimura, leaving him to fend for himself.

The much-vaunted discipline of the Imperial Japanese Army had begun to fray and Nishimura was simply cut adrift.

In the chaos of the withdrawal and without the support of his mates, Nishimura somehow became separated from the main body of troops heading east. He wandered alone in the jungle, lost, and fearful he would at any minute run into Australian forces. For six nights, from 12 to 17 November, he slept on the jungle floor, the bitter cold at night now joining acute starvation on his growing list of discomforts.

After a week of living off the land, the bedraggled soldier stumbled into a tiny village called Mumuni, in Kokoda province, where he ran headlong into the village chief and his wife. Nishimura stopped in his tracks, not knowing whether they would attack him in retribution for the appalling crimes the Japanese had committed against the local people.

Before they reached New Guinea, Japan's soldiers had been told to treat the Papuan villagers well: part of their mission in the Pacific was the liberation of East Asia from white supremacy. In reality, though, the Japanese often treated the Papuan natives very badly. They were press-ganged into working as carriers and stretcher-bearers, sometimes at the point of a bayonet, and often given intolerable loads. They were also ordered to perform the physically punishing work of cutting sago and building roads. Their rations were considerably less than those of the Japanese soldiers, often even less than half, though the work they were asked to do was taxing in the extreme.

Those who tried to run away were punished; collaborators were executed.

Later, when Japanese supply lines were cut, starvation was rife and the death toll was mounting, some Japanese began plundering plantations and stripping villages of every last scrap of food. So they had made more than their share of enemies.

Fortunately for Nishimura, the chief, whose name was Paheki Hojava, and his wife, Tomarako, were more welcoming than he could ever have imagined, and they ushered him into the village. Many years later, Paheki's grandson, John Hojava, a councillor in Oro province, recalled the incident:

> My grandpa, Paheki, told me that both parties were shocked during their encounter. Nishimura just froze a couple of metres away from the couple when they first sighted each other. He was scared that the couple might kill him because the Japanese soldiers in the advance party had killed people, raped women and destroyed food goods along the Kokoda Track on their way to Port Moresby.

Using sign language, Nishimura managed to convey that he was starving. Tomarako roasted a huge taro over the fire and gave it to Nishimura.

Paheki tried to convince Nishimura to stay the night in their village where he would be protected. The Japanese soldier bowed and thanked him, but refused the invitation, saying he needed to catch up with the rest of his fellow troops fleeing to the east. So, after gorging himself on whatever food he was given, Nishimura set off that night, accompanied by Paheki. When they reached the main track, Paheki pointed out directions to the coast and wished Nishimura well.

THE GOAL OF THE retreating Japanese was the coastal towns of Giruwa, Gona and Buna, close to where the Nankai Shitai's advance party had landed four months earlier. When Nishimura finally arrived at Giruwa a couple of days later, he found that the 2nd Platoon had already secured part of the village around the beach. As he staggered into their midst, one of the platoon leaders looked up, and with a hint almost of disappointment in his voice, said: 'Oh, you are still alive.' Nishimura was assigned the most dangerous sentry post on the perimeter of the village, right where the enemy would first attack, and was told to hold the position.

Here he stayed on duty for hours, carrying out his orders, until he was eventually relieved by another member of the platoon. Nishimura went back to company headquarters to report for duty and try to obtain food. But an officer told him curtly that they had nothing to give him. He was sent back to the front line without food, water or sustenance of any form. Now Nishimura realised he was totally on his own.

All along the coast, from Gona to Sanananda, and south to Giruwa and Buna, the Japanese had dug in along the northern beaches, in a series of foxholes, pillboxes, trenches and heavily fortified bunkers. For months, the Japanese Army had been landing fresh troops ashore to entrench this final line of defence.

There, from 19 November until his evacuation on 12 January, Nishimura eked out a terrible existence. The nest of elaborately constructed pillboxes and bunkers were hidden among the coconut plantations and clumps of kunai grass, beyond the steaming sago swamps and delta of criss-crossing streams. Behind the Japanese was the Solomon Sea; in front, marching towards them up the Kokoda Track, were the Allied forces. Nishimura and his fellow troops had nowhere to go, nothing to eat. Outnumbered and outflanked, they were held captive in their own bunkers, their supply lines cut and their troops in advanced stages of malnutrition.

To add to their discomfort, the Japanese troops were soaked to the bone. Nishimura spent much of his time pinned down by enemy fire in a foxhole filled with rainwater. This was the wet season and most nights it rained. Every few days, it *really* rained, 150 or 200 millimetres teeming down in giant drops. Nishimura had found himself in a place so squalid he thought he had arrived at the ends of the earth.

The cloying tropical humidity incubated a rich array of diseases. But for all the discomfort and disease that surrounded him, what occupied Nishimura's mind was more elemental – the need to fill his stomach. When he was called up to the army eighteen months earlier, he was a healthy seventy-three kilograms. He could hold his own against heavier colleagues in sumo practice and was strong enough to run twelve kilometres in full kit in barely an hour.

By the end of the Giruwa debacle, Nishimura weighed thirty kilograms and barely had the strength to walk. His mother would have had to look hard at him to recognise the gaunt, skeletal figure as her son who had left Tokyo little over a year before.

In addition to the half-cups of rice he was occasionally able to scrounge, Nishimura was reduced to picking tiny seedlings out of the mire and eating them. Finally, in desperation, he and his comrades resorted to unthinkable measures in order to stay alive.

The battle for Sanananda, Giruwa and surrounding areas lasted ten weeks, until the middle of January. A fitter, stronger, better-equipped force, impatient for victory, came up against an embedded foe committed to fighting to the death. It was siege warfare of the most punishing kind. All day long, the Australians and Americans kept up their gun-fire and artillery bombardments. Against 2186 Allied soldiers killed or wounded, there were 1600 Japanese deaths and at least as many wounded.

At the Japanese field hospital at Giruwa there had been no medicine for over a month, the wards were under water, and nearly all the medical personnel were either dead or sick or injured. The extreme humidity and heavy rains had caused clothes, bedding and medical equipment to mould, rot or rust away. Timber beds, with patients in them, began to float away. At ground level, dead bodies were floating everywhere.

With the Japanese resistance about to be overrun, the Japanese command had to decide whether to stay and defend the beaches until the enemy swarmed all over their positions, or to cut their losses and make a strategic evacuation. Nishimura remembered that the US Air Force dropped leaflets on their position, reading: 'Give up, because if you don't we will capture you and kill you. If you surrender, you will survive.'

IN JAPAN, SCORN WAS traditionally heaped upon defeated soldiers who didn't fall on their swords. The concept of *bushido*, or the way of the warrior, was still a fundamental code, not merely among imperial soldiers but for many Japanese civilians as well. Despite this, Nishimura's commander at Giruwa, Colonel Hatsuo Tsukamoto, took the unusual step of ordering the withdrawal of his men. He saved his troops' lives but was later publicly derided in Japan.

Nishimura faced a personal dilemma: to obey his superiors and abandon his position, or to stay loyal to his Kochi warrior roots and, in the spirit of *Tosa-jin Kishitsu*, fight until death. But it was a dilemma that did not take long to resolve: in the army, there was no room for personal choice. An order was an order. And it was on 12 January, the day the rice ration finally ran out, that Nishimura was ordered to join the evacuation.

He still finds it difficult to put images of the evacuation out of his mind. Tsukamoto told each officer it was up to them how they dealt with their injured and sick men. Nishimura was horrified that some officers chose to say nothing to the soldiers they had to leave behind. Perhaps because of the ignominy or the guilt they felt, they just took their fittest men and left the rest to fend for themselves, without a word of explanation or apology.

Nishimura could never be so callous. He told his comrades

that he and others in the company were going into the enemy position to get some food to eat. But he promised he would be back to collect them, so as to leave them with a little hope. He remembers the words he used that day: *If you die here, we will collect your bones and bring them back to your families in Japan.* That was the pact he made.

For many Japanese soldiers, this was the most traumatic time of the Kokoda campaign. The stretcher cases or those too weak to walk were abandoned where they lay. Some committed suicide, or were shot on their stretchers by obliging comrades. In some cases, the severely wounded who barely had the strength to lift a revolver were given hand grenades. Pulling a pin was not so taxing.

Nishimura's sergeant told the fittest of the company's wounded: 'We want you to protect this position. We'll leave some machine-guns and ammunition.' The 200 or so injured and sick would soon be surrounded by both American and Australian troops: Nishimura imagined that within two or three days the last vestiges of the Nankai Shitai would be wiped out. But after a further ten days' fighting, more than one hundred remained alive, still defending their position. Finally they were captured, or committed suicide.

In his account, *Battle of Efogi*, Nishimura praised these men who stayed and fought on at Giruwa, protecting those comrades who had abandoned them:

Despite their most remarkable sacrifice, the remains of those who helped us survive were rotten, weather beaten and turning to dust. Those admirable youth, healthy in body and spirit, who haven't done anything wrong – why did they have to endure such miseries? Those wounded soldiers barricaded themselves in and kept fighting. Only their persistence and courage enabled us to escape, and survive. Without them, we all would have died. I could not thank them enough for what they had done.

Two Japanese boats came to shore to evacuate some survivors to Rabaul under the cover of night. The rest of the troops, including Nishimura, who couldn't squeeze on board, had to find their own way to the Kumusi River, some thirty kilometres north-west.

As they left in dribs and drabs, Nishimura was dismayed to hear some of his comrades' conversations. Some men told each other it wasn't their fault the other soldiers had been injured or stricken with disease and had to be left behind. They told each other there was nothing that could be done about those men now. Yes, they'd promised to go back and collect the wounded and maimed, but that was just to ease their torment.

Nishimura did not understand how they could so lightly dismiss their responsibilities. Didn't their word count for anything? He had promised his friends and comrades from the 144th that he would be back, and as he looked over his shoulder at the pitiful scene for the final time, he resolved to keep his word.

Protected by the darkness, and wading shoulder-deep in the sea, Nishimura slowly made his way past the Allied lines and headed north-west towards the Kumusi River. He had noticed some of the Australian positions in the jungle near the beach, and decided it was safest to do most of his walking at night. He was careful not to rush, or make sudden movements, because the swarms of insects that invariably followed him would start flying around in a panic and alert the Australian soldiers.

So he walked slowly, and in the absence of any of his old comrades, he walked by himself. He had been told to get to the mouth of the Kumusi River by the last week in January; that's where the boats would be for the evacuation.

Having finally reached their destination, Nishimura and the ragged crew of survivors boarded eight boats of the Ukai Company, which had been charged with carrying out the evacuation. The fleet slowly made its way north-west but sailed only at night and without lights to avoid attack; every day, the troops sought refuge in the jungle. Still, they came under fire from Allied warplanes. Their boats were badly damaged by strafing and it was not until early April, two months after setting out, that they finally reached the relative safety of Lae, 250 kilometres away, which was a Japanese stronghold until September.

The Imperial Rescript that had been handed to Nishimura and all those who served in the South Seas Detachment in 1941 was quite clear in setting out how each soldier should conduct himself. Issued originally by Emperor Meiji in 1882, it emphasised the obligations of each man who fought under the standard of the Rising Sun.

Five articles in the rescript concerned the qualities of the soul of Japanese soldiers and sailors. These were: loyalty, propriety, valour, faithfulness and righteousness, and simplicity. In expanding on the first article, the rescript said: 'The soldier and sailor should consider loyalty their essential duty and bear in mind that duty is weightier than a mountain while death is lighter than a feather.' Of the fourth article, the rescript spoke no less ambiguously: 'Being faithful and righteous implics keeping one's word and fulfilling one's duty.'

So that was settled then. Nishimura knew exactly what was expected of him. The task of carrying out his duty could well prove weightier than a mountain; but, for Nishimura, it was a burden he'd have to bear. He'd given his word to his fallen comrades and that was the end of the matter: he would be coming back to New Guinea to keep his promise, and to find his friends.

CHAPTER 7

White pork, black pork

IT COUNTS AMONG CIVILISED society's greatest taboos, but the eating of human flesh was so commonplace on the north coast of New Guinea during those three miserable months either side of Christmas 1942 that emaciated Japanese soldiers took to referring to the flesh of Australians and Americans as 'white pork', and the flesh of Papuan carriers as 'black pork', as though they were doing nothing more unusual than reading from a restaurant menu.

There have been other infamous instances of cannibalism in modern history. In 1884, British society was scandalised (and, no doubt, titillated) by the case of the *Mignonette*, a yacht bound from Southampton for Sydney, which sank near the Cape of Good Hope. Its crew took to the lifeboat, and for twenty days survived on tinned turnips. After a further nine days without food or water, the senior crew killed and ate the cabin boy. The captain and a crewman were later found guilty of murder in a highly publicised trial.

Perhaps the best-known recent case of cannibalism concerned a Uruguayan Air Force plane that crashed into the Andes mountains in October 1972. It was carrying a team from a Uruguayan rugby club: of the forty-five passengers, only sixteen survived until they were rescued, after eleven weeks in snow and bitterly inhospitable weather. They did this by eating the flesh of the passengers who had already perished. The survivors, who later published their story, said that they first tried the flesh raw, but found that cooking it briefly made it much more palatable: 'The slight browning of the flesh gave it an immeasurably better flavour, softer than beef but with much the same taste.'

But in terms of widespread practice of cannibalism, few events could surpass the events of those final weeks of Japan's war along the New Guinea coast, from Gona to Sanananda, Giruwa and Buna.

Nishimura said later that only those Japanese soldiers who put aside their revulsion at the thought of eating another human would have escaped from the northern beaches with their lives. *No one who was at Giruwa could have survived that siege without eating human flesh, and that was the truth of it. Nobody wanted to do it, but that was their last resort. It was eat, or die.*

At the end of September 1942, Japanese Army rations had been meagre but acceptable. The standard daily ration, almost 800 grams of rice and some tinned meat, had fallen to 300 grams. By late December, it was down to about 50 grams, or half a cup of rice per day. By 12 January, their rations had disappeared altogether.

Some diaries kept by Japanese soldiers at Giruwa record the scrounging of shellfish and coconuts. 'After boiling the shellfish, you had to cut them out of the shell and this made a noise as the knife hit the shell. The enemy sometimes heard this and fired at us, so we had to be very careful,' one officer said. This man, Sadashige Imanishi, remembered using his bayonet to stab a long swordfish that must have been ill or injured and swam too close to shore. The ensuing feast delighted his men.

Another soldier wrote of catching and eating snakes and raw crabs. A third spoke of his company's few remaining horses gradually being butchered for meat. When they had exhausted these supplies, the Japanese turned to roots and bark and, finally and perhaps inevitably, to human flesh.

The killing field in front of their well-camouflaged bunkers provided them with the raw ingredient required; but, according to Nishimura, the practice of cannibalism evolved almost by accident. When American and Australian soldiers unwittingly walked near their position, the Japanese would wait until they came to within four or five metres and then shoot them, Nishimura said. After a couple of days in the sun, the corpses would begin to smell, so Japanese soldiers would have to crawl out of their foxholes and open up the belly of the enemy soldiers and take out the guts and bury them.

That was how the cannibalism started. Someone took out the liver and ate it raw. Then others did it, including Nishimura. He and the others were surprised that it didn't really taste so bad: Like calves' liver, really, he said. Liver was liver. Other soldiers tried the kidneys and brains and organs like that, but it was very hard to crack open a skull, Nishimura said. A lot of the flesh was very tough, and the men's stomachs at that stage were very weak, so they could eat only soft, tender meat, little by little.

A short distance away, Imanishi's situation was slightly less grim, but only slightly. He had seen one of his soldiers carrying the arm of a dead Australian forward scout, and ordered him to throw it away. It was only when his company began the evacuation west towards the Kumusi River that Imanishi himself resorted to cannibalism. The company had crossed the Kumusi on the way back to Lae. The men stopped at a village where some other Japanese soldiers had earlier killed five local villagers and buried their bodies. Starvation drove some in Imanishi's unit to dig up the bodies, cook them and eat them.

Imanishi was very ill at the time, with vomiting and diarrhoea. One of his soldiers cooked up the liver of one of the slain villagers and brought it to him to eat. He told Imanishi: Don't eat the flesh, just suck the juice. But Imanishi ate a small piece of the liver and sucked the juice, just to stay alive.

SIGNS THAT CANNIBALISM HAD occurred on a large scale were obvious when, in late January, Australian and American soldiers began to occupy the Japanese defences vacated by fleeing troops around Sanananda. So prevalent had the practice been that bodies – mainly Australian and American, but sometimes Japanese – were discovered with great strips of flesh missing. Human flesh wrapped in leaves was found in the mess tins of Japanese soldiers. Sometimes body parts were found, half-eaten, in the backpacks of dead Japanese troops.

In Imanishi's experience, Japanese soldiers did not often eat their own; only the enemy and some local people. But at the battle of Gona, which raged just up the coast from Giruwa, a Lieutenant Muneta was said to have instructed his men: 'Once I die, then you should eat me to stay strong.'

One Australian soldier with the 39th Battalion recalled an incident later in the war, near Wewak on New Guinea's north coast. He was an officer of the 2/6th Battalion when they were ambushed by the Japanese in the Prince Alexander Ranges. One of the youngest members of his unit, aged barely twenty, was captured by the Japanese during the battle. The officer returned the following day with a fighting patrol to rescue him, or retrieve his corpse.

What they found when they came across the Japanese camp was a sight so hideous it made their stomachs turn: the boy was dead and every bit of edible flesh had been sliced off his body.

The evidence Australian and American soldiers saw of Japanese cannibalism enraged them, and helped seal the fate of many Japanese POWs who fell into Allied hands. Some who surrendered were shot; other prisoners were reportedly massacred suddenly, after news of Japanese atrocities reached Australian and American camps.

The celebrated American aviator Charles Lindbergh spent four months flying with American military units in New Guinea in 1944 and was often shocked by what he saw. In his journal, Lindbergh wrote that some American units regularly shot any Japanese who tried to surrender, pushed Japanese prisoners out of planes, tortured them, collected ears and thigh-bones for souvenirs, and tore gold teeth from the mouths of the dying. Such behaviour was justified by the American officers involved as retaliation for Japanese cannibalism and castration of Allied soldiers.

Whatever the extent and frequency of the retaliation, it was clear the unrelenting barbarity of a battle in which the accepted conventions of warfare had been ripped up and thrown away took its toll on even the most fair-minded of soldiers.

CHAPTER 8

Home

ALONE, AND NO LONGER attached to a platoon, Nishimura was among the last Japanese soldiers to be evacuated from New Guinea. He was taken from Lae to the relative safety of Rabaul on 20 June 1943 – fully two months after most of the other evacuees had arrived in New Britain. Nishimura found it bitterly ironic that he was ordered to the front line when there was fighting to be done, but relegated to the tail end of the queue when there was an evacuation going on.

By this time, the exertions of the past few months had really taken their toll. He looked truly terrible, and felt even worse. Scrawny and haggard, his clothes hung off him in rags and his face was gaunt and unshaven. He weighed just twenty-eight kilograms, roughly the optimum weight for a nine-year-old boy, and hardly had the strength to lift chopsticks to his mouth.

In the process of his evacuation, his emaciated body unfit to fight anything more than the most minor infection, Nishimura contracted his first case of malaria. It happened to be the most dangerous strain, falciparum. After four days with a fever, he was carried, unconscious, into the army hospital at Rabaul. His fever continued for more than a week. He was put in a kind of cage in the field hospital after he became violent on the fifth day of his attack.

In the end, he stayed in hospital for about six weeks, and there he enjoyed regular meals for the first time in more than eight months. While his malaria and other ailments were treated, he was fattened up on special meals such as steamed sticky rice and rice with barley.

A recovering skeleton he may have been, but his war was far from over. He could not possibly know it, but he faced another two years of this mayhem. In August, feeling slightly stronger but by no means in peak condition, Nishimura was put on a ship bound for Taiwan, along with other survivors and re-inforcements. The Kokoda Track was no longer a major theatre of combat, but the war raged on elsewhere in the Pacific. And Nishimura, like many other Kokoda veterans, soon found himself in the furnace of battle again.

On the night of 3 September 1943, Nishimura was on watch duty on his troopship, the *Kozan-Maru*, looking out for American submarines near the entrance of Kaohsiung harbour in Japanese-occupied Taiwan. More than a thousand troops from the reinforced 144th Regiment were on board, including the 4th, 5th and 6th Companies and the 2nd Machine-gun Company. Shortly after midnight, within an hour of the end of his shift, the ship's alarm rang, waking Nishimura from a deep sleep. He thought it must have been a routine drill for a sub-marine attack, and jumped from his bed.

But then an American torpedo struck the ship directly

below the dormitory where he and other members of the 5th Company had been sleeping, hitting the third hold. Another torpedo struck the portside engine room. Water started pouring into the cabin. There was a frantic scramble for the door, towards the ladders leading out of the hold.

Nishimura couldn't clearly recall what happened next. Somehow, he was pushed up by the rising tide of water and out of the confines of the ship, and regained consciousness a short time later, as he floated about in the sea. Leaking fuel had caught ablaze and he was surrounded by spot fires. He shouted at those soldiers he could see to dive and swim underneath the flames. Then he remembered floating in a semi-daze and watching the sky, thinking about how dark it looked.

The American submarine that sank their ship soon surfaced nearby. Nishimura, in a barely conscious haze, saw American navy officers and sailors come out on the submarine deck maybe one hundred metres away, to survey the damage. Even though it was dark, they stood out in their brilliant white uniforms. They watched the ocean and floating debris for about twenty minutes before closing the hatch on the submarine and disappearing beneath the waves.

No one had had time to fit lifejackets, so Nishimura and the strongest swimmers pulled together the biggest pieces of flotsam they could find and arranged a makeshift raft. The injured, the weak and the poor swimmers were put on the raft while the fittest of the survivors such as Nishimura, who was a strong swimmer, dangled from its edges.

And that way they stayed until 4.30 pm that day when ten Taiwanese fishing boats appeared over the horizon and began picking up survivors. The boats were operated by Taiwanese fishermen, but had been commandeered by the Japanese Army.

Casualties were surprisingly light given the suddenness of the attack and the speed with which the *Kozan-Maru* had sunk, with only a dozen dead and perhaps thirty seriously wounded.

As he was hauled out of the water, Nishimura realised that his right leg had been injured, and that the shin bone was visible through a nasty wound. He and the rest of the wounded were taken to the army hospital in Kaohsiung, where he stayed for nearly two weeks while his leg healed.

In a way, his injury proved fortuitous. It meant he could again rest up in hospital and eat regular meals. By the time he left hospital, his weight had increased to almost sixty kilograms, somewhere near his best fighting weight. In eleven weeks, including nearly eight spent in hospital, he had gained almost thirty kilograms. He also began to have intensive physiotherapy on his right shoulder for the first time. It helped restore the joint to almost a normal range of movement.

After a peaceful fortnight or so convalescing, Nishimura was once more thrust into the breach. Patched up, issued with a new uniform and weapon, he was packed off to Burma in October with the remnants of the 144th Regiment and other units.

There, near the Indian border, Nishimura's 5th Company was involved in six months of fighting against the British Army, first on the front line with the Zentsuji 55th Division and, later, as part of a diversionary force for the Imphal offensive, as the Japanese pressed over the border into north-east India in April 1944. But, again, the lack of food and medical supplies hampered the Japanese effort. No sooner had Nishimura regained much of his weight, and health, than he was pitchforked into another battle where food was severely rationed, and disease was rife.

One day, a Japanese reconnaissance team discovered that the British had been bolstered by the arrival of an armoured division with dozens of tanks. The Japanese divisional commander, unfazed by the massive firepower now boasted by the enemy, ordered that his battle-fatigued, underfed troops attack the armoured unit. In no time, the hopelessly mismatched Japanese were surrounded by tanks and shelled with massive bursts of firepower.

During the battle, Nishimura was hit by shrapnel from an exploding shell, and received deep wounds to both knees. This meant another visit to a field hospital. Lying there, he looked around the ward and realised that most of the casualties in the hospital were from his re-formed company. It occurred to him that the company, and his own 3rd Platoon, were being given the most dangerous assignments. Incensed, he rose from his bed, checked himself out of hospital and headed straight back to the front where he confronted the divisional commander and, in forthright language, told him to stop sending his troops to the slaughter. This massive show of insubordination, and the argument that ensued, killed off any hopes Nishimura had of promotion.

Burma proved almost as devastating for the Japanese forces as New Guinea, with the death rates roughly similar. Nishimura's 5th Company lost 365 men in both campaigns. Given that a company usually comprises about 160 men, the 5th Company was annihilated more than twice over.

In May 1944, the fighting against the British ceased with the onset of the wet season, as the rain fell so heavily that the entire country seemed to be covered in a thick layer of mud. During this pause, the Japanese leadership decided that the longest-serving soldier from each of the nineteen companies in Burma would be sent home with the remains of colleagues killed on the battlefield. The bodies had been cremated and were neatly parcelled up. Nishimura was chosen from the 5th Company, as indisputably its most senior and battle-weary veteran.

But returning home was not going to be easy.

On 7 July, Nishimura and eighteen other veterans, all carrying their comrades' remains, began an eight-day march through the Arakan Yoma mountain range towards the railway station at Prome, in the south of the country. The range was covered in moist tropical forests, with bamboo outcrops flourishing on the western coastal slopes and teak forests on the eastern side. It also teemed with dangerous predators, particularly tigers, leopards and sun bears. So despite the beauty of the countryside, and the welcome break from the rigours of soldiering, Nishimura and his crew were on constant alert, worried they'd be attacked at any minute.

To add to his troubles, Nishimura was soon stopped in his tracks by another bout of malaria, this one so bad that he could barely move – although still not as bad as his falciparum attack in Rabaul. Afflicted with fever that brought on a searing temperature and pain in his joints, he could do nothing more than simply lie down. Not wanting to be a burden, he said to his comrades, you go on ahead, I'm going to rest here and I'll catch up with you later. And so he lay down in a hut by the track, wondering how on earth he would survive this predicament.

LATER THAT DAY, THROUGH his fever, Nishimura thought he heard the voices of Japanese troops in the distance, and then one of them closer, saying: 'Hey, soldier, what are you doing in there?'

Nishimura looked up and saw the face of Kanichi Ishiyama, his old comrade from Kochi. He wondered whether he was hallucinating. The scene seemed too far-fetched to be real. He called out his friend's name. The soldier walked into the hut and peered into the gloom: 'Nishimura, is that really you? What the hell are you doing in here alone?' Nishimura and Ishiyama had joined the 144th Regiment on the same day, and gone through military training together. He was one of that original group of Nishimura's friends, which had also included

Kubo and Watanabe. Ishiyama was always the one with the coolest head, and could always be relied upon in a crisis. And here he was, just when Nishimura needed him.

Nishimura explained he'd been struck down with malaria and couldn't move. Ishiyama had been appointed as batman to the new commander of the 144th Regiment; he said he would ask his boss that night if he could borrow his car. He told Nishimura to wait until he could return in the morning to collect him. True to his word, the next day Ishiyama picked up his stricken friend in the commander's car and drove him all the way to Prome railway station, passing his eighteen comrades somewhere along the way.

Having been saved a seven-day trek, Nishimura thanked his friend profusely, knowing that without Ishiyama's help, he would have had no chance of surviving alone in the Burmese jungle. It was another good deed that Nishimura would never forget.

He had arrived in Prome days ahead of his colleagues, so he rested, slowly recovering from the ravaging effects of his illness. Together the group boarded a train to Rangoon, and then another to Singapore, carrying the ashes of their comrades carefully packaged up and secured in their packs.

When they finally reached Singapore in mid-July, they discovered that there were no vessels there to take them home. This came as no great surprise to the men: by now Japanese troops were accustomed to official botch-ups. Four ships damaged in air-raids were somehow salvaged from shallow water and repaired, work that took almost three months to complete. In October, the makeshift fleet set sail for Japan, Nishimura's vessel capable of a top speed of barely four knots.

As if on cue, danger presented itself, this time in the form of American bombers that flew close to the fleet near Hainan Island in the South China Sea. An inexperienced seaman on board his ship tried to douse the fires underneath the boiler so the smoke wouldn't be spotted, but he succeeded only in blowing up the boiler and nearly sinking the vessel. They limped into Taiwan for repairs, and then managed to sail to Japan, docking at Moji port in Kyushu on 7 January 1945. It was six months to the day since Nishimura and his eighteen companions had set out from Burma.

Most servicemen who reached dry land after six months in a leaky boat might have felt entitled to some R&R. But that sort of self-indulgence held little appeal for Nishimura. Without resting, he took a train to Kochi and presented himself to his senior officer at the 144th Regiment's headquarters at Asakura. It was 4 am on 8 January when he reported for duty, and delivered the ashes of the Kochi warriors back to their home town.

Somehow on his journey, in his weakened state, he'd contracted a third bout of malaria and was sent to hospital immediately to recuperate. Seven months later, Nishimura was again laid low by the disease. Recovering from his fourth attack, he was bedridden in a Kochi hospital when the Americans dropped atomic bombs on Hiroshima on 6 August, and on Nagasaki three days later.

Lying in the army hospital, Nishimura remained unaware of the terrible conflagration taking place not far from Kochi, on the southern tip of Honshu, and then further south, on Kyushu. Like many Japanese people, it was many days, even weeks, before Nishimura learned the full story of Hiroshima's destruction and the Emperor's ensuing surrender to the Allies.

THESE, THEN, WERE THE circumstances in which Nishimura returned home to Japan as the only survivor of his 56-man platoon, and one of the few hundred members of the Nankai Shitai able to walk, stagger or limp away from the carnage.

According to Japanese analysis of the casualty rates, of the 5586 combat troops of the Nankai Shitai sent to New Guinea (excluding the 41st Regiment), and of the 1797 reinforcements who arrived later, 5432 were killed in action. The South Seas Detachment, the elite unit from Kochi who had left home with hopes of conquering the Pacific Ocean, had, for all intents and purposes, been obliterated.

It is difficult to gauge accurately the mortality rate among the original members such as Nishimura and his friends, because reinforcements arrived in dribs and drabs after the early fighting. But, even on the most conservative estimates, eighty per cent of the original force perished in New Guinea, and the actual figure could be upwards of ninety per cent. Its astonishingly high mortality rate was on a par with some of the key military conflicts of modern history: the American Civil War, the Battle of the Somme in 1916, and the Battle of Stalingrad, which raged almost concurrently with the Kokoda campaign.

The 144th Infantry Regiment suffered similarly. Of the 3500 troops who headed off to war in 1941 under its banner, 3264 did not make it home to Japan. The regiment absorbed another 1150 troops in the following three years. Once again, it is difficult to obtain an accurate mortality rate among the original conscripts, but eighty per cent would be a conservative estimate.

What is certain is that Kochi and the surrounding townships that produced these men suffered terribly. Altogether, 4894 men from Kochi died in New Guinea and New Britain, the vast majority of them not yet aged thirty. Given that it was not a populous district in the 1930s, the deaths of so many of its young men was a great price to pay in human potential, and amounted to almost a lost generation.

CHAPTER 9

Work

NISHIMURA FELT NO EXULTATION at having survived the war, just an abiding emptiness. Nearly all his friends were dead, and he had come as close to death as humanly possible. His regiment had committed horrific war crimes, and he had witnessed scenes so vile that he couldn't in his mind reconcile them with life in the civilised world of post-war Japan.

Nishimura had been thrown into disarray by his war experience. And, suffering from what today might be known as post-traumatic stress disorder, he found it difficult to assimilate into civilian life.

After he was demobbed, he wandered the countryside for almost ten years, drifting from place to place, working odd jobs here and there. Allied war interrogators, chiefly the American Military Police, wanted to ask him about the Tol Plantation Massacre at Rabaul in 1942, because there were precious few Japanese left from the 144th Regiment who could help shed light on the atrocity. He was not able to offer much assistance. His battalion had been fifty kilometres away from Tol and he hadn't witnessed the killing of any POWs.

But he didn't trust the Military Police and the tactics they might resort to if ever they caught up with him. While he had nothing to hide, Nishimura decided he never wanted to be in a position where these men could get him alone in a room and use their tricks to interrogate him. So on and on he moved, never more than four or five months at any one job, covering his tracks as he went, a fugitive in his own country.

Nevertheless, despite his itinerant lifestyle, late in 1945, Nishimura married. He was introduced to a young woman in Kochi by the name of Yukiko; the matchmaker was a former classmate of his mother's. It was the first, and last, time he had agreed to an *omiai* – an arranged date with a view to marriage, the basis of most marriages in Japan in the 1940s. Yukiko was twenty, five years younger than her future husband.

Nishimura's only condition for marriage was that he must, at some stage, make a trip back to New Guinea to recover the remains of his wartime comrades. Yukiko agreed to that, and her parents promised she would cooperate with him. So, without any courtship to speak of, Nishimura and his bride took their marriage vows in a traditional Japanese ceremony, in the presence of the matchmaker.

It was common practice at that time in Japan for a bride not to be added to the groom's family registry until she bore a child. If the wife failed to produce a child, she could be sent back to her family and the marriage annulled. Nishimura thought the practice dishonourable, so Yukiko was added to his family registry on the day of their wedding. He felt it was a sign of respect, too, for the woman who had chosen to spend her life with him.

Over the next six years, the couple had four children – a girl, Sachiko, and three boys, Akira, Makoto and Osamu. While Nishimura was wandering the countryside like a gypsy, he sent any money he earned back to his young family, who were living with his mother in Nagahama, the suburb where he grew up. Nishimura was occasionally able to slip back into Kochi and visit Yukiko, but he never felt safe enough to stay long.

In order to eke out a living, he took on a swag of menial jobs. He dug wells, made salt on the beach at Tanomachi and Yasudamachi near Kochi City, was a logger in the mountains, helped repair the cabling that carried logs from the mountain down to the trucks, and worked as a mechanic fixing fishing boats on the coast.

At one stage, Nishimura even set up the Kochi Kennai Kyodo Kumiai, or Kochi Prefecture Cooperative, which arranged jobs for unemployed war veterans, widows, and families who had lost a father or brother in the war. He made himself the co-operative's managing director. The work was often menial, such as transporting soil and sand to reclaimed land at Kochi harbour. Nishimura paid the workers based on how many round trips they did, to and from the harbour. But his average payment was about 1000 yen per day, considerably more than the government's minimum daily wage of 240 yen. More than 180 people were given jobs as a result of the cooperative; not just former soldiers and widows, but even some fatherless children who came and worked with their mothers.

Yet, all the time, Nishimura was a prisoner on his home island of Shikoku, unable to leave because the Military Police had set up checkpoints at every port and railway station. He never once made it across to Honshu, the main island of Japan. In this lost decade, he worked in every prefecture of Shikoku – Kochi, Ehime, Tokushima and Kagawa – waiting for the time when he could resume a normal life.

Even after the San Francisco Peace Treaty was signed by Japan and the Allied powers in 1951, Nishimura stayed in hiding because the Pacific island of Okinawa was still under American occupation and swarming with Military Police. It was 1955 before Nishimura's friends in Tokyo finally convinced him to return home. The Military Police had wound up their border patrols, his nightmares had started to subside, and the siren wail of the Australian soldier he killed in hand-to-hand combat had stopped waking him at night.

He moved back to Tokyo and made plans to capitalise on his talent for civil and mechanical engineering. What Nishimura loved doing most was inventing new products and solving insoluble building problems. He wanted to start his own factory and be the boss of his own company.

During his time working at a foundry before the war, Nishimura made a point of taking on jobs that other people couldn't or wouldn't do. He developed a reputation as a trouble-shooter. In 1940, when Japan had been at war with China for three years, Riken, one of the country's leading science and technology research companies, came to the factory where he then worked with a challenging problem. They were developing armaments and wanted to design an artillery shell that travelled noiselessly and did not produce a fire-flash at night. The shells in use attracted attention, assisting the enemy to identify the position from which they had been fired.

In his spare time, the nineteen-year-old Nishimura had tinkered with developing a linear motor for a train that worked on the principle of using electro-magnetic forces to overcome gravity. One part of the motor was on the train, the other on the guideway. A year later, Nishimura saw that he could adapt this technology to artillery. He placed electro-magnetic coils inside the barrel of the gun, and the conductive power of the magnets fired the shell silently and without a fire-flash. His gun was tested at the army's range at Tokai village, where a 300-millimetre shell flew several kilometres. The experts from Riken were amazed that someone so young could develop such a sophisticated solution.

Now, fifteen years later, Nishimura founded the Nishimura Machinery Research Institute, a factory-cum-laboratory in the Ota district, near Haneda airport in Tokyo's south-west. Here he went to work, his brain fizzing with ideas. One of the first things his company produced was ultralight steel beams and rods for use in the construction of housing frames. They were strong and safe, and proved an enormous success during Japan's post-war construction boom.

His views on construction mirrored his view of the world: *compromise was death*. Nishimura knew other people sometimes said one thing when they believed another, just to be diplomatic. But when he believed something, he said it. When he needed to do something, he did it. His experience as a designer and engineer had taught him that if you made a single mistake, or cut corners and compromised even a little, you destroyed everything.

Soon his reputation as engineering's go-to man began to spread. The technical people at Sony would call when they came across a problem that had their brightest boffins scratching their heads. In order to circumvent the bureaucracy in his burgeoning company, the founder of Sony, Akio Morita, would often call Nishimura directly if he wanted a problem solved.

Morita appeared on the cover of *Time* magazine in May 1971, under the coverline 'How to Cope with Japan's Business Invasion'. In the process of building up Sony as one of the best-known brands in the world, he met just about every dignitary and eminence in the West, from Queen Elizabeth II to Henry Kissinger. But back in Japan, his list of favourite VIPs included a certain Kokichi Nishimura, of the Nishimura Machinery Research Institute.

For as Morita was on the way to becoming the highest-profile Japanese citizen on the planet, he developed a friendship with his personal trouble-shooter, a relationship that defied their vastly different backgrounds and positions in Japanese society: the wealthy, well-connected founder of Sony and the merchant sailor's son who had left school at eleven. Morita liked to visit Nishimura in his factory, where the two of them would sit and talk about their mutual love, machinery and electronics. Despite the differences in their social and financial status, Nishimura saw it as a relationship of equals. He loved how Morita called almost everyone, even British Cabinet ministers, by the more informal title of *Kun*, rather than the more respectful *San*. Yet Nishimura he called *San*, as a sign of veneration. Soon, Nishimura refused to deal with anyone else at Sony. Unless Morita called him personally, the job would remain unfixed.

One day in the middle of summer, Morita telephoned Nishimura with a note of urgency in his voice. The airconditioning unit at Sony headquarters, a massive piece of machinery located on the roof of the building, had broken. The main shaft had fractured and the entire unit had collapsed on to the roof. If it wasn't repaired within a day or two, Sony's entire intricate cabling network and computer system could overheat and go into meltdown. The manufacturers of the cooling facility said it would take two weeks to fix, probably too long, so Morita asked Nishimura whether he would do them the honour of paying a visit and seeing what he could do. Of course, Nishimura said, and duly went around to one of the tallest skyscrapers in Tokyo with his toolbox and set to work. Toiling away by himself on the roof, Nishimura was able to re-attach all the broken parts to the unit, weld the shaft together, and make the airconditioning function again.

Nishimura never sent Morita an invoice; his work was a gift not just to his friend but to Japanese industry. Of course, Morita never accepted the present without payment and, within a day or two, money would be deposited into Nishimura's bank account.

Soon, Nishimura's reputation began to spread far beyond the Nishimura Machinery Research Institute and the work he did for Sony. The president of Hitachi sought his assistance. His technical team had been trying without success to drill 24 holes sideways through an iron plate 10 centimetres thick. The size of each hole needed to be 30 millimetres in diameter and 2.7 metres in length, a task that destroyed conventional drill bits every time. Within three days, Nishimura found a way to get the job done.

He enjoyed a special relationship, too, with the Hitachi president who was always very respectful and called him 'Mr Nishimura'.

In the late 1950s, he began tinkering with a rotary engine for motor vehicles. After refining his design, Nishimura could get his car to 4000 or 5000 revolutions per minute without a problem. He took it out on the highway and drove the car at almost 200 kilometres per hour. Its efficiency was reasonably good too, requiring 11 litres of fuel per 100 kilometres.

Word of his invention leaked out, and in 1958 a delegation from Isuzu brought 20 million yen to the factory and asked him if he'd sell them the technology. A company chauffeur from Isuzu lived in the same apartment block as Nishimura, and Nishimura suspects he somehow got wind of the plans. As they were discussing the finer detail of the deal, one of the Isuzu officials asked Nishimura whether they could do whatever they liked with the technology once it had been purchased. Nishimura smelt a rat. He asked whether Isuzu was planning to sell the information to a foreign company. The group fell silent and Nishimura knew then that his technology was not going to be used for the benefit of Japanese people but for foreigners. His sense of patriotism would not allow such a betrayal. He shouted at the men to leave his factory.

Nothing came of Nishimura's design. He was too busy filling orders for his ultralight steel beams and did not have time to devote himself fully to the project. But in the 1960s, he read in a magazine that Mazda had just purchased a patent from German motorcycle-maker NSU and was on the verge of launching its own car with a rotary engine. When he saw pictures of the proposed new model, Nishimura could tell straightaway that Mazda would have problems with a certain part of the engine, as he had done.

A Mazda serviceman happened to come to his house to fix his car a short time after the article appeared, and Nishimura told him what he thought of the company's plans. Within days, a team of Mazda specialists appeared on his doorstep. They demanded to know how Nishimura knew so much about the rotary engine and the intricate details of how the engine worked. Because, replied Nishimura, I made my own rotary engine about ten years ago. The men were staggered. But this was a top secret of the company, they said, and all the technical experts at Mazda had been working on solving this problem.

According to Nishimura, Mazda's early engines were inferior to his own, and were just a variation on a piston engine rather than a true rotary engine. He even bought a Mazda Familia car to compare its engine to his own. He said the early Familia models struggled to do 6000 rpm, fewer than his own, later, creations. Mazda, of course, went on to refine the technology further, producing the RX sports car series, which became a familiar sight, even on Australian roads.

At the Nishimura Machinery Research Institute, the inventions came in a steady stream: a machine that turned dung into feed for livestock; a new material that helped seal roads more tightly; the constant tinkering and reworking of engines to make them more efficient. One of the machines of which Nishimura was most proud was an odour measurement device, the only one of its type in the world, which scientifically measured industrial smells, the size of the particles responsible for their odour and their characteristics. He sold it to several corporations, including the Tokyo Metropolitan Livestock Experiment Station and Takasago International Corporation, Asia's biggest manufacturer of fragrances and flavours.

While his success brought him pleasure and no small amount of money, Nishimura was preoccupied with other thoughts. Even when he was talking to Akio Morita, or dreaming up a new way to improve the efficiency of rice farming, his focus tended to drift. Every day, and often several times a day, he would think of the war, and the soldiers whose remains were left behind in New Guinea. The Imperial Rescript to Soldiers and Sailors that decreed duty was weightier than a mountain while death was lighter than a feather kept repeating in his head, a mantra he could not be rid of.

IN THE YEARS HE spent on the run in Shikoku, and on subsequent visits, Nishimura made it his duty to visit the graves of the soldiers he had outlived. The graves were mostly empty – the bones still lying somewhere in the New Guinea jungle – but they were a memorial focus for the grief and prayers of the soldiers' bereaved families.

While Nishimura was working on the beach making salt at Tanomachi in the late 1940s, he met the sister of his first grenade launcher, Zenzaburo Ushimado, who happened to live in the town. Together, they visited Ushimado's grave where Nishimura stood and silently prayed for his troubled friend who had led such an unhappy life.

Much later, he sought out the family of Harukazu Oka, or Karl, his friend who had once been a dog handler. Nishimura travelled to the family home in Ochimachi Town, in Kochi prefecture. Oka's mother, who was in her eighties, answered the door, and could not believe her eyes when she saw her son's friend standing there. You came back alive, she shouted. She fawned over him, as though her own son had suddenly appeared back in her life. I am so glad you came. Please stay healthy. Mrs Oka took Nishimura to her son's grave, where she choked back sobs while he prayed for Harukazu's spirit.

There was an even more emotional reunion at the home of Satoshi Watanabe, the dear, dependable and steadfast friend he felt he had inadvertently killed. When he visited the Watanabe family home, he was greeted like a long-lost son. Watanabe's parents were in tears. They knew from Satoshi's correspondence how close their son had been to Nishimura. They told him that Satoshi's bedroom had been left exactly how it was when he set off to war in 1941. His clothes were still in their drawers, the bed still made. His mother then asked Nishimura if he would please wear some of Satoshi's clothes and stay the night in his bed. It would bring them great comfort if he would do that for them, they said. It was an emotional wrench for Nishimura, sharpened by the acute sense of guilt he still felt over Watanabe's death, but he did as they wished, putting his head on the same pillow where his great friend had once slept.

He felt a debt to his comrades, not just because he had lived and they had not, but because they had helped him to survive. Mitsuo Itahara leaned out of his trench at Ippongi to try and protect Nishimura, with little thought for his own safety. His bravery cost him his life. Captain Fujisaki rescued him from the tree stump at Ippongi when Nishimura was perhaps a day away from dying. Kanichi Ishiyama had appeared like a vision before him in Burma and helped transport him to safety when, again, his fate appeared sealed. Without them, he surely would not have survived. How could he ever forget these men?

Twenty-five years after the war had ended, Nishimura felt increasingly irritated by the attitude of his countrymen and government towards Japan's war dead. Hundreds of thousands of men had sacrificed their lives for their country and the Japanese Government, now fully engaged in its post-war revival, seemed hesitant to acknowledge them, as if ashamed of the country's role in starting a war that had caused death and destruction on such a profound scale.

Nishimura, though, chose to remember. In quiet moments in his office, he began to outline a plan to return to New Guinea to try to find his friends' bodies. After all, he had given his word to them, and his word was inviolable. The job now was to plan every last detail of his trip. Sometimes, doodling on paper at his desk, he would design a boat, made from empty drums tied together, with a small engine and big sail, which he would use to transport the bones from beach to beach along New Guinea's north coast.

Even though the Imperial Japanese Army had ordered its soldiers to hand back every document and bit of paperwork they were given during the war, Nishimura had kept the lot. He was helped in no small part by the clerk from the 5th Company, a man by the name of Kuroda, whose job it was to record the names of comrades who died in New Guinea, when and where they perished, and how they died. Kuroda had to make three copies of the same log – for the company itself, the regimental HQ and the divisional HQ. But Nishimura somehow prevailed upon him to write a fourth copy for his own records. In the end, that was the only copy to survive the war; the other three were lost somewhere in New Guinea.

There were other items, such as maps, records of battles, operational directions and so on, which were going to be burnt by the army in the dying days of the war but some of which Nishimura stole, and smuggled back into Japan under his shirt, even though he knew he'd be arrested if caught. These records formed a crucial part of his planning. They included drawings of battle sites, the topography, and each company's position and movements.

Nishimura had begun doing his own exhaustive research as well. He filled up exercise books with descriptions and details of his experiences in New Guinea, but chiefly with details of the battlegrounds and the whereabouts of those soldiers he'd had to leave behind. He listed the dead by name in one book, by place of death in another, by date of death in a third, and by their respective units in yet another. In the absence of many of the official records, which had been lost or destroyed, Nishimura's notes and research, and the records compiled by Kuroda, became an integral part of the official archive, the 144th Infantry Regiment Record of Battle.

As his plan to return to New Guinea took shape, Nishimura read and re-read his materials. He was able to retrace his steps and pinpoint key sections on the track where his company had fought and where they had lost many men. Soon, he had drafted a thorough map of the areas where he would need to dig, starting at the villages of Giruwa and Gona in the north and working his way down the track to Efogi, where his platoon was wiped out at the Battle of Ippongi.

He resolved in his mind to leave Japan in 1979, as soon as he retired at the age of sixty. He was thinking big. This was a mission that couldn't be completed in six or eight months; if it took him five years or ten, or even fifteen, well, so be it. That's how long he'd have to be away.

In preparation for his project, Nishimura contacted the

Japanese Defence Agency in Shinjuku and asked if he could buy a landmine detector. The agency was not accustomed to dealing with such requests from members of the public. The man at the other end of the phone told Nishimura he must be mistaken; this was not some sort of discount machinery shop in a mall. But Nishimura persisted. He needed a landmine detector for a project he was about to undertake which involved locating buried metallic objects. The man laughed. But in what was to become the pattern of his mission, Nishimura persisted, bombarding the staff at the agency with requests for the detector until finally someone there, who could take no more of the harassment, relented and sold him one.

The detector was packed with the few personal belongings Nishimura planned to take with him, along with a shovel, tomahawk, machete and garden hoe. These were to be the tools of his new trade: bone collector.

CHAPTER 10

Holdouts

THE JAPANESE COINED A term for those soldiers who kept on fighting long after the war had ended. They were called holdouts. From Saipan to the Solomon Islands and Iwo Jima to Indonesia, these holdouts fought on for years after the Japanese surrender, some unaware the war had ended, others refusing to believe the Emperor would ever capitulate to the Americans. Some hid in the jungle alone; others fought in groups and continued to launch attacks against anyone that lived nearby, especially the local police. The enemy, in their mind, was still everywhere.

The holdouts were a manifestation of the Imperial Army's relentless indoctrination of its troops. To surrender was unthinkable; a soldier's destiny was to die for the Emperor or to kill himself in the shameful event of being captured. This fanatical devotion to duty meant World War II did not end neatly when Japan surrendered on 2 September 1945. In some cases, small, misguided pockets of resistance lasted another thirty years.

Perhaps the best known of the holdouts were Sergeant Shoichi Yokoi and Lieutenant Hiroo Onoda, soldiers who spent almost three decades fighting their own private wars thousands of kilometres from Japan. After his unit was obliterated by American tanks in Guam, Yokoi went into hiding on the island, living alone in an underground cave for twenty-eight years until his existence was discovered in 1972. Onoda emerged from the jungle of Lubang Island in the Philippines in 1974 after conducting his own one-man guerrilla campaign against the local people for twenty-nine years.

Both men returned to Japan amid extraordinary fanfare, just as Nishimura was putting together his master plan to return to New Guinea, and their feats left an indelible impression on him. If these two men could serve Japan, doing their duty for more than a quarter of a century, then surely he could too. He did not know how long his digging campaign would take, but if it also took twenty-eight or twenty-nine years, so be it.

The strident patriotism shown by both men struck a chord with Nishimura. Onoda, who refused to believe the pamphlets that had been dropped in the jungle to announce the end of the war, wept openly when he was told of Japan's surrender. Yokoi, his trusty rifle at his side, said upon his return: 'It is with much embarrassment that I have returned alive . . . I am sorry I did not serve His Majesty, the honourable Emperor, to my satisfaction.' The remark became a popular saying, quoted ironically by younger Japanese who had been taught little about the war and undoubtedly found quaint such devotion to royalty.

Year by year, the experiences of Japanese who had served in the war slipped further from public consciousness. The war was becoming a distant memory for his countrymen and that dismayed Nishimura. A national cemetery, Chidorigafuchi, had been built by the Japanese in Tokyo in 1959 to house the nation's unknown war dead, but even that had a strangely detached and dispassionate feel about it. Hundreds of thousands of Japanese soldiers and civilians were interred there, their bones reduced to anonymous ashes that were compressed into tiny cubes and stored in one of the cemetery's three underground ossuaries.

The remains of about 351,000 Japanese soldiers and civilians have ended up at Chidorigafuchi, but they represent a fraction of the nation's casualties in World War II. Out there in the vast war zone of the Pacific region and beyond, lie another 1.16 million Japanese, some just where they fell in battle, others buried by comrades.

To Nishimura, the exploits of Yokoi and Onoda served as an inspiration and breathed fresh life back into his campaign to recover those comrades who had perished in New Guinea. Yokoi actually turned up at Mount Chachao in Guam, the very place where thirty years earlier Nishimura's 5th Company had come across the three unarmed American soldiers who knew nothing of the Pearl Harbor attack.

Yokoi had survived for all those years on a diet of coconuts, breadfruit, papaya, snails, eels and rats. Sometimes he stole vegetables from nearby farms. Before the war, he had been a tailor's apprentice, and so was somehow able to fashion crude items of clothing from the fibre of wild hibiscus plants.

Forced to endure enormous privation, Yokoi – in much the same manner as Nishimura – became an advocate for an austere lifestyle, devoid of luxuries and Western extravagances. He was surprised and a little saddened at how his country had changed since he had been away. 'The glories of nature that I used to know have all disappeared,' he said. 'Instead, up in the sky, we have this thing called smog. On earth, cars are killing more people than war.' The biggest change he noticed was in Japanese women, no longer the demure and subservient wives of an earlier period.

He died in 1997 of a heart attack, aged eighty-two, and was buried at a Nagoya cemetery, under a gravestone initially commissioned by his mother in 1955, when he had been officially listed as dead.

While Yokoi hid in the remote Talofofo area of Guam and seemed more intent on surviving rather than fighting, Onoda made a pest of himself with the Filipinos right until the bitter end. In the grand samurai tradition, he was committed to going down fighting.

It took an extraordinary encounter with a young Japanese university dropout named Norio Suzuki before Onoda was persuaded to give himself up. Suzuki was travelling the world and told his friends before leaving Japan that he was 'going to look for Lieutenant Onoda, a panda, and the Abominable Snowman, in that order'. Somehow, he managed to track down the soldier on Lubang, and the two developed an unlikely friendship, but Onoda said he was staying put unless ordered otherwise by one of his commanders.

Suzuki offered his help, and returned to Japan with photographs of himself and Onoda as proof of their encounter. The Japanese Government became involved and located Onoda's commanding officer, a Major Taniguchi, who had become a bookseller after the war. Taniguchi flew to Lubang with Suzuki and informed Onoda of the defeat of Japan, and ordered him to lay down his arms. Which Onoda duly did on 9 March 1974, in his dress uniform and sword, with his Type 99 Arisaka rifle still in operating condition, and carrying five hundred rounds of ammunition and several hand grenades.

Though Onoda, who was trained in guerrilla warfare, had killed some thirty inhabitants of the island and engaged in several shoot-outs with police, his peculiar circumstances were taken into consideration, and he received a pardon from the President of the Philippines, Ferdinand Marcos.

Like Yokoi, he returned to Japan to a hero's welcome, and was hounded by curious members of the public wherever he went. He wrote about his experiences in a book, *No Surrender: My Thirty-Year War*, then moved to Brazil to raise cattle. Later, he married a Japanese woman and returned to Japan to run a camp for children.

WHILE NISHIMURA WAS AN unabashed admirer of the holdouts' survival skills, durability and devotion to their country, he held vastly differing views about the way they conducted themselves while still in uniform.

Because Yokoi hid in the jungle and did not continue to fight, he had – in Nishimura's mind, anyway – betrayed the noble tradition of the Imperial Japanese soldier, who would always fight to the death. Conversely, by waging his own private war after three of his fellow holdouts were killed in skirmishes with Filipino forces, Onoda had upheld the samurai code. Or so Nishimura thought.

He didn't like the way that Yokoi was treated like a hero when he returned to Japan. He felt Yokoi was a chicken, an NCO who had ordered his men to charge the enemy, but himself hid shamelessly in his hole. He stayed there for almost thirty years. Nishimura thought his crime was much worse than murdering someone, because he had brought no honour on himself or the Japanese Army. This was similar to the disdain Nishimura felt for the Japanese POWs captured and interned at Cowra, in New South Wales. They had shamed Japan, he felt, and the fact that 231 of them died in 1944 while trying to escape was not any mitigation.

On the other hand, Lieutenant Onoda was a real soldier, and a real man. He never compromised his principles and kept fighting until ordered to surrender. Onoda became even more of a hero in Nishimura's eyes when he tackled a young television journalist who tried to interview him shortly after his return to Japan. The journalist, who would not have even been born when Onoda began his 29-year odyssey, made the mistake of wearing dark glasses during the interview, a Western affectation that raised the hackles of the old warrior. Onoda was very angry: 'Take your sunglasses off or I won't speak to you. You're very rude, what kind of education did you have?'

And that summed up Nishimura's uncompromising attitude to duty, respect, pride, honour and self-sacrifice. They were virtues, inviolable and indestructible, that had made his country great. Like key points on the moral compass, they should be pinned up in every home and office in the country, and taught to schoolchildren from the time they first entered a classroom.

During the war, he had been indoctrinated to believe that duty was everything, while death was 'lighter than a feather' – just a minor concern. Now he saw evidence that the order of things had irrevocably changed. In September 1977, a Japan Air Lines flight with 156 passengers on board was hijacked by Red Army terrorists en route from Paris to Tokyo, and forced to land in Dhaka, Bangladesh. The Japanese Prime Minister, Takeo Fukuda, caved in to the terrorists' demands, paying the US$6 million ransom and agreeing to release six Red Army members from jail.

Fukuda famously said, *Jinmei wa chikyû yori omoi*: human life is weightier than the world. So that was how much times had changed. Once, it had been duty that was exalted over life. Nishimura was not impressed with this new, expedient morality.

He would uphold his own moral code, even if the country was abandoning its ideals. The virtues he believed in would soon drive him back to New Guinea. He was a survivor of the war and he had given his word to his comrades at Giruwa that he would return to collect them and bring them home. And he never broke a promise.

Yokoi and Onoda arrived back in Japan when Nishimura was in his mid-fifties, and spending a lot of time thinking about and planning his return to New Guinea. He dreamt about making good his promise. The holdouts' tenacity left a lasting impression on him and Nishimura drew great strength from their resolve. It invigorated him, and he felt he couldn't wait to get back to the tropics and carry out his duty.

But there were one or two serious matters to attend to in Japan before he embarked on his quest.

CHAPTER 11

Family

NISHIMURA LOVED ALL OF his four children, but was especially proud of his eldest son, Akira. He was a boy who honoured the family name with the noble and dignified way in which he carried himself. What Nishimura especially liked about Akira was his impeccable manners. He never swore and was always polite and respectful to his elders. Yet he was no pushover, for he shared the same fierce inner determination as his father.

Akira became president of the student council in his first year in junior high school in Tokyo. Someone so young had not been given the leader's role before; normally, it was taken by a third-year student. Akira was popular with the other boys at school, and adored by the girls. Every Sunday, a procession of girls came to visit Nishimura's son at home.

When he finished school he came to work at the factory that bore his father's name. There was one particularly prickly employee at the Nishimura Machinery Research Institute, a university graduate who thought he was somehow superior to his fellow workers. His arrogance annoyed everyone on the factory floor and often led to disputes. Nishimura always turned to Akira who, calm and reasoned, was able to talk sense to the man. Soon the crisis would be over.

Then one day in 1966, when Akira was just twenty, the car in which he was driving was hit hard from behind by a taxi. The young man was taken to hospital with terrible injuries and, after six days in a coma, he died.

The taxi company that owned the cab was one of the biggest in Tokyo. In ploughing into a stationary car in front of him, the driver had clearly been negligent. Nishimura could have raised merry hell and received substantial compensation from them. But he didn't. Instead, he asked the president of the company to come to his house and light a stick of incense for Akira's spirit, which the executive duly did.

The driver of the cab came from distant Kagoshima, and had only been working in Tokyo for three weeks. He had a wife and children. Nishimura knew if he reported to police that someone had died in the accident, the driver would lose his licence, possibly even go to jail, and his family would be without a source of income. He told the driver he wouldn't do that. He simply asked the man to promise he would never make the same mistake again, and to work hard for his wife and children.

So desensitised was Nishimura by his war experience, in which death became a fact of life, and so accustomed was he to internalising his feelings, that he decided the most important thing at that time was not his son's death but the welfare of the taxi driver and his family. The tragedy ended without police action, an insurance claim, or a court case, and with not even so much as a reprimand.

Life went on, but Nishimura was devastated. The old warrior, who had spent twenty-five years bottling up his emotions, had no idea how to express his despair and heartbreak. He tried to rationalise the accident by telling himself it was fate and there was nothing he could do about it. He also told himself that he had seen hundreds of men of a similar age killed during the war, and that there must be parents all over Japan who had lost sons in their prime. But it was little comfort.

Akira's death left his entire family grief-stricken for years. The equilibrium of their little unit had been thrown into disarray and it took years before any sense of normalcy returned. That was why Nishimura felt apprehensive about raising the subject he had been putting off for months: telling his family he would be leaving them to travel to New Guinea. Possibly, for a very long time.

One night after work, with his wife, two sons and daughter all at home, he finally broached the issue. Clearing his throat, he called them around and said he had an announcement to make. Many years ago, he said, he had promised his friends in the army that, if they died and he survived, he'd go back and collect their remains from New Guinea. Now he wanted to deliver on that promise. Soon, he would give up work, leave Japan and set up base in New Guinea, where he would begin his mission. He did not know how long he would be gone, but probably many years.

His wife, Yukiko, sat there silently watching him, mouth agape. What do you mean you're going to New Guinea, she finally said. Your life is here, in Tokyo, with us, your family. And we don't want you to go anywhere. I didn't think you were serious when you said visiting New Guinea was a condition of our marriage. If I knew that, I would never have agreed to this thirty-five years ago. His surviving children – Sachiko, thirty-two, Makoto, thirty, and Osamu, twenty-eight, were equally stunned. Nishimura's sons also urged their father to reconsider this rash decision. It would be such an expensive and difficult project, they said.

Sachiko remembered that when she was a child her father had sometimes talked about New Guinea and how he planned at some stage to head back there to recover his friends' remains, but she never paid much attention, thinking it was idle talk. As she grew older, Sachiko realised her father was not given to making idle boasts; if he said he was going to do something, it was generally done. So, while the announcement still came as a surprise to Sachiko, it was not a total shock.

The Nishimura household ran along fairly conventional Japanese lines, which is to say that the man of the house was king of his domain. Whatever Nishimura said, generally went. And he didn't brook any nonsense or insubordination from his family. Yukiko was a traditional Japanese wife who, while not walking three steps behind her husband, may have been half a step adrift.

So the show of dissent from his wife was unusual and it displeased him. He said that the trip had always been a condition of their marriage. *I only let you be my wife if you agreed to me going to New Guinea at some stage in the future. You and your father agreed to that. But if you say no now, well I'm not going to let you come into my house. If you complain, that's it, no more, the marriage is over.*

But Yukiko could not contain her feelings. Again, she said: Please don't go. It is a ridiculous plan. We want you here. I need you at home.

Knowing her husband as she did, she realised this show of defiance could only have one ending.

She recalled the time when Kokichi had just returned from the war, and the two of them were newlyweds. There was a dreadful scene at his home one day when Nishimura's younger brother, Toyoichi, who had just returned from serving in Korea himself, called out to their mother: *Omae!* (Hey, you!) Nishimura was enraged that his brother could be so disrespectful. For the first and last time, Nishimura punched his brother hard in the face. Toyoichi reeled from the blow. And so shocked was he by the exchange that he never again talked to his elder brother. Their relationship, which till that time had been free from bickering and fighting, ended then and there.

So Nishimura was no stranger to family bust-ups, and Yukiko could sense that this scene was also going to end unhappily.

Nishimura knew she didn't want him spending the family fortune on some crazy trip to New Guinea. She wanted him to keep working in Tokyo so that he could earn a handsome income and together they could lead a comfortable life in his retirement. So he said to his wife: OK, if that's the way you feel, I will give you everything I have – all my savings, my property portfolio, my business, every asset I own, even my samurai sword – if you leave the house.

The elaborate samurai sword had tigers forged into its blade and was an enormously valuable antique, almost a national treasure; Nishimura had been offered ten million yen (A$110,000) for it in 1965, but had declined. Now, because he didn't want Yukiko to complain about being left with nothing, he was prepared to give it to his wife, along with just about every other possession he owned.

In the tumultuous exchange that night, the family split in two. Makoto and Osamu sided with their mother. Sachiko, the quietly spoken daughter, went with her father. You're too cruel, she shouted at her mother. Nishimura handed over the keys to the Nishimura Machinery Research Institute to his sons, a special blessing for Osamu, the youngest child, who had not long graduated from university where he had studied engineering and construction. Then his wife and two sons walked out of his life.

The old soldier, who never knew the meaning of compromise, never allowed himself to regret his decision, nor did he dwell on its wisdom. And never once did he think about attempting a reconciliation. What was done was done.

Afterwards, he did not enquire whether the Nishimura Machinery Research Institute was still managed by his sons, or even if it was still operational. If people asked, he said he could barely remember his wife's name. *I don't know where she is, or whether she's dead or alive. I prefer to think about other things. My policy is: do what I say, follow me. If you don't have a strong enough stomach for that, too bad. I'm not diplomatic at all, I never compromise. All I know is my own way, I know nothing of the outside world.*

Faced with the choice of living out his days in suburban Tokyo or doing his duty, there could only be one decision. The call of duty overrode his love for his family.

Usually, no one dared to ask him whether his family was too high a price to pay for fulfilling his promise to his comrades, but if they did, he answered: You might see it as a big sacrifice to lose your family, but what sort of sacrifice is it against that made by the soldiers who died in New Guinea? Compared to them, I live in heaven. I believe it is the duty of survivors like me to honour the dead by keeping their promise.

I don't believe in saying one thing and doing another – of speaking with a forked tongue. I never made a promise I didn't keep. *When I left Giruwa, I promised I would return. I never tell lies.*

AND SO THAT WAS how, in the course of a single evening, the Nishimura family unit was split asunder.

From that night in 1979 onwards, Nishimura never again saw his wife or sons, much less spoke to them. That chapter in his life was closed, locked and sealed shut.

Bone Man

CHAPTER 12

Touchdown

TRYING TO IGNORE THE residual bitterness surrounding his family affairs, Nishimura began to make his final preparations to return to New Guinea. Thirty-seven years after he first set foot on the Salamaua Peninsula with the 5th Company, he would land on the same stretch of coast alone. This time, his hair would be thinning, his eyesight fading and, instead of khaki battle fatigues and helmet, Nishimura-san would be dressed in a T-shirt, loose-fitting cotton pants, sensible shoes and hat. And rather than carrying a grenade launcher and rifle, he would be armed with a landmine detector, shovel and garden hoe.

Before he set off, though, he had some loose ends to tie up with his business before his sons officially took control. In late April 1979, Nishimura went up to Hanyu City in Saitama prefecture north of Tokyo to install a machine that would reduce air pollution at the local poultry farm. Nishimura had three of his young colleagues from work with him and, because he wanted the job finished before the national holiday on 5 May, he recruited three more workers from the office in Tokyo to help get the machine installed on time. They worked hard all day on the 4th to finish the job, and late in the afternoon when everything was close to being completed, Nishimura took his straw mat and laid it out between the rice fields nearby and had a nap.

But he was well concealed, and no one had told the local farmer that Japan's great war survivor was asleep on the pathway between the paddies, so Nishimura woke up just as the 1.3-tonne tractor used for ploughing the paddies began to drive over him from head to toe. His screams alerted his younger colleagues, who ran over and pulled him out from underneath the plough.

An ambulance took him into the emergency section of the hospital in Kazo City, the Nakada Byouin. Doctors there thought 59-year-old Nishimura would not live. There was an imprint of a tractor tyre on his groin, and his head had been lacerated by the plough behind the tractor and required many stitches. He had also sustained some minor fractures of his skull, and suffered severe whiplash where the vertebrae in his neck were jolted out of place.

None of his ribs was broken, however, meaning his vital organs had escaped damage. Nevertheless, the doctors could not understand how he had not been killed instantly.

His accident was a major setback to his travel plans, since it meant he would be in and out of hospital for the next fifteen months. Some people might have been discouraged from going, but Nishimura was bursting to get to New Guinea and told his doctor how he'd been planning this trip for a decade. The doctor looked at him strangely, but when he realised

Nishimura was deadly serious, he said: OK, you can go, but only on a brief reconnaissance mission. I want you gone for no more than a week.

And so, barely two months after his life-threatening accident, Nishimura boarded a plane for Papua New Guinea, still wearing his hospital identification collar under his shirt.

Shortly before leaving, Nishimura had received a phone call from a local government official in Kochi. He told Nishimura that a parcel of land he owned in Kochi was still registered in his name and a local developer wanted to build an apartment block on it. Would he be prepared to sell it? No, it's not me you should be talking to but my wife, Nishimura said. I've given everything I own to her. But the official said she could not own the land while it was still in his name. Nishimura had no desire to track down his wife and have another scene with her, so he asked Sachiko if she wanted the proceeds from the land sale. No, she said, she didn't need the money. So Nishimura thought: What the hell, I'll use the funds to help pay for my trip to New Guinea.

He shook his head ruefully. Wasn't life strange? Even when you wanted to do the right thing and give everything away, something stopped you. Fate intervened and handed the money right back.

Armed with his unexpected windfall, on 24 July 1979, Nishimura boarded an AirNiugini flight from Kagoshima, on the island of Kyushu, and headed off to Port Moresby. Such was the lack of demand for seats to New Guinea, Japanese travellers had to fly from Haneda airport in Tokyo down to the southern-most tip of mainland Japan, before they could board the AirNiugini flight.

He took almost nothing in his bag, except a few changes of underwear and an extra shirt and pair of pants. During the week he was there, he tried to get a feel for the country again, to cram in as much travel as he could and visit as many battle sites as time would allow. He also tried to find the elderly couple from Mumuni village in the Kokoda district, Paheki and Tomarako Hojava, who fed him and showed him such kindness when he was lost and starving during the Japanese retreat in late 1942.

He managed to get word to John Hojava, their grandson, that he would dearly love to meet up with them again. Alas, Hojava informed him, both his grandparents had died during the 1960s. Nishimura was saddened: he had desperately wanted to thank them for their bravery and generosity. So that was one debt he could not repay personally. He would have to make restitution with Mumuni instead, and to make sure his philanthropy extended into the heart of Oro province.

When Nishimura returned to Japan a week later, he went straight back into hospital. His neck and back were causing him terrible pain, and required intensive physiotherapy. He would go back to New Guinea for further reconnaissance several months later, in early 1980. By the end of that year, when he was finally given a clean bill of health and allowed to take off his patient's smock and identification collar, Nishimura knew where to look and how best to tackle his mission. He was primed and ready to go.

After much research, Nishimura decided he would make Popondetta his base in New Guinea. The village had several advantages. First, it was on the Sanananda Track between Giruwa to the north and Kokoda to the south, giving him equally good access to the places he'd identified as Japanese gravesites. Second, the village was elevated, about one hundred metres above sea level, and was therefore cooler and more comfortable than Port Moresby. Third, and most important, it would give him the chance to repay an old debt of gratitude on behalf of the South Seas Detachment.

When the beach campaign had ended in January 1943, with the Allies finally winkling the Japanese out of their pillboxes and bunkers, an atrocity reportedly took place that does not feature in any of the military histories of the campaign. Nishimura claims American troops rounded up the bedraggled remnants of the Japanese Army, those dozens of men who had been left behind in places such as Buna and Giruwa because they were so sick and weak, took them to an airfield, lined them up, and drove over them in tanks or bulldozers.

The village chief at Buna was horrified by this massacre and managed to hide one of the wounded Japanese officers. The Americans discovered the soldier was being given safe haven, found him and killed him, and then executed the chief for protecting the enemy. Nishimura believed the story was true, and could be corroborated by local villagers who had witnessed the massacre.

After the war, the chief's daughter married a villager by the name of Iewago Torosian, who still lived in Buna, not far from Popondetta. Nishimura wanted to pay his respects to Torosian and thank him for the help his father-in-law gave to the Japanese. He wanted Torosian and his wife to know that the chief's supreme sacrifice had not been forgotten and that, indeed, he was seen as something of a hero by the dwindling band of Japanese survivors.

Nishimura's greatest anxiety in moving to New Guinea was not the mechanics of conducting his bone-collecting project, or the prospect of sleeping out in a one-man tent for weeks on end. It was more elementary: how he would be received by the local people, and how he would get them on side. The Japanese, both during the war and for a long time after it, were reviled by Papuans for their cruelty.

Even now, they were viewed with distrust. There had been reports of Japanese visitors who arrived by bus on the north coast of Papua New Guinea in the 1970s and 80s to visit the land where their relatives had lost their lives, being beaten by bands of locals and sent scurrying back to their buses. Not surprisingly, a national census in 1998 revealed that precisely 212 Japanese nationals had taken up residence in the country.

But not all such encounters between Japanese and Papuans ended badly. On one of his first visits back to New Guinea, Nishimura was accompanied by a friend from the 144th Regiment, Masataro Kitamura, who owed his life to local people who had hidden him in 1943. Kitamura had been stationed in the village of Kui; from there his role was to help evacuate Japanese troops. When Australian soldiers searched the village, some locals threw him into a latrine, and he hid there uncomfortably, but undetected. In 1979, Nishimura and Kitamura visited Kui, and Kitamura thought he recognised one of the villagers. The man, who had been just a boy when Kitamura knew him, was one of those who had risked his life for Kitamura during the war. Now the boy was a middle-aged man, with children of his own. The old veteran hugged the man, bowed to him and thanked him for saving his life.

Like Kitamura, Nishimura knew of some of the atrocities that had been committed against the villagers and wanted to show the Papuans that the Japanese were not all pitiless warmongers capable of unspeakable barbarity. He was partly on a mission to win over hearts and minds.

Soon after arriving in Popondetta, Nishimura bought a hectare of land on the other side of the road from the village. He built a two-storey house out of the local hardwoods, a relatively grand structure with windows on the second floor overlooking a tropical garden with mango trees and banana palms. He also set aside a plot in his garden to grow vegetables. No point in going to the market and paying a farmer good money for something he could grow in his backyard.

He had running water, a fridge and a small stove in the kitchen. But he didn't need much in the way of cooking utensils: a pot to boil water for his rice, a spoon to stir powdered milk, a knife to cut up mango and spring onions, and a pair of chopsticks. In one corner of the house, he began to build a shrine. This was where all the bones he found would be kept.

Over time, and after a lot of hard work by Nishimura, the initial reserve towards him gave way to acceptance by the local community. He would always hand out extra food to the villagers if he had any spare. And he decided to build a school on the land he'd bought, to educate local children whose families couldn't afford the modest monthly stipend for primary school.

Nishimura applied to the Japanese Embassy in Port Moresby for a government grant to help with its construction. Because mending relations with the Papuans had become a priority after the war, the Japanese Government gave Nishimura a ten million-yen grant for his project, an extremely generous allocation.

Nishimura asked a young man whom he had befriended, Miichin Sarigari, to be the principal of the school. To pay for some of the equipment he knew he'd need, Sarigari hired a grader and built some roads that were necessary for a palm oil company in Popondetta to expand its operations.

In the summer of 1981, Nishimura's daughter, Sachiko, spent an extended break with Nishimura in Popondetta and brought boxes of crayons and pencils and stationery with her to give to schoolchildren. They even arranged a meeting with Michael Somare, the former Prime Minister who was MP for East Sepik province, to talk about which schools were in direst need of their help.

Nishimura also began helping to train locals to become mechanics at the vocational centre in Popondetta, his vast mechanical knowledge and improvisational skills more than making up for the centre's rudimentary equipment and resources. Later, he built a car workshop and driving school at Akomuta village near Popondetta for Eric Torosian, the son of his friend, Iewago. This was done on the condition that Torosian took no fees from his students. He would be paid for the work he did as a mechanic in the workshop.

Iewago Torosian was about the only person in Popondetta that Nishimura felt total confidence in. He was an honest, serious and trustworthy man, who went out of his way to help Nishimura. One of the qualities Nishimura most appreciated was that Torosian was never blinded by the lure of money or other benefits the friendship might bring him. The pair exchanged brotherhood vows, and Nishimura became his elder brother. This did not involve a special ceremony, just a verbal agreement. Iewago, who could hardly read or write and only spoke Pidgin English, may have been poorly educated but he still understood the values that Nishimura held dear, and at the top of that list were loyalty and honesty.

Apart from Torosian and Sarigari, Nishimura had one other truly reliable friend in Papua New Guinea. Not long after becoming established in Popondetta, Nishimura also got to know Kikue Miyake, a young Japanese woman who first came on holiday to Papua New Guinea, and would later take up a job at the Japanese embassy. Whenever he flew down to Moresby from Popondetta, Ms Miyake met him at the airport – the rampant crime in the capital meant not even the most adventurous entrepreneur was prepared to risk setting up a taxi service – and took him shopping. She also helped him facilitate the grant money for his school, and generally assisted him with the sort of problems that can confront a foreign resident in a sometimes dangerous land. Much of her help was given voluntarily, and in addition to her embassy work.

Australian troops and Papuan carriers look north along the Kokoda Track in August 1942 where they would soon engage the Japanese troops heading their way. Nishimura was among the first Japanese soldiers to land in New Guinea.

The village of Kokoda is destroyed by Allied aircraft attacks during the Japanese retreat in late 1942.

At the height of the siege on the northern beaches in January 1943, M3 Stuart tanks, such as this one at Buna, were used by the Australians to help break open heavily fortified Japanese bunkers and pillboxes. Nishimura was entrenched nearby at Giruwa.

The bodies of four Japanese lie beside a pillbox after being killed in action at Buna.

An Australian soldier gives a Japanese POW, who was found starving and exhausted at Nauro in October 1942, a drink from his water bottle. Three months later, with Japanese supply lines cut and starvation rife, Nishimura's own weight had fallen to twenty-eight kilograms.

At Gorari, Australians bury Japanese soldiers in a mass grave. More than 600 Japanese died in fierce fighting here in November 1942. Many years later, Nishimura was to find dozens of bones in the area.

Nishimura, centre, with wounded comrades at the Japanese Army hospital in Taiwan in September 1943. His leg was badly gashed when his ship was torpedoed and sunk by an American submarine outside Kaohsiung Harbour.

Nishimura poses in uniform after leaving hospital in Taiwan. After nearly dying from starvation in New Guinea, the hospital diet of soft, sticky rice helped increase his weight to almost sixty kilograms.

At Wewak on 13 September 1945, the Commander of the Japanese 18th Army in New Guinea, Lieutenant General Hatazo Adachi, signs Japan's formal surrender document and hands over his battle sword to Australia's Major General Horace Robertson, symbolising his country's defeat.

Nishimura, seated, third from left, in Tokyo in 1961 with colleagues from his company, Tsunoda Electric, an offshoot of the Nishimura Machinery Research Institute, the eponymous engineering firm which he built into one of Tokyo's finest.

Shoichi Yokoi, Japan's second-last 'holdout' from WWII, was captured by two villagers in Guam in 1972 after hiding in a cave for twenty-eight years. His devotion to the Emperor struck a chord with Nishimura.

Hiroo Onoda, the last of the 'holdouts,' who finally surrendered in the Philippines in 1974 after waging a one-man war in the Filipino jungle for twenty-nine years. His sense of duty and refusal to surrender also made a huge impression on Nishimura as he finalised his plans to return to New Guinea.

These folders contain Nishimura's painstaking and detailed war research. The top one reads, '144th Regiment Battle Record by Names, Dates, Place and Unit'. The fifth one down is entitled 'List of Dead Men by their Birthplace and Date'; the sixth one, 'Name List of 15th Independent Engineer Regiment and 41st Infantry Regiment'.

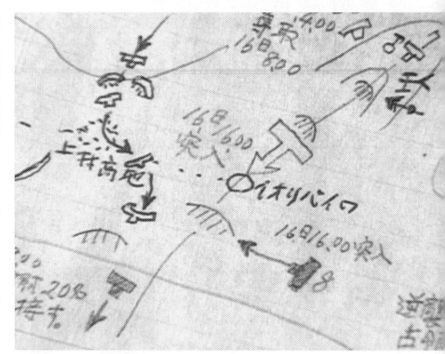

A drawing from his records shows detail from the key Japanese operation at Ioribaiwa, the most advanced position the Japanese reached on the Kokoda Track before their retreat. The circle at the centre of the map denotes Ioribaiwa the markings to the left show the Japanese attacks at a place called Kamimura Hill. It reads: 'Attack was conducted at 1600hrs on September 16th'.

Nishimura talks to his interpreter, go-between, house-sitter and friend, Miichin Sarigari. Sarigari became a crucial mediator for Nishimura whenever they entered villages for the first time.

Nishimura camped on the Kokoda Track outside Efogi during his dig in July 1988. He slept in tents with local villagers who came out to help his project. This was where the remaining forty-two members of his platoon were killed in September 1942. The decimation of his platoon played a large part in Nishimura's decision to return to New Guinea. In the left foreground, Ippongi – or One Tree – is visible as a vine-covered stump.

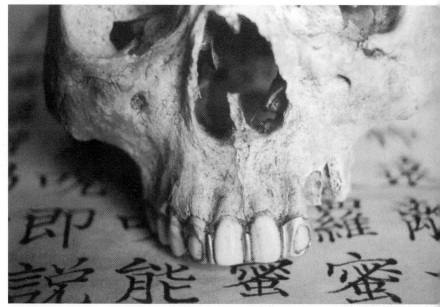

The skull with four gold teeth that Nishimura unearthed at Giruwa in 1989. The search for the soldier's family back in Japan, which lasted fifty days, proved one of the more remarkable episodes in Nishimura's 26-year bone-collecting crusade.

These two Japanese skulls are part of a macabre tourist exhibit at Giruwa, one of many such displays on the northern beaches. The skull on the left, with silver teeth, is believed to belong to Colonel Shigeaki Yamamoto, who became commander of Nishimura's 144th Regiment late in the Kokoda campaign.

This 'dog tag', or identification disc, (bottom) was found by Nishimura in 1982 and reads, '8426 First-Lieutenant Munenori Kuwabara'. He was a medical officer with the Nankai Shitai, the same unit that Nishimura fought with. Nishimura returned the dog tag to Kuwabara's son, Kanta, in Matsuyama City. The top picture was sent back by him with a letter of thanks to Nishimura. Kanta holds the dog tag and a Buddhist plaque on which his father's Buddhist name is written.

This flag belonged to a young soldier named Tadayoshi Morita, of the 18th Army, who fell ill with malaria and died while being cared for by villagers near Wewak. As was the custom in Japan, friends and family members wrote their name and messages of good luck – or *yosegaki* – on the flag before Morita departed for war.

Returned to Japan by Nishimura, the *yosegaki* flag – patched up and framed – is hung at the Riasho Temple in Komatsu City, where Morita's family register was kept.

The biggest of the three boats Nishimura brought from Japan, the *Okino-shima*. He sailed it to PNG, having just sat his test for a skipper's licence in Kochi City. The trip, one of Nishimura's grandest adventures, took nineteen days.

The remains of Japanese soldiers being cremated in Popondetta in 1995, with food, drink and incense laid out on the table as an offering for the spirits of the war dead. That year, the 50th anniversary of the war's end, the Japanese Ambassador in PNG personally asked Nishimura to hand over his bone collection to the government.

Sei-ichi Yano, right, at Buna in 1996 with the water pump that played a central role in another of Nishimura's great undertakings. Yano was the elder brother of Daizaburo Yano, a naval officer from Hokkaido, who died here early in 1943. Sei-ichi wanted to take the pump back to Japan as a memento of his brother. The man on the left is another member of the veterans association from Hokkaido.

Reunited at last, Nishimura with Sei-ichi Yano and the water pump he transported back to Japan. Yano holds a photograph of his younger brother, Daizaburo, as witnessed by a Hokkaido newspaper. The water pump was delivered to Yano's family on 2 January 1997, fifty-four years to the day since Daizaburo died.

（○年）１月３日（土曜日）

ニューギニア在住の元日本兵

命日に戦友の

足寄の遺族にポンプ渡す

遺品の弁当箱遺族へ

ニューギニアでの戦死から５５年ぶり

The metal lunch box belonging to Lieutenant Morimoto is returned to the soldier's brother (who was not present) in 1997. Nishimura, left, had carved Morimoto's name into the lunch box in 1941. Astonishingly, he found it fifty years later while digging at Waju, near Kokoda.

Nishimura with the then Prime Minister of PNG, William Skate (in dark shirt), in 1998. Skate was visiting the hospital in Nishimura's village of Popondetta. The Japanese became a celebrity of sorts as word of his campaign spread from village to village and all the way to Port Moresby.

Aboard a boat with Kazuko Sasaki, a Japanese woman who lost her brother, Naoyuki, during fighting on the northern beaches in 1942. With Nishimura's help, fifty-five years later she tracked down the spot where he is thought to have died.

The double-storey home built by Nishimura not long after arriving in Popondetta in 1981. In the garden he grew spring onions and mangoes. Over time, though, he had to barricade up the windows and erect a barbed-wire fence to prevent burglaries.

Back in Japan, this was Nishimura's home in suburban Tokyo, where his daughter Sachiko lived. Note the perspex hut on the roof, built by Nishimura so that he could sleep under the stars on a sheepskin rug and pretend he was back in New Guinea.

Posing for a newspaper article in Tokyo in 1999, just before setting off on his epic journey around Hiroshima Prefecture in search of the family to which the soldier's skull belonged.

Nishimura's daughter, Sachiko, and Masaaki Izawa, the president of the Association for War-Bereaved Families, pose next to the tomb in Shobara City where the skull with four gold teeth is buried. The 2.5-metre stone structure bears a statue of the Goddess of Mercy, or Kannon, as she is referred to in Japanese.

Nishimura's friend, Sadashige Imanishi, aged ninety-one, standing in front of the altar bearing gifts and food for the war dead at the annual Kochi-New Guinea Association memorial service in October 2006.

The 86-year-old Nishimura and his daughter, Sachiko, sit either side of the author at their home in Kazo City, Tokyo.

Initially, when people asked him why he had come to Popondetta, Nishimura was cagey. He didn't want to arouse suspicion or opposition. He told Ms Miyake he wanted to build roads from Popondetta to the coast, and from Wewak to Madang in the north west, just to help the local infrastructure. He also said he wanted to buy a boat to transport coconuts from one beach to another and sell them at the market in Moresby. Both stories had a grain of truth in them but were revealed over time to be thinly disguised reasons to help his bone-collecting project.

Word began to spread through the villages, and all the way to Port Moresby, of this strange, bespectacled Japanese man now living in Popondetta, building schools for local schoolchildren, teaching young men to become mechanics and trying to find the remains of Japanese soldiers. Eventually, it reached the government's offices in the capital. Somare and the Science, Culture and Tourism Minister, Stephen Tago, were intrigued – and a fraction concerned – by the reports coming from the other side of the Owen Stanleys. They sent word to Nishimura in Popondetta and called him to a meeting at their offices in Port Moresby.

But Nishimura was not overly concerned. He'd heard that Somare had grown up in a village in East Sepik province and his earliest education was in a Japanese-run primary school at Kauru during the war, where he learned to read, write and count in Japanese. Even though his father, a police officer, hid in fear for his life, Somare was said to remember the Japanese with affection. Nishimura thought he might be a beneficiary of the goodwill the former Prime Minister felt towards his countrymen. But he was sadly mistaken.

Somare and Tago welcomed him into an office, where Somare said little. Nishimura noticed immediately that Tago was eyeing him suspiciously. What's this I hear about you collecting the bones of Japanese soldiers? Tago asked

Nishimura. The bones are the property of Papua New Guinea, and are not to be removed under any circumstances. There are certain penalties for breaking this law. I hope I make myself clear when I tell you this.

It was true that a macabre industry in displaying Japanese skulls and bones, and war memorabilia such as pistols and swords, had sprung up in various places along the northern beaches. Skulls would be lined up in rows on a table or bench and the display would be garnished with bones and Japanese ordnance. Ghoulish entrepreneurs would charge tourists a few kina to view the decaying remains of the Japanese Army, spruiking their displays.

The Japanese Government had turned a blind eye to this practice, allowing the men who once wore the Imperial Japanese Army uniform with distinction to become nothing more than a sideshow. The government's appalling negligence in this regard made Nishimura's blood boil.

So he was not fazed in the slightest by this veiled threat from yet another man in a crisp suit and tie. It would only make him more determined. Nishimura fixed his stare on Tago and said: But these are my friends' bones. I want to collect as many as I can and pray for their spirits. Then I want to identify them and take them back to their families in Japan. You can punish me if you like, or put me in jail, but you will not be getting any bones that I find. Do you understand?

Tago was not used to being addressed in such a disrespectful way. The two of them had a heated row that shook the walls of the pre-fab office building where their meeting took place. Eventually, when Tago realised the sort of irresistible force he was dealing with, he calmed down a little.

OK, I understand your position, he told Nishimura. I understand how you feel. But the law is the law, and we can't change that. However, we'll look the other way and you can continue digging, because we understand why you're doing the work. You can keep the bones on the condition that you don't cause any problems with the local people. And you mustn't take any bones back to Japan without permission. If you do all that, I guarantee no one will touch you.

And that was that. This meeting took place in August 1981, about two years after Nishimura had made his first brief trip to New Guinea, and by this time, he'd still barely scratched the surface of his project. His priorities had been getting the locals onside, building himself a house and planning a new school. Now, he'd received an official imprimatur to go ahead with his shovel and box of tools and dig Kokoda's sticky red earth to his heart's content.

CHAPTER 13

Breaking ground

WORD OF NISHIMURA'S WORK also trickled back to Japan over time. A documentary filmmaker heard about it and dispatched a crew to Popondetta, to shoot a television documentary. The program was aired in Japan a short time later, and among the hundreds of thousands of people who watched it was one of the country's biggest businessmen, the president of Shinko Trading, Yoshiki Miyaji. Miyaji was so moved by the project to repatriate the bones of Japanese soldiers that he immediately volunteered his help. He offered to ship a bulldozer, road-grader and other heavy earth-moving equipment from Japan to New Guinea, free of charge. It was a gesture that was crucial in getting the Nishimura show off the ground.

With this machinery, Nishimura helped grade decent roads between Popondetta and villages on the northern beaches, such as Giruwa and Buna, and also in places from Madang to

Wewak in East Sepik province. Now, the trip from his home to the northern dig sites would take only forty minutes or so, a vast improvement on what it had been over the unmade tracks.

When he had last seen the coastal township of Giruwa in 1943, the war had taken a heavy toll on the surrounding environment. Its jungles had been completely mown down by artillery and aerial bombardments, and only the stumps of coconut palms poked out from the barren plain. Now lush foliage covered everything, making it completely unrecognizable from the place where the Nankai Shitai met its end. There were no telltale landmarks from which to get his bearings. The stakes, rock piles and other grave markers hurriedly erected by Japanese troops had all disappeared under a cloak of dense jungle.

One day, though, a little further inland at the Cape Killerton track junction, Nishimura came upon the rusting hulk of an Australian tank in a field and from that key discovery, he was able to calculate exactly where battles he knew of had been played out. In January 1943, three Australian tanks had attacked his unit's entrenched position. A Japanese soldier destroyed one by jumping on to its turret and detonating an anti-tank landmine. Nishimura was confident this was the tank he found near Cape Killerton junction, a clapped-out, overgrown shell with caterpillar tyres.

Having pinned down his location, Nishimura found his unit's old anti-aircraft position and then, after hacking away at the undergrowth, the tracks that led to the supply depot. There, consulting his own records and maps, Nishimura used a machete to clear away the positions he'd identified as possible burial sites. And then he began to find his bodies.

Small indentations in the earth usually signalled foxholes. When he found them, he would get out his landmine detector and run it over the ground nearby. If that did not set off the machine's telltale squeal, Nishimura would produce a long thin spike from his pack and drive it into the soil. The softer the soil, the more likely it was to contain a body. If it yielded to the spike, that usually indicated decomposed remains and there was a chance he'd find what he was looking for.

Then Nishimura would go to work with his shovel and garden hoe, removing sand and soil which had built up over forty years. The bodies were rarely buried deeper than a metre. Often, soldiers just dropped where they were shot; occasionally they were spreadeagled on top of each other.

Most of the Australian bodies from the siege of Giruwa had been collected by Australians before the end of the war and taken to Bomana Cemetery, a short car ride from Port Moresby. So Nishimura knew that not many of them should still be in the ground. There were also some important clues to the identity of the bones Nishimura found, and whether they were Australian or Japanese: the tibia and fibula were often still connected to army boots, and the boots were clearly identifiable as Japanese. So well preserved were some of the remains that skin from the soles of the feet were still stuck to the inside of the boots.

As well, Australian bones were as a rule much larger than the Japanese ones. And Japanese dog tags, or identity discs, could provide cast-iron evidence that the remains he was recovering belonged to his countrymen, not the Australians. When Nishimura found these dog tags they were not always attached directly to a body. Feral pigs or other forces had disturbed the remains, but at least they gave him a vital clue about the site.

When the landmine detector began its high-pitched squeal, Nishimura would begin to dig, usually without a great sense of anticipation, for it often turned up something minor – belt buckles, knives or tin cans. But one day he dug up a dog tag inscribed with the name Lieutenant Munenori Kuwabara. Nishimura discovered later that Kuwabara had been a medical officer assigned to the Nankai Shitai's HQ. He came from Matsuyama City, in the north-west section of Kochi prefecture.

Although Nishimura had not known Kuwabara, he felt a strong kinship with the former Nankai Shitai man, who would never have been far away from him during the New Guinea campaign.

He was not able to reunite Kuwabara's family with the disc until a year or so later, when television reporters from the broadcasting company TBS came to seek him out on the Kokoda Track for an interview. Nishimura showed them the tag and asked them if they could help find Kuwabara's family when they returned to Japan. They tracked down his son, Kanta, in Matsuyama City. Nishimura sent Kanta his father's identity disc and later received a heartfelt, if formal, thank-you letter from him. The letter enclosed a photograph of Kanta holding the oval-shaped tag.

The sense of satisfaction Nishimura got when he was able to bring a fallen soldier together with family was immense. For it not only gave the soldier overdue recognition at home, and provided some closure for the family, but made Nishimura's long hours walking and sweating over a shovel seem worthwhile.

Intrigued by his search, local people began turning out to help him dig. As word spread, farmers and landowners began to come to him and say: I've got bones on my farm, too, Nishimura. In these early days of his mission, Nishimura was rarely alone. He was beginning to learn Pidgin English, and soon knew enough to make his intentions understood. Sometimes, he had Miichin Sarigari by his side, and the Papuan, who had learnt a little Japanese, was able to act as an interpreter.

If he found bones on the property of a local landowner, he would bury them again and then go to talk to the owner. There are bones on your property here, can you please not plant crops over the top of them, or use a plough? Nishimura would say.

Please respect the fact there are Japanese soldiers there. He would return when he could to recover them.

In all, Nishimura returned to Giruwa four or five times over the following years. Of all the places he searched in New Guinea, this stretch of land proved the most fruitful, for this was where hundreds of Japanese soldiers were corralled into a small area and fought to their deaths.

It was during a later visit, in 1989, at a place on the beach he reckoned would be rich with Japanese bones, that Nishimura's landmine detector started beeping madly. Digging down almost a metre, his shovel clunked into something hard. Nishimura got down on all fours and began scraping away the sand. Suddenly the richness of his find was revealed: a perfectly formed skull with four gold teeth. Four other bodies lay nearby, two of them on top of each other.

In all, Nishimura found almost 120 bodies, or parts of bodies, along the stretch of beach at Giruwa. He recovered more remains than he ever thought possible in this part of the country. At Buna and Gona, two other townships along the coast from Giruwa, he retrieved another sixty skeletons.

After two years of digging, a back room in Nishimura's house was transformed into a kind of Aladdin's Cave of relics. Rows of bones and skulls were lined up neatly on the shelves, testament to the early success of his campaign. But he was careful to keep the treasure trove hidden from prying eyes. No one was allowed to see them except the Japanese families on pilgrimages to find out information about a lost relative.

Quite a few of these families, having heard of Nishimura's work, would visit him. They always asked the same questions: had he found bones at such and such a battlefield where their relative had fallen; and had he been able to identify those bones as belonging to a Corporal Sato or Private Takahashi or Lieutenant Watanabe. No, I'm sorry, he usually had to say, I haven't been able to identify many remains yet, but leave your address with me and if I find your relative, I'll let you know straight away.

As the years went on, the question of identifying the bones came to preoccupy him more and more, particularly with the advent of DNA testing. Such identification work would have to involve the Japanese Government, and he knew from experience that would not be easy. Still, he'd cross that river when he came to it; the important thing now was to keep adding to his collection.

CHAPTER 14

The lunch box

THE ONE DARK CLOUD on Nishimura's horizon concerned his work with the locals in Popondetta. The presence of a man of means in a remote part of a developing country was always going to present problems, and his attempts at philanthropy were slowly beginning to unravel. It had not helped that word of Nishimura's lucrative grant from the Japanese Embassy had begun to circulate.

Nishimura's house was repeatedly burgled, not that he had an awful lot to steal. Sick of the thefts, he erected a large wire fence around the perimeter of his block, topped with barbed wire. He also placed security bars across his windows. He was happy to share everything he had with the locals, he just didn't want them to help themselves.

He seemed prey to all sorts of low-lifes. A Japanese man appeared out of the blue one day in 1983 and introduced himself as Hirozaku Yasuhara. He was from a right-wing nationalist group in Japan, and also claimed to be chairman of an organisation that was recovering the remains of dead soldiers. It was called Ikotsu-shu-shudan, or Remains Recovery Association, and was also involved in bone-collecting in Okinawa and the Solomon Islands and other World War II battlegrounds.

Yasuhara said he was keen to help Nishimura with his mission but, after a while, the old soldier smelt a rat. And indeed, Yasuhara was not all he seemed. The man asked Nishimura if he would hand all his bones over to him, in the interests of helping Ikotsu-shu-shudan.

The reason for his request soon became clear. Yasuhara, in effect, had made a ransom demand of the Japanese Government through the embassy, telling them: give me sixty-four million yen or you won't get any of these bones back.

He promised all the landlords and village chiefs around Popondetta that they would get a slice of the ransom if they supported his scheme. Nishimura had been double-crossed. He confronted the troublemaker, who said to him: You're old, this is all mine now. I'm taking over this land and building and keeping the bones. We don't need you any more, get out. Nishimura did not take kindly to this attempt at intimidation.

But to his distress, some of the bones stored in his house were stolen by Yasuhara's men as part of this cock-eyed plan. Yasuhara also tried to convince the locals to establish marijuana plantations, saying he could help them sell the crops. Nishimura tried to tell all the chiefs they were dealing with a gangster, but he sensed that the kina signs were flashing before their eyes. Of course, the government flatly refused Yasuhara's demand for money, leaving him to deal with a group of very angry, empty-handed locals.

The trouble Nishimura was experiencing in Popondetta made the time he spent on the Track all the more appealing. It became his sanctuary. There, he could be alone with nature, and leave behind the human race. As he headed inland, away from the northern beaches, Nishimura increasingly performed his work in isolation. Just him, his tools, his one-man tent and his Sony World Band Receiver radio, which kept him company at night.

At Soputa, a village between Giruwa and Popondetta, he found two part-skeletons. This made sense. Although there had been no battle at Soputa, the Japanese stationed a medical unit for sick and wounded soldiers there, and two men had died there. He was directed to their remains by a local man, Champion Torosian, the elder brother of Iewago. The bones he carefully arranged in his backpack.

Crossing back through Popondetta, where he deposited the skeletons and stocked up on supplies, Nishimura headed west towards Kokoda and the start of the Track. On the way he stopped at a village called Waju, or Baribe as it was referred to by the Japanese, one of the villages that featured most significantly in Nishimura's wartime experience.

It was here that most of the remnants of the 144th Regiment were wiped out in the first two weeks of November 1942, as the Japanese retreated to the northern beaches. The 2nd and 3rd Battalions had been based at Waju, as had the regimental headquarters. More than 600 Japanese died as they made their last stand against the Australians here and around the neighbouring villages of Oivi and Gorari. Several more were captured as prisoners of war.

At Waju, the chief of the village was the owner of the local cocoa plantation and he let Nishimura stay on his land. Nishimura slept in his tent, but when it was really wet, he moved inside to a small storage room for cocoa.

Waju proved to be a productive site, as Nishimura had expected. Looking over his records, poring over his maps, then setting his landmine detector to work, Nishimura found first one, then two, then three Japanese bodies, all belonging to men who died during the fighting retreat.

Scratching around in the dirt one day, Nishimura came upon a metallic object that looked like nothing he had unearthed before. It was an aluminium lunch box, just like the one owned by his former training instructor, Lieutenant Yoshiyuki Morimoto. Surely it couldn't be the same one, surely not. That would be just too much of a coincidence.

He cleaned away grime from the lid and there, indeed, was the name of Yoshiyuki Morimoto, the Kanji characters carved by Nishimura himself in May 1941, more than forty years earlier. Nishimura felt elated, for the wheel had turned full circle: he was now recovering the bones and possessions of his comrades-in-arms.

Nishimura opened the lunchbox; it was empty. He recalled the day that Morimoto leant across during a break from training drills and asked him to inscribe his name on it. He remembered how much he admired the young officer, who had once accepted responsibility for Nishimura's accidental loss of part of a grenade launcher. Morimoto was a generous man, he reflected, and one of his superiors in the army that he admired most. To be reunited with this memento from the war, and all the memories it evoked, brought a tear to Nishimura's eye.

When he returned to Popondetta laden with his fresh collection of bones, Nishimura immediately took steps to discover the whereabouts of Morimoto's family. As far as he could tell from his research, the officer had died at Waju on 11 November 1942. Nishimura knew that he would need the help of a veterans association to trace Morimoto's relatives.

Nishimura was a long-standing member of the Kochi–New Guinea Association, a dwindling band of Nankai Shitai survivors who attended an annual remembrance ceremony in

Kochi each August, keeping alive the legend of the Shitai warriors who had fought one of the most dirty and dangerous campaigns in the Pacific. But it might be difficult to convince the organisation's leaders to help him, for his decision to return to the Track had disturbed them. When he outlined his plan to live in New Guinea and search for the remains of his comrades, it was not received well.

There were rules about these things, the association's president, Masura Moriki, had told him, official channels through which you need to go. We will not sanction your trip, nor will we recognise it. This is against our rules. If you go, you go on your own.

Another veteran, Sadashige Imanishi, with whom Nishimura had become good friends after the war, had returned to the jungles in 1969 as part of an official delegation from the Ministry of Health. They had stayed for three weeks at Popondetta, which was then under Australian control and a very beautiful town, quite different from its condition post-independence. Their group, with the help of locals, recovered dozens of bodies. The remains were burned completely and packaged up and brought back to Japan for internment at Chidorigafuchi, the magnificent cemetery in Tokyo for the unknown war dead.

But that trip was sanctioned by the government; Nishimura's one-man maverick campaign was not. Nishimura, never known to be cowed by orders from anyone, said: Fine. I'll go on my own then.

Moriki had been one of those soldiers who had seen out the war as a POW behind the wire at Cowra, in New South Wales, having been captured at Oivi, just near Waju, in late 1942. Some families refused to attend the regular reunions in Kochi because they thought he should have done the honourable thing and committed suicide rather than remain a POW. So he was no stranger to controversy himself.

Nishimura wrote to Moriki, telling him he had found Morimoto's lunch box and asking for help to locate his family. Moriki soon sent back word that he'd tracked down Morimoto's elder brother in Kochi City.

The brother, who was a very private person, said he would love to have the lunch box back in his family's possession but he did not want to be involved in any publicity. Nishimura and Moriki said: Of course. If that is your wish, so be it.

When the Morimoto family was finally reunited with the relic, the occasion was notable for the absence of the dead soldier's elder brother. In September 1997, the *Kochi Shimbun*, a local newspaper, reported the story prominently under the headline: 'War dead's lunch box finally returned to the family 55 years after his death in the Battle of New Guinea'. The reunion was held at the offices of Komatsu Construction, in Kochi, after Nishimura approached the company's president, Mr Komatsu, who had become a friend, and asked if the media conference could be held there. The photograph accompanying the report showed Nishimura, Moriki and Mr Komatsu with the lunch box, but no sign of Mr Morimoto.

If this event typified the sorts of frustrations Nishimura experienced in the course of his work, it also gave him great pride. His project, while painstakingly laborious, was occasionally bearing fruit. And now it was being recognised nationally, way beyond the small circle of Japanese families whom Nishimura had visited since 1981.

MESS TINS AND LUNCH BOXES had been used during, and just after, the war to transport ashes back to grieving families in Japan. Occasionally, the entire body of a dead soldier would be cremated, but when this proved impossible – as often it did – an arm or finger would be amputated, then cremated, and the ashes placed in the soldier's mess tin. It would then be wrapped in paper for transport back to Japan. In New Guinea and other theatres of war, such as Burma, there was often not the time or resources even to conduct a proper cremation ceremony. So, comrades would amputate a finger from their dead friend's hand and return it to his family for burial in Japan.

When there were no remains, the soldier's identity tag or disc was sent home in his mess tin. Occasionally – as in the case of Morimoto – the lunch box would arrive home with nothing in it. But that was generally immaterial to relatives who considered the deceased's spirit to be residing within. Still something, no matter how small, was better than nothing.

All told, Nishimura recovered thirty to thirty-five bodies from Waju: the number is vague because it was often impossible to tell which bones belonged to which body. Unless the skeleton was lying there virtually intact, it became like a jigsaw puzzle trying to match up the right bones with the right bodies. It did not help that, over such a passage of time, feral pigs and other wild animals had been allowed to snuffle and dig among the corpses, disturbing the rest of the dead.

He had been hoping to find the body of Yoshiaki Yamamoto, the lance corporal in the medical unit who had helped Nishimura dress the body of platoon commander Inoue at Efogi. Putting himself in great personal danger, Yamamoto had removed Inoue's clothes, cleaned the four bullet wounds to his head, torso and arm, applied bandages to the wounds and then re-clothed Inoue. Two months after that, Yamamoto was shot dead himself, at the battle of Baribe, on 8 November 1942.

Nishimura was desperate to find the body, take it back to Japan and give him the decent burial he deserved. But he never turned up so much as a dog tag that identified Yamamoto, so he was never able to tell whether the medic's remains were among the thirty-five or so bodies he collected or not. He just liked to tell himself they were.

From Waju, Nishimura walked west towards Kokoda. He knew almost all of the Japanese bodies at Kokoda had been picked up by Allied forces and transferred to Buna, but wanted to have a look around anyway. Supported by a sturdy pole fashioned from a branch, Nishimura then walked on to Deniki. He remembered seeing six graves there forty-four years earlier, containing the bodies of men from the 1st Battalion. Nishimura was able to find the location where he'd seen the graves, but though he scoured the site for hours, he was only able to turn up two skeletons.

Isurava, further down the Track, had been the scene of ferocious fighting in 1942 but, for once, Nishimura's unit was not involved. They had been engaged at Abuari, to the east. Because Nishimura wanted to confine his search to places where his 5th Company had fought, he chose not to search at Isurava, concentrating his efforts instead on places where he knew the terrain.

He was aware that Imanishi had tried without luck to find bodies at Abuari during his brief government-sponsored dig in 1969, so he skipped the village and headed south along the Track, stopping here and there where the scenery evoked a memory or the terrain sparked a flashback.

Each time, the routine would be the same. He'd study his maps and research, work out the most likely places the soldiers fell, and then pitch his tent. With the landmine detector, he would go to work, sweeping it across the top of the ground, waiting for the telltale beep. The discovery of knives and belt buckles and tin cans was often a good guide; bones would usually not be far away. If there was no signal, he'd plunge his spike into ground that looked like an old foxhole and hope it sank down without much resistance. That was usually a positive sign.

The longest time he spent alone on the Track was twenty-five days. His standard uniform during the day – forty years after discarding his army-issue khakis and cap – was a loose-fitting cotton T-shirt, money-belt, baggy cotton pants and lightweight Japanese farmer's boots, a calf-length design with rubber soles.

Each day, he'd be up at the crack of dawn, and breakfast on rice, perhaps with some tinned fish, although that was something of a luxury because most tinned tuna and sardines in Papua New Guinea had been imported from Japan, and cost more than double what Nishimura was used to paying.

The rice he bought in PNG was an Australian long-grain variety. He ate a lot of roasted banana, some of which he had grown; he also consumed an edible tree leaf that the locals called cabbage. Mangoes picked from his garden formed a large part of his diet and, as a vitamin source, he also grew fresh spring onions. Sometimes when on the Track he would buy home-grown fruit and vegetables from local villages. Papua New Guineans did not like raw fish in the sashimi style, so any fish he ate was generally cooked. And Nishimura, who had never done much cooking when he was married and living in Tokyo, busied himself over a fire each night when on the Track, producing simple and inexpensive dinners that would sustain his digging.

At night, in his tent, in the jungle darkness so black that it had unnerved him as a young soldier, he'd switch on his short-wave radio set and listen to the news service of Radio Japan. Light entertainment and music he considered a waste of time. When he turned his radio off after the eight o'clock news, there was barely a sound to be heard.

First-time visitors to the jungle might imagine it was alive with the songs and whistles of birdlife. But the villagers were so proficient with a slingshot or bow and arrow that there was often precious little birdsong at all. The creatures had either been scared away from village gardens or ended up in a pot.

Occasionally, a young bureaucrat from the Japanese Ministry of Health would be sent from Tokyo to supervise Nishimura's digging, the government wanting to both monitor his collection and give the appearance to the New Guinea Government that they were sensitive to local concerns about him. Hauled out of an air-conditioned office in Tokyo and dragged into this jungle dripping with humidity, the man was ill-equipped for his task. He started drinking in the morning to dull his pain and by lunchtime was a physical wreck, unable to climb any hills of note, let alone keep up with Nishimura.

Up in the mountains, local people would sometimes come out of their villages and help Nishimura. They were tireless workers and an invaluable help. But they were more inclined to walk at night when it was cooler. A rope would be tied to each member of the group and they'd troop off together in the pitch black. It reminded Nishimura of the war, when the Japanese did so much of their walking – and fighting – at night.

This had taught him to be able to sleep anywhere, at any time. If one of his officers said, we need to leave this position at 3 am, Nishimura developed the knack of going straight to sleep and then waking just before the appointed time, as if fitted with a mobile alarm clock. In Tokyo, he used the same trick when riding on trains, falling into a deep sleep before jolting upright at his station, as if prodded by an unseen ghost.

After every extended stopover on the Kokoda Track, Nishimura would lug his booty back to Popondetta, sort the bones out on his shelves and decide which ones he had the best chance of identifying. Occasionally, he would have to cremate some of the remains because they were too badly decomposed to transport home. Then he would keep the ashes, package them up in special boxes tied with a ribbon and take them back to Japan as well. If he couldn't identify every bone, then he would at least give the ashes to Chidorigafuchi, where they would be entombed with the hundreds of thousands of other, nameless Japanese war dead.

Strangely, and he could never work out why this might be, it was the leg bones – tibias and fibulas – that he found more often than any other parts of the body. Often the legs still had boots on their feet. Nishimura ascribed a special significance to this: his friends were waiting for him. Their upper bodies had gone, but the legs and boots were waiting to be returned home to Japan.

ALL THIS WORK BEGAN to cost a substantial amount of money. Nishimura needed digging equipment and basics such as clothes, medicines, batteries for his radio and landmine detector, petrol and oil for his bulldozers and heavy machinery, a tent and groundsheet. And then, of course, there was his food, small though that outlay was.

Nishimura had never received a war pension. He had been made platoon leader late in 1942, and promoted to Lance Corporal, so that should have entitled him to quite a decent pension. But American planes bombed Kochi City late in the war and all of Nishimura's records were lost when a government building was destroyed in the raid.

It was only much later, after he had managed to establish his credentials by way of his war record in New Guinea, that he was paid his rightful government benefit. The pension was only worth A$5000 a year (480,000 yen), or maybe $400 a month, but in New Guinea that modest stipend could be stretched to go a long way. He had relied heavily, too, on the fortuitous windfall he received from the sale of his parcel of land in Kochi. Together, those two streams of income, plus the help of benefactors such as Yoshiki Miyaji, funded his campaign – not that he wanted for much, living as frugally as he did – and his philanthropic work with the locals.

But his generosity was barely being reciprocated. For all the success of Nishimura's campaign, and the mounting count of bodies recovered, his problems in Popondetta persisted. He began to entertain the idea of moving to a small village on the Track, somewhere like Efogi where he had such close emotional ties.

CHAPTER 15

Ippongi

NISHIMURA REMEMBERED MOST OF their names, and how they died. But by cross-referencing Japanese and Australian war records, he was able to compile a definitive record of the fate of his forty-one colleagues killed or mortally wounded at Brigade Hill on 8 September 1942.

The list showed not only which men had perished in each wave of the battle, but the cause and time of their deaths – to within five minutes accuracy, he proudly said. All of the dead were from his native island of Shikoku. Thirty-eight were from Kochi prefecture, and three from Ehime prefecture, a neighbouring region.

Nishimura carried this list in his pocket in July 1988, when he walked down the Track from Efogi towards Brigade Hill. With ease, he located a massive, rotten stump covered in vines that was the remains of the tree he and his friends had known as Ippongi. This was the most obvious landmark of battle he'd found during his entire expedition, and he took it as an auspicious sign, for the dig at Ippongi was the most important part of his mission. He hoped that, from here, finding and digging up his friends' remains would be easy.

Nishimura enlisted the help of a number of villagers from Efogi and soon established a good rapport with them. They knew about his project and were only too willing to follow him up the Track when he started his dig. In its first phase there were often five and six tents on the Track, housing this group of amateur archeologists trying to find the remnants of the 144th Regiment.

Progress was slow. Nishimura knew exactly where most of his friends had fallen – he could remember details of the battle as if it were last week, as well as the location of his platoon's foxholes on the east side of the track – but the mine detector stayed silent and the red earth defiantly yielded nothing. Day after day, he swept the machine across areas he knew contained Japanese bones, without results. He and his helpers began digging trenches to find something – anything – but still they came away empty-handed.

The frustration was intense. As morale dissipated, the villagers began to return to Efogi, thinking Nishimura was not just wasting his time but slowly going out of his mind. He was almost losing faith in the project himself. But he remembered that the platoon had been told by its officers that the Australians sometimes dug up Japanese corpses to see whether they'd been killed by gunfire, illness or starvation. Nishimura and his fellow soldiers had been ordered to be extra careful in burying bodies: to do it so they would never be found. So he kept hoping.

One day, Nishimura began to dig up some black soil. Close by, he found five leg bones still wearing Japanese Army boots. They had been scorched by fire. Then he realised what had happened in the weeks after the Battle of Ippongi. The killing field had been littered with hundreds of bodies and parts of bodies. Under the intense tropical sun, incubated by humidity, the remains became so putrefied that the stench was overwhelming. The Australians returned to the area sometime later and, repulsed by the abominable smell, burnt the Japanese bodies en masse on a funeral pyre. That was why the soil was blackened with ash.

As he surveyed the area, and dug around the edges of the mass cremation, Nishimura realised he would never find the remains of his friends. There were no bones – not even identity tags or knives or lunch boxes – just a layer of dark grey ash sandwiched between the ochre-coloured soil.

This was the greatest blow he had suffered in his campaign so far. In all those years he had been daydreaming and scheming about his return, Ippongi had always featured large in his plans. This was where he had seen almost his entire platoon wiped out, including old friends from Kochi. It was as if a section of his life had been erased, just like that, and now he had no chance to retrieve it. His friends would remain forever in New Guinea, abandoned in the shadows beneath the impenetrable jungle canopy. Nishimura was devastated. A hollow feeling of depression ate away at him for days.

Trying to come to terms with his disappointment, Nishimura decided to dig up a couple of shovelfuls of the ash and put them in his backpack, ready to be stored in his house at Popondetta. He cremated the five leg bones he had found, and packaged those ashes up in a separate container. For the next five years, he kept these blackened remains in two aluminium tins, the sort you buy powdered milk in from any supermarket. As it happened, the two he used were for milk-powder made in Australia. He placed the tins on a Buddhist altar in his home and, each day before breakfast, he lit incense sticks and prayed for them. On top of the altar were rusting Japanese ordnance, including a pistol, as well as forks and spoons he'd recovered. He always set out offerings of food to the spirits of the dead – rice, tea and water. Under the shrine were plastic bags full of Japanese bones he'd collected.

Those milk tins carrying the cremated bodies of his friends watched everything he did. It was meaningful to have them by his side, sharing his life. People who had only known peacetime couldn't hope to understand his reasons for collecting and keeping the decaying bones of soldiers, nor the fanaticism with which he had attacked his project. His wartime friends would have understood, though, and it was comforting to have them close by.

There was no cheap sentimentality about recovering those remains and bones. He could not do the work if he started thinking in emotional terms: the work had become his life. *Some of those men died to save him. In a way, those ashes were more important to Nishimura than the bones of his own family.*

Before his next trip back to Kochi, Nishimura decided it was time to return the remains of his friends home to Shikoku. So he loaded the ashes into two bags, and packed them tightly into his suitcase. He rationalised that he wasn't carrying bodies as such, just a light, powdery human form, so he didn't feel the need to tell the government about his baggage, or declare it on his Customs form. Yes, there'd be some explaining to do if his suitcase was accidentally jolted open and travellers at the airport were suddenly covered in the fine grey dust of dozens of Japan's exalted war dead, but he figured he'd take the risk.

Nishimura landed the ashes safely, and delivered them to Kochi, where they were interred at the Gokoku Shinto shrine – Gokoku, meaning 'protect the nation'. The ghosts of the 3rd Platoon of the 144th Regiment were back where they belonged.

WALKING IN THE DAPPLED light of the Kokoda Track, visitors have to adjust their eyesight to the intense variation between light and dark that filters down from the jungle canopy. In such conditions, monuments to fallen soldiers can catch trekkers by surprise. Between Isurava and Alola, they run almost headlong into a monument to the Australian soldier Lieutenant Harold 'Butch' Bisset, a handsome metal plaque attached to a huge rock that sits right on the edge of the track. Bisset, from Melbourne, was a larrikin jackaroo and amateur boxer who became one of the spiritual leaders of the 2/14th Battalion. Here, in August 1942, he was caught by a burst of Japanese machine-gun fire and died soon afterwards in the arms of his younger brother, Stan.

Across the river near Menari, another plaque chiselled into rock commemorates the life and work of Australian camera-man Damien Parer, who won an Academy Award for his wartime documentary *Kokoda Front Line!*. He died at Palau on 17 September 1944: keen to get shots of the faces of advancing soldiers, Parer was walking backwards behind a tank, filming a group of marines advancing under fire, when he, too, was felled by Japanese machine-gunners.

Then there are the official Australian memorials – an imposing one recently built at the major battlefield of Isurava, to honour all the Australians and Papua New Guineans who died there, and the eerily beautiful Bomana Cemetery near Port Morseby, evidence of the Australian nation's readiness to remember the enormous sacrifices made by its soldiers in the hellish PNG campaign.

The Japanese lost many more men than the Allies in the Kokoda and northern beaches campaigns – approximately 13,000 against the Australian and American total of 3095. But visitors to the Track soon notice that monuments to the Japanese dead are few and far between.

One of the most conspicuous Japanese memorials was erected at Buna by the government of Japan, not long after the end of the war. But after Papua New Guinea's independence in 1975, a tax was levied on the land where the memorial stands. The landowner didn't want to pay for the upkeep of a Japanese war memorial, so when Nishimura later appeared on the scene, he turned to him for help. Never one to shirk his duty, the former Nankai Shitai man agreed to provide 10,000 yen (A$110) annually to maintain the monument and cover the land tax bill. Although it was not a huge amount, Nishimura resented paying when the government should have been meeting the bill: he felt that he was already doing the government's work with his bone-collecting.

In all, the Japanese Government built seven memorials in this corner of the Pacific – two large ones, at Rabaul in New Britain and Wewak on the north coast of New Guinea, and five smaller ones including the monument at Buna. It continues to pay two million yen (A$22,000) each year to have the Rabaul and Wewak memorials maintained, but contributes nothing towards the upkeep of the other five, which are in various states of disrepair.

Which is why the handsome Japanese monument at Efogi, about 1.7 metres high and made from smooth river stones, is so notable. Nishimura built this himself, without permission from the government or the Kochi–New Guinea Association, because he felt some sort of permanent tribute needed to be made to his fallen comrades from the 3rd Platoon, 144th Regiment and Nankai Shitai. They were all buried here, sleeping the sleep of the dead, thousands of kilometres from the whale-meat restaurants and sake bars of their beloved Kochi. And they deserved better than to be left, ignored and anonymous, in a mass grave.

With the help of local children, Nishimura fetched five

dozen or more large river stones and lugged them up the hill to the village. He organised two Cessnas to fly in several bags of cement to the Efogi airstrip from Port Moresby. Then he and some of the villagers put the bags over their shoulders and carried them from the grass runway of the airport up to the memorial site. Mortared together, the river stones formed the four-sided base of the monument.

The headstone he had been thinking about for a while. On a previous trip to Japan, to Okinoshima Island in Kochi prefecture, Nishimura had found a large rock, a smooth, light-brown, oval-shaped beauty; this, he decided, would be the one to sit atop his plinth. He had been at Okinoshima visiting one of his old friends from the army and thought it only fitting that the headstone should come from Kochi, the home of the 144th Infantry Regiment. But he decided it would carry a non-denominational tribute in order to honour all those who fell in New Guinea, regardless of which side they fought on, or of race or creed. In striking Kanji characters, the headstone would read simply: *To The Loyal War Dead*.

Nishimura transported the stone to Tokyo, where he knew the monks at Zenshoan Temple, one of the most famous Zen temples in Japan, could engrave the inscription. Zenshoan happened to be the temple where Japan's Prime Minister at the time, Yasuhiro Nakasone, regularly prayed and practised Zen meditation. Somehow, the Prime Minister came to hear of the work the head monk was doing with Nishimura's headstone. He was fascinated by the brief account he was given of Nishimura's story, and asked to meet the former soldier.

Nakasone listened, captivated, as Nishimura described his project, and told him he was honoured to meet such a great patriot. In fact, so taken was he by the cause, Nakasone offered twenty million yen (A$220,000) of his private funds to help Nishimura with his campaign. This money would be used to travel around Papua New Guinea, and to update some of the equipment he needed for digging, but it was also intended as a de facto salary in recognition of the work Nishimura was doing on behalf of the Japanese nation.

Nishimura was flattered by the offer, and the government leader's interest in his work, but respectfully declined it. He told Nakasone that he was not doing the work in the hope of any financial gain; that was never his motivation. He had given his word to these soldiers that he would come to collect them after the war, and now he was carrying out his promise. Nothing more, nothing less.

Privately, Nishimura was also worried that if news of the payment ever leaked out in the public domain, it would spell political trouble for Nakasone, whom he had come to see as a friend. If the Communist Party found out, for example, and painted Nakasone as a supporter of the war who was using money to keep alive the memory of this shameful episode in Japan's past, his reputation might be sullied.

So, Nishimura bowed and said: Thank you for your kind thoughts, but I must refuse your offer.

A short time afterwards, Nakasone sent the former grenadier a card expressing regret that he could not be of any assistance. In it, he wrote: 'Please accept this message card instead. I am sure this luggage won't be as heavy for you as your headstone.' Nakasone signed the card with the salutation *Issho soshin*, which translates roughly to 'Always with a straight, honest and pure mind.'

It was because of his unflinching honesty and unbending principles that Nishimura attracted disciples wherever he went. People soon realised they were in the presence of a dynamic force who simply fizzed with electricity. He exerted a kind of mesmerising power over all those around him. Leading Japanese industrialists such as Akio Morita, Mitsuo Yokota and

Yoshiki Miyaji, and now top-level politicians such as Yasuhiro Nakasone, were drawn to him, intrigued by his views on life and the uncompromising way he pursued his ideals, and swept up by his boundless energy.

When he returned to Papua New Guinea armed with his freshly inscribed headstone, Nishimura headed off down the Kokoda Track to Efogi once more. A local landowner helped Nishimura put the finishing touches to the monument and, on 5 July 1989, it was finally completed.

Efogi, which had figured so large in Nishimura's war experiences, was a pretty village, the huts built on stilts with roofs of a thatched broad leaf. The common area between the huts was swept clean and tropical flowers were planted around its perimeter. Nishimura ended up spending so much time there, that he built a hut for himself.

He organised for tools and building materials – timber, galvanised iron, shovels and so on – to be transported from Port Moresby in one of the Cessnas that brought him the bags of cement. Local women weaved him bamboo walls for the hut, while the men helped in its construction. It was built about a hundred metres away from his memorial, at the edge of the village. Here he came regularly, walking the five or six days from Popondetta, to rest and pray for his dead comrades from the 3rd Platoon. While he never moved to Efogi permanently, it offered a much more tranquil existence than crime-riddled Popondetta.

Because the Japanese have still not been forgiven by some for their role in the war, his monument is occasionally vandalised by Australian trekkers or aggrieved locals. But each time, Nishimura or the local landowner has gone back and repaired the damage. Nishimura can understand the resentment. The war did strange things to people: to the soldiers who fought the battles, and to the citizens back home who held life-long grudges years after the final bullet was fired. Unbreakable bonds were forged between the men who fought alongside each other; lasting enmities were created between foes.

Nishimura had to concede that the war had done strange things to him as well. With each passing year, he seemed to grow more frustrated with the rules and conventions of living, and more reckless in the pursuit of his personal mission.

CHAPTER 16

The sailor

IN 1984, FIVE YEARS into his stay in Papua New Guinea, a revelation came to Nishimura: boats. We need boats. It was as if he had suddenly remembered the rafts he used to sketch when he had first started planning his project, back in his office in Tokyo.

Boats could be used to transport locals from village to village, to ship coconuts and other produce from the beaches to the market, and to ferry the people of Popondetta from the northern coast around to Port Moresby, saving them a ten-day walk. Boats could also be used for carrying skeletal remains, but that was another matter. Nishimura decided to buy a boat and give it to his friend Iewago Torosian, and Iewago's son, Eric, on the condition that it was available to him whenever he wanted.

So that was how Nishimura came to be in Japan in April

1986. He had flown back to Kochi City in 1984 and begun his search for the right vessel. Now it was time to seal the deal. The boat had to be cheap, of course, that was the main priority. Its condition was of less concern. It had to be seaworthy, but he was not looking for something in mint condition; it was not going to grace the commodore's mooring at Royal Port Moresby Yacht Squadron.

Nishimura had no idea how to sail or navigate. He had rowed a dinghy about on Urado Bay when he was maybe nine years old in Kochi, and been a passenger on plenty of troopships during the war, but piloting his own boat was one thing Nishimura had not yet done in his life. Still, he wasn't going to let that faze him.

One day, in Sukumo City, in the west part of Kochi prefecture, he came across a vessel that seemed to suit his purpose. It had been used by the Port Maritime Authority as a ferry between the small islands off Kochi. It was twenty-three metres long and weighed more than eighty tonnes, so it was not an insubstantial craft. It would have tested the skills of a far more experienced skipper, let alone a novice yet to sit his licence. And the ship's condition was about as far from mint as possible. The hull was rusty, and above the waterline her white paint was flaking off. She looked like what she was — a vessel that had been decommissioned after many years of solid service. Still, she was a bargain, and that was important.

Nishimura went to the Coast Guard office at Kochi and asked them if he could sit an exam for a first-class skipper's licence. He studied various training manuals for three weeks, until he felt ready to sit the test. He taught himself how to read a nautical map and find his way around a boat, what the various buttons and levers were for, and how to respond in an emergency.

But after sitting the test and passing, he discovered that it only gave him a licence to operate a twenty-tonne boat. He was furious, and lambasted the Coast Guard officials for making him sit the wrong exam. Frustrated and impatient, Nishimura said he would get around the problem by buying a four-tonne boat to tow his eighty-tonne ship out into international waters. The official told him that a four-tonne boat was only allowed to go eight kilometres from shore. In an even more obstinate mood than usual, Nishimura said: That's fine. As soon as I am eight kilometres from shore, I'll switch the engines off and drift until I get close to another country, then I'll switch the engines on again. And I'll do this until I drift all the way to Papua New Guinea.

The official looked at him with a pained expression, wondering how it was that he came to be lumbered with this pest, this demented old man who would not take no for an answer. He told Nishimura his plan was so ridiculous, he wanted nothing to do with it.

The old soldier was frustrated by the small-mindedness of these petty officials. Couldn't they see the big picture? He stormed back into Coast Guard headquarters and said: Right, I'm leaving on my eighty-tonne ship and if you shoot me out of the water, you shoot me. I don't care, I'm going anyway.

The bureaucrats were confused by this very un-Japanese display of obstinance and rebellion. Finally, in exasperation, one of them said to Nishimura: OK, as long as you deregister the nationality of the ship, you can go. That means as soon as you untie the ropes and pull up anchor, the ship no longer belongs to Japan. Then you are not bound by Japanese law. But you run the risk of being arrested by another country's Coast Guard for piracy. And there's one other condition, too: you'll need at least one crew member as a minimum to accompany you on your voyage, otherwise it'll be far too risky. If you do those two things, we'll let you sail out of here.

Normally a ship of the size of Nishimura's ferry would

require a crew of three or four experienced sailors – not a 66-year-old skipper with zero hours on his sailing log, and a stranger he had found on the street as his first mate. But that's how the *Okinoshima-Go* started her new life as a vessel on the high seas.

Nishimura scoured the bars and shops around Sukumo City asking if anyone was interested in crewing a ship that was sailing to New Guinea. Several people expressed interest but quickly changed their minds when they clapped eyes on the rusting hulk moored in the harbour. Word began to spread about the slightly deranged old man who was planning to sail this rustbucket over the equator. But, one day, a man named Morita who owned a dive shop in Sukumo came to see Nishimura. He said he had long hankered to dive the reefs and shipwrecks around New Guinea and that he would love to accompany Nishimura on the trip. He confessed he had no experience of sailing a ship of this size. No matter, said Nishimura, we can work it out together as we go. It'll be an adventure.

At 5 am on 14 June 1986, Nishimura and Morita waved goodbye to Kochi port and chugged out of Urado Bay on the *Okinoshima-Go*, setting a course for Papua New Guinea. Behind them trailed a 3.9-tonne fishing boat, the *Ichiryo-maru*, which had been given to Nishimura by a local bonito fisherman. She, too, had been put out of service for being too old, but Nishimura wanted to bring the boat along as a gift to the good people of Buna.

The *Okinoshima-Go*, however, wasn't equipped to navigate the South Seas. The vessel carried no radar, gyrocompass, long distance communication equipment or nautical charts. In his total naivety, Nishimura had looked at a map and seen that Papua New Guinea lay due south of Japan, so his plan consisted of a single idea: keep heading due south and sooner or later we'll bump into PNG.

Of course, the scheme was so incompetent, and so hopelessly optimistic, that Nishimura and his crewmate ran headlong into trouble, and very nearly disaster. Only a few days out of Japanese waters, they sailed straight into a summer typhoon which whipped up great walls of water, much higher than the ship. The *Okinoshima-Go* listed first one way, then the other, at an angle of thirty degrees. It was night, and the novice skipper did his best to control the ship in the pitch black. But the rope holding the *Ichiryo-maru* snapped and the fishing boat disappeared into the distance. A short time later, the anchor on the port side also came adrift. Nishimura had to change the ship's direction to avoid being swamped, running it up the face and down the back of waves rather than across them.

When a watery sun rose the following morning, Nishimura – by now, drenched and exhausted – could see a dark shape on the horizon. It proved to be an island, and he eventually navigated the ship around to its sheltered side where they anchored in a bay.

In the turmoil of the previous fourteen hours, Nishimura had become hopelessly lost. He could not be sure, even approximately, where they were. From the deck, he and Morita could see a house among the palm trees about a kilometre away, and a man on the beach waving his arms at them. Nishimura said to Morita: Put your dive gear on, jump in, and go and ask the man where we are, and how we get to Papua New Guinea from here.

Morita was initially reluctant but, after some persuading, he donned his wetsuit, flippers and mask and dived into the water. A short time later, Nishimura could see him waddling up the beach towards the man, and the two of them were soon waving their arms about, pointing and gesticulating, as if Morita had done nothing more unusual than alight from his car and ask directions of a traffic policeman.

It transpired they were anchored off Anatahan Island, south-east of Iwo Jima, and maybe 1100 kilometres south of Kochi. The storm had blown them well east of their planned course. But the lone inhabitant of Anatahan Island said to Morita: Just follow this chain of islands, which are called the Mariana Islands, go past Saipan and Tinian, and keep going south until you hit Guam. From there, set your compass for due south and in no time you'll find yourself in Papua New Guinean waters. Morita was unconvinced.

ALTHOUGH NISHIMURA DID NOT know it at the time, Anatahan Island had been the scene of one of the more remarkable episodes involving Japanese holdouts – almost in the league of the famous Sergeant Yokoi and Lieutenant Onoda. In June 1944, American forces sank three Japanese ships, and a group of thirty survivors found their way to Anatahan, a small volcanic island about nine kilometres long and three kilometres from one side to the other. Among them was a woman, an Okinawan.

Early in 1945 a B-29 Superfortress plane crashed on the island, killing the aircraft's crew. The life of the holdouts improved dramatically. They used metal from the American bomber to fashion crude implements such as pots, knives and roofing for their hut. The oxygen tanks were used to store water, and clothing was made from nylon parachutes. The cords from the parachutes became fishing line, the springs from machine-guns, fish hooks.

Later that year, the Americans dropped pamphlets on the island, telling the Japanese the war was over, but the holdouts rejected the pamphlets as American propaganda. The group spent another seven years living on the island, eking out a sparse existence, eating coconuts, taro, wild sugarcane, fish and lizards. They smoked crushed, dried papaya leaves wrapped in the leaves of bananas and made an intoxicating local brew known as 'tuba' – or coconut wine.

The holdouts were equipped to survive on Anatahan indefinitely, but personal differences were growing among them, inflamed by drinking and competition for the woman's favours. Eleven of the holdouts died, six as a result of violence. Eventually they were convinced to give themselves up. Two American commanders went ashore by rubber boat on 30 June 1951, and formally accepted the last group surrender of World War II.

NOT LONG AFTER LEAVING Anatahan, a similar tale of anarchy began to unfold aboard the *Okinoshima-Go*. Morita, who apparently thought he'd signed on to work on a small luxury liner, where he'd be required to swab down the decks once in a while, soon discovered he was being press-ganged into action, day and night. This was not what he'd expected at all. Soon, the two men were arguing incessantly. Morita was an easy-going fortysomething, not accustomed to such a strict regime; Nishimura was a tyrant for whom the phrase 'ran a tight ship' might have been invented.

Somehow, bereft of even the most rudimentary navigational gear apart from a compass, Nishimura and Morita managed to dodge the reefs, quays, rocks and wrecks and reached their destination. At 5 pm on 3 July 1986 – almost three weeks after they set out – the pair anchored the *Okinashima-Go* at Madang, on the north coast of Papua New Guinea. They'd completed a 4500-kilometre voyage in a decommissioned rust-bucket, a remarkable feat of seamanship that owed as much to luck as to Nishimura's extraordinary determination and tenacity. The journey took nineteen days, most of which Nishimura spent at the wheel; he lost seventeen kilograms in the process.

At anchor in the deep-water bay outside Madang, Nishimura raised the yellow flag, signifying he wanted a health inspection. But Customs officials assumed the ship had sailed from another port in PNG and ignored the signal. Eventually, two Customs men came out to meet them. They asked Nishimura where he'd come from. Japan, said the crusty old salt. They said it was impossible that such an old wreck could have come that far. Where are your charts, they asked? And if what you say is true, how on earth did you manage to avoid the hidden reefs and rocks in the area? It's a miracle you landed here safely. Nishimura, whose one fairly rudimentary map showed the Admiralty Islands and Bismarck Archipelago and, closer to shore, Karkar Island and Long Island, said they had brought no other guides with them.

Then one of the men in crisp white uniforms asked how many people were on board. Just the two of us, replied Nishimura. The man shook his head. Two? It's impossible to control a ship of this size with a crew of two. Nishimura assured them they were not telling lies and asked them to stamp his passport. They refused, thinking the Japanese visitors were up to no good. After checking out their story and confirming they had indeed left Kochi City on 14 June, Nishimura and Morita were allowed ashore.

Before leaving the ship, the Customs men insisted Nishimura take a detailed nautical map of the area, free of charge. Then they gave him directions to Oro Bay, further east along the coast near Popondetta, bade him good luck and departed, still shaking their heads.

Madang, the headquarters of the Japanese 18th Army in 1943, is one of the prettiest towns in Papua New Guinea, certainly more safe and pleasant than Port Moresby, Lae and Popondetta. Because of this, some non-government organisations, among them Save the Children, World Vision and the

World Wildlife Fund, have chosen to locate their national offices there. But neither of the *Okinoshima-Go*'s crew was able to enjoy his visit. By now, relations between the ship's captain and first mate had deteriorated to the point where they were not communicating at all. When they went ashore, Morita, who had worked himself up into something of a state, said: That's it, I'm not staying here for one day longer than I have to, I'm going back to Japan. I've got a dive shop to run and a family expecting me back home.

Nishimura said: But, after all the trouble we've taken to get here, after everything we've been through, don't you want to do some scuba diving first? No, Morita replied, I am leaving as soon as I possibly can. And after their paperwork was finalised, and passports stamped, Nishimura watched as his one-time ally – with his bag and scuba gear slung over his shoulder – walked down the road towards Madang airport.

Two days later, on 9 July, Nishimura sailed 250 kilometres east along the coastline and berthed the *Okinoshima-Go* at Oro Bay. He handed the vessel over to Eric Torosian and she began her second life as a ship-of-all-trades.

Recalling this voyage many years later, Nishimura would laugh, but say that it hadn't seemed like a funny experience at the time. He had lifejackets on board, so he wasn't too scared. He figured bad things happened, whatever you did, and you had to deal with them. But even by his own standards, this was an unbelievable adventure.

Apparently undeterred by the difficulties he had encountered, Nishimura returned to Japan twice in the following decade in order to buy more boats. The next vessel was an eight-tonne fishing boat, the *Fukuyo-maru*. This time he wasn't required for piloting duties. The boat was transported from Osaka to Madang in the hold of a freight ship, thanks to the managing director of Goyo Construction, Mitsuo Yokota, who had heard about Nishimura's story and was anxious to help out. The *Fukuyo-maru* arrived at Madang port in January 1995 and is still being used to catch bonito around the islands.

The second trip, later that year, was more problematic. Nishimura was at the helm once more. He left Ishinomaki port in Miyagi prefecture on 11 November 1995 skippering a 63-tonne fishing boat, the *Dai-Ichi Tsune Maru*.

A local businessman in Popondetta who was a freight forwarder required the vessel for his business. Who else to procure it but Nishimura, now seventy-five, and perhaps past his best seafaring days? Again, the adventure nearly cost him his life, for Nishimura inadvertently sailed the vessel into United States waters around Guam. Soon after he unwittingly crossed the twelve-mile international border, he spied a US Navy warship looming up on his bow, the sizeable barrel of its main gun trained on the ageing fishing boat and its septuagenarian skipper. Once again, Nishimura's craft was not carrying the flag of any country. And, as he had no radio on board, he couldn't communicate with the Americans. He felt lucky that he was not blown out of the water – but because he hadn't declared his identity, or the purpose of his trip, he wouldn't really have blamed them if they'd sunk him.

How very different it was from his previous trip to Guam as a uniformed soldier fifty-four years earlier, when the Imperial Japanese Army had enjoyed the run of the island, and Nishimura had spent his down time watching his friend Kubo knocking back coconut liquor inside the village chief's hut.

CHAPTER 17

Ashes

WHILE NISHIMURA CONDUCTED THE most extensive, expensive and lengthy bone-collecting campaign in Papua New Guinea, he was by no means the only Japanese who became involved. Often, sons went searching for the fathers they had never known, but sometimes the searchers were women hoping to find the remains of husbands, fathers or brothers.

As Nishimura's project became well known in his home country, he was contacted by more and more Japanese families who wanted to visit Papua New Guinea and requested his help to find the remains of their loved ones. In 1997, he received a call from a 68-year-old woman, Kazuko Sasaki, whose brother, Naoyuki, had perished in December 1942. His war experience was tragically brief. He was killed in a beach battle as he came ashore with the 170th Regiment, and was just twenty-two when he fell.

The 170th had been disbanded, supposedly for the crime of losing its regimental flag, a disgraceful offence in the Japanese Army. Perhaps as a result, there was no public record of how and where its members died. His sister discovered none of the detail of his brief experience of war until many years later, when a comrade of Naoyuki's sent her a letter describing his final days, and where he was buried. By the time Mrs Sasaki finally received this letter, she had already travelled to Papua New Guinea three times to search for her brother's remains. On a fourth trip, armed with this new information, she enlisted Nishimura's help to locate Naoyuki's final resting place. The letter she had in her possession said Naoyuki had died on Napopo Beach, 'near a big tree'.

Since this stretch of coastline was inaccessible by road, Nishimura set off with Mrs Sasaki and two of her Japanese friends in a boat from Sanananda. Once they came ashore at Napopo, they enlisted the help of villagers old enough to remember the fighting. Eventually, they found a large tree jutting out into the beach that seemed to satisfy all the criteria listed in the letter. Here, Mrs Sasaki laid out a small table and made a shrine for her brother. She propped up a framed photograph of him, then laid out plates of rice balls, red peppers and vegetables, and cups of green tea and water as an offering to his spirit.

Mrs Sasaki then opened up a bag full of small origami paper cranes, a symbol of peace in Japan, and handed them out to the crowd of locals that had gathered around the impromptu ceremony. She said it was a small way to thank them for not developing or destroying this part of the beach. They sang a hymn, then the New Guinea national anthem. Having made her final goodbyes to her brother, and satisfied that his spirit was now at peace and well fed, Mrs Sasaki returned to Popondetta with Nishimura, then left New Guinea for the final time.

Other Japanese women have been equally determined to find

their relatives. Keiko Tatsumi, sixty-eight, has made several trips to eastern PNG to track down her father, Tatsuo, who was killed in action in 1943. She refuses to give up hope she will one day find him. In an echo of Nishimura's work, Tatsumi said: 'I promised my father that I'll come back and look for him. I just want to be where he spent his final days.'

A man of a similar age, Kokichi Morimoto, has also been on a crusade to find his father, Toshio. Morimoto knew him only as a kimono-clad man in a black-and-white photograph dated 25 December 1942, the day he joined Japan's war in Asia, never to return. The family later received a military letter confirming Toshio had been killed on 3 December 1944, on patrol in Boikin in northern New Guinea. His body was not recovered or identified.

Like Nishimura, Morimoto was sixty, and newly retired, by the time he was finally able to undertake his own mission in New Guinea. He joined a Japanese Government-sponsored trip in October 2003. A group excavated a vegetable field and uncovered the remains of more than one hundred unknown Japanese soldiers. The remains were so decayed that it was impossible to determine if Morimoto's father was among them.

'The skeletons appearing from the soil just broke my heart,' Morimoto said later. 'Just imagine how it must have been to be abandoned for so many years in the middle of nowhere so far away from home.' He has joined other bereaved families fighting to repatriate and identify the remains of lost soldiers.

Japan's national war cemetery, Chidorigafuchi, was built in 1959 to house the remains of the unknown war dead. Given that Japanese soldiers and sailors fought in a massive area across the Pacific, and died in horrendous numbers, the bones kept coming back to Tokyo each year as if on an assembly line.

By the end of 2006, the official body count at Chidorigafuchi was precisely 351,324, but only 611 sets of remains interred there had been formally identified. The dead had been collected from former battlefields as far flung as Mongolia, India and Burma in the west, New Guinea and the Solomon Islands in the south, Hawaii in the east, and Sakhalin and the Kuril and Aleutian Islands in the north. If there was a land mass of any size in the Pacific, there was a fair chance a Japanese soldier set foot on it at some stage during the war.

Some of the remains were recovered in a series of government-sponsored missions that began in the 1950s. In 1954, the Japanese Government requested permission from the Australian Government to send a vessel to recover Japanese war dead from New Guinea, which was then an Australian territory. The *Taisei Maru* visited New Guinea and other territories in February and March of 1955 and took back the remains of 5093 Japanese war dead. The authorities could so precisely put a number to the remains collected because barely a decade had passed since the war, and most of the bodies were still intact. In black-and-white archival footage of the *Taisei Maru* returning to dock in Tokyo, Ministry of Health officials marched down the gangway carrying white boxes full of cremated bones while members of the soldiers' families stood nearby, barely able to contain their distress.

Other remains were brought home after the war by returning military units and, of course, one-man rescue crews such as Nishimura's. Then, for decades after the war, a farmer might be tilling a field in Manchuria, a builder using earth-moving equipment in Okinawa, or a villager digging a well in Borneo, and they would disturb remains that were later found to be Japanese. Consular officials would be notified and eventually the body would be transported to Tokyo.

Chidorigafuchi's original charnel house, Rokkakudo, reached capacity in 1990. Two others have had to be built to accommodate the remains of soldiers that keep being returned, year after year, in a steady and unrelenting stream. Rokkakudo is located beneath a five-tonne ceramic coffin at the centre of Chidorigafuchi's main hexagonal hall. One of the largest ceramic objects in the world, it is made from stones and pebbles gathered from major war zones around the Pacific, including New Guinea.

To the left of the hexagonal shrine, there is carved in stone a *waka*, or traditional Japanese poem, composed by Emperor Hirohito in 1959, the year of the cemetery garden's construction: 'For the country / they gave their lives – / thinking of them / our throat / constricts.'

And this is where, much later, Nishimura would occasionally spend time, sitting beneath the gingko and elm trees, lost in quiet contemplation in this serene garden, outside the walls of which traffic noise and Tokyo city life pulsated.

IN LATE 1994, AS his digging entered its fifteenth year, Nishimura was approached by the Japanese Ambassador in New Guinea, Tadashi Masui, and asked to come to a meeting at his Port Moresby residence. Masui sat Nishimura down and told him he been briefed on all the work Nishimura had done. He said he greatly admired the bone-collecting project, and praised Nishimura: You are a true patriot, he told the former soldier.

The following year marked the fiftieth anniversary of the end of the war. Masui said the Japanese Government would like Nishimura to hand over all the bones and ordnance he had collected. They belonged back in Japan, he said. It was time to draw a line underneath the work Nishimura had done. The ambassador said he would finish his Moresby posting in mid-December that year, and would like to have Nishimura's agreement to such an arrangement before he returned to Tokyo.

Nishimura felt unsure. His project was half-complete. He wanted the bones he had retrieved to be identified: he wanted the government to DNA-test them, and then he planned to return each soldier's remains to their family. Now his loyalty was being torn between an appointed official of the government – not a bureaucrat as such, someone more senior than that – and his deceased friends and fellow-soldiers.

Initially, he protested, telling Masui he would like to keep his bones and continue his work. He had much more to do. The project would only be complete when he could see the delighted faces of family members reunited with the father or brother they had given up as lost forever. Masui said: Maybe you can keep on digging. We'll see. We just want all the bones you have collected so far, now that 50 years has passed since the end of the war. 'It will be an important symbolic gesture,' he said.

Eventually, Nishimura was swayed. He felt he would lose face by refusing a formal and respectful request from a high-ranking Japanese official. So he handed over all the bones he had collected to the Japanese Ministry of Health. His house in Popondetta, which had been a makeshift ossuary for thirteen years, a repository for maybe 200 bodies, or parts of bodies, was cleaned out.

He could not remember receiving a specific reassurance from Masui that his bones would be DNA-tested by the Ministry. But he left the meeting with the strong feeling that efforts would be made by the government to identify them.

In recent years, DNA-testing has been successfully used by several Western nations to identify wartime remains. In 2007, the Australian Army employed the technology to identify Diggers who were killed in World War I battles in Belgium. It was a surprising, and often moving, development for their surviving closest family members, some of them now in advanced years. Since Japan introduced the technique for war remains in 2003, only sixty-seven sets of remains have been identified. The effort has been hindered in part by the lack of testing facilities in Japan able to handle such decayed bones.

Back in 1994, DNA-testing was still a fledgling science. And there was the time, expense and effort associated with DNA-testing the bones, then tracking down and testing all the living family members. In the end, it was too much for the Ministry of Health to grapple with. A government official from the ministry rang Nishimura early in 1995 and gave him the bad news: the remains he had collected would not be DNA-tested; they would instead be interred at Chidorigafuchi.

Nishimura was dismayed. He felt hoodwinked. He told the Ministry of Health official that his only purpose in going to New Guinea was to find remains, have them identified and then returned to their families. But he was told the exercise would be too costly and take too much time.

If he'd known that, he would never have given back the bones. He was deeply disappointed. He had a list of names detailing where each soldier died, and a great deal of information about who was lying where, but the government, it seemed, didn't want to do the work in identifying them.

There was also a diplomatic difficulty with the government of Papua New Guinea. The government had made a law forbidding the removal of remains from the country; it considered the Japanese bones to be PNG property. Clearly, it was best if the Japanese Government could have Nishimura's collection cremated quietly in New Guinea, then packaged up and transported back to Tokyo. Much less confronting than transporting great palettes of skulls and ribs and clavicles and leg bones still attached to army boots, and much less likely to cause an incident.

The decision made Nishimura furious. He had even shown the Ministry of Health officials his trust, by revealing to them the location of some bones in faraway fields that he had learnt about but was unable to reach alone. Together, they had travelled there and dug them up. Nishimura felt as though he had taken the government into his confidence, and made them a partner in his plan, only to be betrayed.

For Nishimura, the government's attitude was tantamount to contemptible negligence. These young conscripts died for Japan, but they were treated no better than criminals. Their remains were now decayed and weather-beaten. He could not help but feel that the attitude of the government, and the Japanese public at large, was heartless.

And indeed, it seems true that since a flurry of official activity in the first twenty-five years after the war, successive governments have been guilty of a lacklustre, piecemeal approach to the recovery project. Nishimura felt as though the government just wanted the issue of soldiers' remains to quietly go away. Which, soon enough, when all the bones turn to dust, it surely will.

CHAPTER 18

Relics

THE GOVERNMENT'S HIJACKING OF his bone collection left Nishimura feeling deflated and disillusioned, but not defeated. It was now 1995, he was not yet seventy-six, and he still felt as fit as a Kobe bull. He figured he had plenty of years of digging left in him, and resolved to use his remaining years in New Guinea as profitably as he could. The thought of returning to Tokyo never crossed his mind.

He was still searching far and wide. Often, when he entered a village for the first time, he brought his friend Miichin Sarigari with him to act as interpreter and guide. Sarigari's own father had died when he was a child, and since Nishimura and Sarigari had first met, fourteen years earlier, the young Papuan had come to look upon the old soldier as a father figure. Sarigari had a great aptitude for languages, and he soaked up Nishimura's Japanese lessons like a sponge.

Soon, he was able to speak the language, on top of English, Pidgin English and his own tribal dialect, and he proved an invaluable ally to Nishimura as he negotiated with village chiefs about building new roads nearby or, more importantly, about digging rights.

'After I got to know Mr Nishimura, I came to think of him as my father,' Sarigari explained in a 1997 Japanese television documentary about the old soldier's life. 'When he was collecting Japanese bones or visiting friends or negotiating with villagers, I would take him as my father. So if there are any problems he comes across, I try to represent him and help him. That is the relationship between Mr Nishimura and myself.'

The Japanese documentary showed one meeting with a village chief who wanted to charge Nishimura ten kina (less than A$5) for the privilege of looking for bones on his land. Sarigari had to interpret for both sides, in an increasingly fraught discussion. Eventually, Nishimura walked away in disgust, saying: 'But they are my friends' bones, they are not your family's. You can't ask for money to show me my friends' bones. You can't profit from their misery. You'll never get one kina from me.'

At a place called Ambasi, about sixty kilometres further up the coast from Giruwa, Nishimura uncovered five bodies. Nearby, at the mouth of the Mambare River, he found the remains of two more. The search kept throwing up surprises. Further north again at Salamaua, near Lae, Nishimura noticed the wreck of a Japanese ship on a reef no more than 200 metres from shore. He went out to investigate and discovered, to his shock, that it was the *Kotoku Maru*, the ship which had transported him and the 5th Company to New Guinea in July 1942.

After unloading Nishimura's company, the *Kotoku Maru* had been attacked near Gona by American A-24 bombers. The ship was badly damaged, but was able to steam back to Lae under reduced power. Barely ten days later, the ship was bombed again and drifted, before running aground near Salamaua. She now sits in twenty-five metres of water, the bow section still clearly visible above the waterline, and is a popular site with divers.

Nishimura's discoveries energised him and convinced him to resuscitate his bone-collecting program. The Japanese Embassy thought they had persuaded him to abandon his project after the fiftieth anniversary of the end of the war, but they were sadly mistaken. That date meant nothing to him. It was irrelevant. Why should he stop trying to find his friends just because of some arbitrary date on a calendar? He felt his work was timeless, that it shouldn't be shackled by the constraints of a clock and calendar, especially those monitored by government bureaucrats. He also felt he owed the government nothing after the Ministry of Health deceived him into giving up his bones then decided not to DNA-test for positive identification. So his search would go on.

IT WAS NOT JUST bones that enabled Nishimura to make a connection with the soldiers' families. A pile of rusty relics was also mounting at a great rate: belt buckles, spoons, knives, bullet casings, lunch boxes, mess tins, swords, pistols and bayoncts among them. And then, a water pump.

In 1997, as he broadened his expedition from Buna north-west along the coast to Wewak – trailing in the footsteps of his final evacuation from New Guinea in 1943 – Nishimura was contacted by a Japanese man, Sei-ichi Yano, who asked if he would help carry out a special mission.

Yano told Nishimura he had recently made a trip to New Guinea to find out more about the fate of his younger brother,

Daizaburo, a naval officer from Ashoro in Hokkaido who had died at Buna. Because he had been given Daizaburo's diary by one of his comrades after the war, Sei-ichi knew much about his brother's life in New Guinea, and the work he did each day until his death, aged twenty-six, when his unit was obliterated in an Allied attack on 2 January 1943.

On his trip to Buna, Sei-ichi had discovered a broken, rusting water pump in an overgrown field, still standing in its original position at a place where the Japanese command centre was once situated. He immediately knew it to be the pump Daizaburo had referred to many times in his diaries. On the day before he died, Daizaburo had described how he had pumped water for that evening's meal, which he also helped to cook.

Sei-ichi asked Nishimura, whom he knew to have influence in Buna, if he would talk to the village chief on his behalf: he was seeking the water pump as a memento of his younger brother. Nishimura thought the request slightly unusual – a rusting water pump was hardly the most noble souvenir of a much-loved and honoured brother – yet he understood Sei-ichi's reasons and pledged to help him.

So, Nishimura travelled to Buna to speak to a man by the name of Bunani, the local landowner and counsel of Buna. When Nishimura put the proposal to him, Bunani said that he would happily let Sei-ichi Yano have the water pump – as long as he replaced it with a new one. So the deal was done.

Nishimura then called Yano in Japan and told him that he would need to buy a new pump to replace the one he wanted in Buna. He told Yano he would fly out in the next few days to collect it.

Nishimura now had a tricky week ahead of him: he had to negotiate his way from Popondetta to the wilds of Hokkaido to pick up the pump and bring it back to Buna. Then he had to retrace his route and find a way to get this twelve-kilogram lump of metal all the way from Port Moresby to Yano's house in suburban Ashoro. It was to become another of Nishimura's great expeditions.

Nishimura realised it would have been far cheaper, and easier, if he himself had bought the equipment from a store near his home in Tokyo, rather than travel all the way to the northern tip of Japan to collect it. But that was not the right way of doing things. The replacement pump must be purchased by Yano for the deal to be properly consummated.

When they met, the two old men embraced. Yano said he could not sufficiently express his thanks to Nishimura. The former soldier had done his family a great service by facilitating this trade and pledging to bring the old pump, such an identifiable part of Daizaburo Yano's wartime experience, to their home. Now, they would have a focus, no matter how impersonal, for their grieving.

Yano had wrapped the glistening new pump in a thick covering of paper. He presented it to Nishimura who, after stopping for barely long enough to down a cup of green tea, bade him farewell and headed back to Obihiro airport. I'll be back soon with the old pump, he said, as he waved goodbye from the taxi.

From Narita airport in Tokyo, Nishimura took a flight to Port Moresby, catching some sleep along the way, and reflecting with satisfaction on the pump stored safely in the hold of the jet.

He couldn't know that his minutely planned operation was about to hit a hurdle. Without warning, Nishimura began to bleed heavily from the nose as soon as he arrived back in New Guinea. Try as he might to staunch the flow, the blood kept pouring. In the end, the Japanese Embassy had to call in a doctor, who sent him to hospital. He was treated and told that he could go home, as long as he didn't over-exert himself. He was, after all, seventy-eight, the medico reminded him.

Nishimura wouldn't have minded slowing down right then, but – although he didn't mention this to anyone at the hospital – he was determined to complete his operation first. People were waiting for him, relying on him. He needed not to slow down but to move faster. He was trying to ensure he returned the old pump to the Yano family before 2 January, the anniversary of Daizaburo's death.

Weakened by his ailment, Nishimura felt he couldn't take a commercial flight from Moresby to Popondetta, so he hired a helicopter instead, the chopper landing next door to his two-storey house. Here, Bunani was waiting for him, along with Miichin Sarigari, and the new pump was exchanged for the old. By now, Nishimura was feeling so off-colour that the helicopter pilot lugged the pump off the chopper and into the yard for him.

Armed with his hard-won relic, Nishimura returned to Port Moresby by helicopter and stayed there for a night to catch his breath. He had been on the go for two days. But his sense of utter exhaustion was worth it. If he could help a Japanese family who had lost a father or brother in New Guinea by reuniting them with everyday objects from the South Seas battlefields, be it a soldier's dog tag, a lunch box, or a water pump, then that was a reward in itself. He could think of no greater joy than providing these families with some comfort and succour after all these years.

The following day, with his nose still inclined to pour blood at odd intervals, the 78-year-old caught a commercial flight back to Narita. Eschewing an expensive taxi fare, he caught the public bus service into Tokyo – a ninety-minute trip – then switched to a Japan Rail train out to Kazo City, where his daughter Sachiko lived, another ninety-minute journey. All the way, he lugged the rusty twelve-kilogram relic, as well as his luggage. When he got to Kazo City, he immediately went to the local ear, nose and throat clinic to have the haemorrhage investigated and treated. By the time he reached home, it was late and he was in an advanced state of fatigue. It was now New Year's Eve, and he wanted to spend the evening with his daughter, although he was far too tired to see in the new year.

On 1 January 1998, after stiffly getting out of bed, Nishimura boarded public transport again for the tedious three-hour trip back to Narita airport, with the rusty pump under his arm. After flying back to Obihiro airport for the second time in three days, Nishimura was met by Yano's son and driven to the family home. Then, following a performance by Nishimura that could safely be categorised as above and beyond the call of duty – even by his exacting standards – the old pump was delivered to its destination. The Yano family finally experienced a tangible connection with the last days of Daizaburo's tragically shortened life.

A memorial service was held for the naval officer the next day, the anniversary of his death. When Nishimura officially presented the water pump to Sei-ichi Yano, the moment was captured by a photographer and reporter from a local newspaper. Their coverage appeared under a long headline that read: 'Memorabilia of the Dead Comrade to be returned on his Death Anniversary. Japanese Veteran Living in New Guinea. Returning the Pump to the Family of the Deceased.'

The newspaper photograph showed Nishimura, his hair still black, dressed in a smart suit and wearing black-rimmed glasses, holding the water pump. Alongside him sat Mr Yano, clutching a picture of his brother Daizaburo in his sailor's uniform.

THE CONNECTION BETWEEN A Japanese soldier and his equipment was almost an unbreakable one, since the equipment was considered to have been a gift from the Emperor. Sometimes soldiers went to extremes not to be parted from it.

In one notable case, which Nishimura knew of well, since it occurred not far from Popondetta, the barrel of a Japanese mountain gun was uncovered by villagers at Gorari after the war. Gorari, at the northern end of the Track, was the location of the last major engagement of the Kokoda campaign: as many as 600 Japanese soldiers were killed there during their retreat north in early November 1942.

The villagers who found the gun barrel took it to the house of Bert Kienzle, an Australian who had lived in New Guinea since before the war, and who had organised the Papuan carriers known to the Australian troops as the Fuzzy Wuzzy Angels.

The ordnance remained at Kienzle's place until 1968, when a former Japanese Army company clerk by the name of Nakahashi, who had served in New Guinea, and was the author of one of the 144th Regiment's most comprehensive war diaries, returned to the Kokoda area to help recover the remains of his fallen comrades.

Nakahashi immediately identified the gun barrel as belonging to his friend, First Lieutenant Yoshijo Takaki. He recalled how Takaki, while preparing to evacuate from Gorari towards the northern beaches, had received orders to help the wounded over the Kumusi River, which was swollen with recent heavy rain and difficult to cross, and to leave his gun behind. Yet because the artilleryman's manual said the soldier and his gun are as one, Takaki knew he couldn't be separated from his weapon.

He asked his commanding officer if he could take the gun, while still helping casualties across the Kumusi, but his request was refused and he was ordered to bury the weapon. So Takaki, who was just twenty-four, called his friends around and bade them a final farewell, then sat down on the spot where the gun was freshly interred, took out his pistol and shot himself in the head. Such was the brainwashing of the Imperial Army's troops, that a young man felt he should sacrifice himself rather than abandon his gun. Nakahashi wrote in his diary that news of Takaki's gesture 'spread throughout the force and did much to lift the flagging morale of the Japanese troops which had been showing signs of stagnation'.

Later, recalling his 1968 trip to New Guinea, Nakahashi felt that it was divine intervention he had been reunited with a piece of equipment that had once meant so much to his dear friend.

When I saw the barrel of the gun which had been abandoned under such distressing circumstances, I was filled with deep emotion. Remembrance of those times brought about a flood of tears. I, who had a lifetime of friendship with the officers and men of that unit, had been strangely destined to discover this gun barrel. I must have been guided by the spirit of First Lieutenant Takaki.

The barrel of the mountain gun – minus its chrysanthemum crest, presumably removed by Takaki before he killed himself – now sits atop a Japanese memorial in the small museum at Kokoda. Along with Nishimura's stone cairn monument at Efogi, it is one of the few structures along the Track devoted to the Japanese campaign.

CHAPTER 19

Skull II

DURING ONE FLIGHT BACK to Japan in the late 1990s, Nishimura happened to read a review of a book, written by an emeritus professor of forensic odontology at Tokyo Dental College about the secrets that teeth could reveal in post-mortem investigations. Excited by this unexpected development, Nishimura decided he must get in touch with the professor, Kazuo Suzuki, as soon as he landed. He wanted to explain to him the peculiar circumstances surrounding the skull with gold teeth that he had found on Giruwa beach during the first years of his dig, and to ask Suzuki whether he would be prepared to examine his treasure.

Which is why Nishimura found himself in Tokyo in August 1999 with the skull in his hand luggage, wrapped in a Japanese flag, and an appointment beckoning with one of Japan's leading forensic odontologists. After examining it, Professor

Suzuki decided the skull was likely to have belonged to a male of between twenty and twenty-five years, judging from the state of the forehead, the lower front teeth and the general health of his teeth. He also suggested that the soldier had hailed from a wealthy family, given that the four gold crowns were attached to teeth that appeared to have been healthy.

The rest of the information supplied by Professor Suzuki helped confirm what Nishimura had already gleaned from his own research.

Hoping to capitalise on Suzuki's findings, Nishimura sought out and gave an interview to the *Mainichi Shimbun* evening newspaper, one of the largest in the country. He appealed for information from anyone who might have had such a relative killed in the Kokoda campaign, or otherwise knew something about the skull's identity. The article was accompanied by a dramatic photograph of Nishimura cradling the skull in his lap. It closed with a plaintive plea from the former soldier: 'Family members of these remains are getting old, as am I. I hope I can get some information on the identity of this skull as soon as possible.'

But no one came forward, so Nishimura decided to set out on his odyssey alone, armed with the list of names and addresses of surviving relatives, which he had narrowed down to seventy. On 14 August 1999, four months shy of his eightieth birthday, Nishimura began his search in Hiroshima prefecture for the rightful owners of the skull.

After fifty days and nights, Nishimura found himself in the mountains outside Shobara City, driving up a gravel driveway of a traditional rural estate.

There had been times over the past seven weeks, as he shivered under the flimsy bedding in the back of his car, when even Nishimura began to think of his quest as hopelessly quixotic. But the feeling of futility was usually only fleeting.

Invariably, his thoughts turned back to the war, as they had without fail every day since he returned home from the Pacific, and that had the effect of firming up his resolve. He thought of the dead friends he had left behind along the Kokoda Track, sometimes where they lay, sometimes in shallow graves, sometimes on funeral pyres. And of those he left behind on the northern beaches, as the final, frenetic Japanese evacuation was carried out under nightfall.

The pitiful look on the faces of those abandoned men was what he remembered most. The wounded, disease-ridden and dying lay on stretchers or in hospital beds, skeletons the lot of them, too weak to get up, too debilitated to do anything except watch through dull eyes as the fittest of their comrades were evacuated by sea. They were being left on that godforsaken coast to die. These images were seared into Nishimura's brain. Sometimes they woke him at night. The experience of having to turn his back on his brothers-in-arms had scarred him more deeply than any of the bullet and shrapnel wounds that pocked his small body.

The discipline of the Imperial Japanese Army was respected and feared the world over, but it had begun to fray as disease, hunger and Allied firepower overwhelmed it. To Nishimura, it didn't matter how dire the situation was, the Japanese Army was not supposed to abandon its own. If it had lapsed into a form of anarchy, he wasn't going to go the same way and compromise his principles. He was going to embody the *bushido* spirit, the way of the warrior, and devote the rest of his days to making good the injustice suffered by those men.

Sometimes, his extraordinary life began to play out in monochrome before his eyes, as if shown on an old slide projector. He thought of his family and the ugly scene that erupted on the day of his retirement in 1979 when he told them of his decision: he was going to leave Tokyo and their comfortable suburban life to go and live in New Guinea. New Guinea, of all places. Home to poverty, malaria, tropical disease, rampant gang crime and leeches. Are you completely mad, his wife had shouted at him. No, he said calmly, not mad, just doing my duty.

As he lay in the car, he sometimes chuckled to himself as he remembered the official from the Japanese Ministry of Health, a young man in his early thirties, who had been assigned by the government to observe Nishimura's one-man bone-collection project. The government had become worried by reports coming out of the New Guinea jungle that this maverick former soldier was conducting an unauthorised digging campaign, hoarding the bones in his hut and trying to identify them himself. The Papua New Guinean government was making noises, too.

The man from the Ministry of Health happened to be along-side Nishimura when he uncovered the skull, and four other skeletons, in 1989. They were on a part of the north coast called South Giruwa. The bureaucrat had been given orders to demand the return of every bone that Nishimura unearthed. Nishimura did not think much of this idea.

Soon enough, and sure enough, a standoff ensued. The Ministry of Health man said: If you don't give me the bones and skulls, we must force you. Nishimura said: If you want the bones, come and get them. But he added: As long as my two eyes are open, as long as I'm alive, I'll never let you touch the bones. If you want them, you'll have to kill me first. Are you ready to fight me right here and now? I might be sixty-nine, but I'm a former soldier and even young bucks like you couldn't get close to me.

The young man in his suit blinked nervously behind his glasses, as the old warrior, who had been fighting battles with one person or another for most of his life, stared at him defi-antly. It was a contest only one of them could win. Nishimura got to keep his skull, although he agreed to part with some of the bones that lay nearby, just to let the young bureaucrat save face.

Ten years later, when Nishimura was ready to return the skull to Japan, he took the box containing it under his arm to Port Moresby airport. He had decided it was best not to declare its contents to Customs, so he boarded the AirNiugini flight to Tokyo and stowed the skull in the hand luggage compartment above his seat. He hoped no one would bump his precious cargo to the ground, or accidentally knock the plywood top off the box. Then there'd be some explaining to do.

The trip unfolded uneventfully, but there was strife waiting when he arrived. The government of Papua New Guinea had somehow discovered his mission and complained, through its embassy in Tokyo, to the Japanese Government. This man Nishimura was illegally transporting human bones back from New Guinea, they said. He must be stopped. The bones were found on New Guinea soil; therefore, they were not Japanese, but the property of the PNG government. Nishimura assured the Japanese Customs official everything was in order. The Ministry of Health has processed all the legal formalities, he said, so just confirm it with them. Eventually, Nishimura was allowed on his way.

And now, fifty nights – and sixty-seven family visits – later, here he was, in the courtyard outside an imposing old house, in the middle of a cedar plantation outside Shobara City.

The older man standing in front of him gently cradled the skull in his hands, his face contorted with grief. Between sobs, he explained that the skull belonged to his younger brother, Takashi. There was no mistaking it. After composing himself, the man introduced himself as Hajime Yokokawa. He asked how Nishimura had found his brother, and how he knew where to look for his family back in Japan. When Nishimura regaled Yokokawa with the abridged version of his epic journey, Yokokawa thanked him profusely for all his work and for bringing Takashi's remains back to his family.

Takashi, he said, had belonged to the 2nd Company of the 41st Regiment and had attained the rank of lance corporal. Yokokawa said he knew straight away from the distinctive dental work that it was his brother. The reason for such elaborate orthodontics was that Takashi had suffered a bad accident the day before he was due to leave for war, when his family decided to celebrate his last night at home by having a big fish dinner. They went down to the river that flowed in front of the house to catch some fish, but Takashi slipped on mossy rocks, fell forward on to his face and his front teeth were all pushed back. The gold was inserted behind, and in-between, the four front teeth to hold them in place.

Yokokawa lived with his son's family and, hearing the conversation outside, the family got up from the table where they were about to have dinner and came out to find out what the commotion was about. And then a strange thing happened. When Yokokawa explained the purpose of Nishimura's visit and said that the skull he was holding actually belonged to Takashi, Nishimura noticed a peculiar reaction among some of the family. Instead of widespread wailing and tears of joy and jubilation, as he had hoped, there was a much more muted response, almost as though he had brought some sort of curse with him to the house.

The family retired inside to discuss what they should do. After an animated discussion, Yokokawa came back to Nishimura and, with an earnest and despairing look, announced: No, I'm sorry, we don't want to keep the skull. You take it.

Nishimura was stunned. Why on earth not, he asked.

It transpired that Takashi had been a party boy, a ne'er-do-well who drank too much, kept company with women of questionable morality, and was said to have sold off some family heirlooms to pay for his lifestyle. His rabble-rousing had brought great disgrace upon the family.

Dumbfounded, Nishimura reluctantly took back the skull. The family, sensing his dejection, asked Nishimura if he wanted to come in and share dinner. But he said: No, thank you. I've had some tinned fish and biscuits already, so I'll be on my way.

Numb with disappointment, Nishimura manoeuvred his car down the driveway towards Shobara. He was consumed with the thought: How could they behave like that? How could they turn their back on someone who was not only a member of their own family but a soldier who died fighting for Japan? The whole episode was anathema to him. Nishimura decided to stay on in Shobara to see if he couldn't find a more satisfactory resolution to his problem. He'd come this far, he wasn't going to quit now and slink back home to Tokyo a beaten man. The skull, returned to its box, was restored to its usual position on the passenger seat.

The following day, after combing his hair and tidying himself up as best he could, Nishimura began searching in town for someone associated with the 41st Regiment. Eventually, he was directed to the chairman of the Bereaved Family Association of the War Dead, Masaaki Izawa, a man in his fifties with kind eyes. When Nishimura explained what he'd been doing in Hiroshima prefecture over the past seven weeks, and how his mission had been totally derailed by the unexpected events of the previous evening, Izawa was furious: How dare they reject one of their family like that.

Izawa then said to Nishimura: Please, give me the skull and I will take care of matters.

Finally, after seven weeks of driving up and down Hiroshima prefecture, of visiting strangers, sleeping in his car, and being constantly tired and hungry and worried, Nishimura felt a surge of elation. His mission was done, his work complete. One Japanese soldier had been brought home, if not to the bosom of his family then at least to his home town. And now, in Japanese Buddhist tradition, he could be worshipped with all the other war dead as a divine spirit.

Nishimura thanked Izawa profusely, bowed deeply from the waist and got back in his car. In Izawa, he had found someone who shared the same feelings of pity as he did for the thousands of war dead, and the same unbridled and steadfast sense of duty in trying to set their troubled souls at rest.

Izawa kept his word, as Nishimura sensed he would. Today, standing proudly in the cemetery at Shobara City, is an imposing 2.5-metre stone memorial, bearing a life-size statue of the Goddess of Mercy, or Kannon, as she is known in Japan. On the statue's pedestal is inscribed the name, Takashi Yokokawa. The 41st Regiment's veterans association in Hiroshima helped organise the building of the tomb, but, although he'd never take any credit for it, much of the money to buy the plot of land and commission the elaborate monument came from Izawa's own pocket – almost thirty million yen (A\$330,000).

The skull is interred in a charnel under the statue.

THERE WAS A FOOTNOTE to the story of the skull. Although the newspaper article about Nishimura's find produced no new leads, it piqued the interest of a leading Communist Party MP and former diplomat, Miyo Inoue.

Ms Inoue was fascinated to read of Nishimura's two-decade-long project in New Guinea and of his quest to discover the identity of the skull, and she undertook to help him. In 2001, she raised the issue in parliament, at a public hearing of the Health, Welfare and Labour Committee. One of the agenda items was a discussion on remains recovery efforts in Papua New Guinea, the former Soviet Union and Mongolia.

Researching the issue, Ms Inoue had become increasingly annoyed by the government's tardiness in recovering the remains of Japan's dead soldiers, several hundred thousand of whom were still known to lie in makeshift graves across the Pacific. At the committee hearing, Inoue, in formidable fashion, demanded some answers from the Minister of Health, Labour and Welfare, Chikara Sakaguchi, and his bureaucrats, while bereaved family members watched intently from the public gallery.

She outlined Nishimura's work in Papua New Guinea, and praised his efforts to improve the lot of the local people. As well, she demanded that the government of Japan meet its financial responsibilities to maintain the memorials to Japanese war dead that had been built in PNG, instead of letting this duty fall on citizens such as Nishimura. 'Though this is such a small amount of money, I believe it is important for the Japanese Government to be engaged in this type of support,' Ms Inoue said.

Admonished, the Health Minister defended the low recovery rate of Japanese remains in Papua New Guinea, but he applauded Nishimura's efforts, and said he would discuss the issue of the Buna memorial with the Ministry of Foreign Affairs:

I have never heard of Mr Nishimura personally, he said. Having read the newspaper article, I can just bow my head for his efforts for his dead friends at the old age of seventy-nine. I feel we shouldn't waste the efforts such as those made by Mr Nishimura.

So Nishimura, who had never received so much as a certificate of appreciation from the government, let alone a civic award for patriotic duty, was finally given some official recognition in parliament. While he was pleased that his work was finally acknowledged, it was too little, too late. Imagine what sort of success he would have had if the government had supported him in the early stages of his campaign. With its backing, and the DNA-testing of his hundreds of bones, he could have given scores of servicemen's families some peace of mind.

CHAPTER 20

Government man

ALL HIS TRAVELLING TO and from Japan, and all his walking and digging in eastern Papua New Guinea, was beginning to take its toll on Nishimura. The truth was becoming difficult to mask: he was slowing down. He could feel a tiredness in his bones, and his mind had lost that alertness which had helped him survive almost six decades of crises. Papua New Guinea was a difficult enough place to work anyway, without the added burdens of being old and infirm. Nishimura was now eighty.

He also had to concede that, for all his determination and attempts to foster goodwill with the locals, life in Popondetta was becoming more difficult by the month. His bone-collecting project had proven more fruitful than he could have imagined, but his attempts at assimilating into life in Papua New Guinea were far less successful.

One wing of his primary school had been built and fitted out with desks, chairs and a blackboard. Local villagers used the building at weekends for karate practice, but the school as such had never opened. Ill-feeling grew between the school teacher, Nishimura's friend Miichin Sarigari, and the Japanese nationalist, Hirozaku Yasuhara. Sarigari believed that the troublemaker from Tokyo was trying to sabotage his project and get hold of the government school grant.

It was a dispute that not even Nishimura could successfully mediate and, in the end, it was resolved dramatically while Nishimura was away from the village. Sarigari, the registered proprietor of the school building, pulled the structure down and took the building materials with him to his village of Farigi, to use them there. Nishimura's Popondetta utopia was in danger of becoming a pipedream.

Ten million yen (A\$110,000) had been directed from the Kusa-no-ne-kikin (Grassroots Fund) for the school. The Japanese Embassy requested a report on the progress of the building. It never received a reply. To Nishimura's embarrassment, it was one of those failed projects that would simply be filed under the heading: Only in PNG.

And by now, Nishimura was being robbed blind. Almost everything he brought to PNG was taken by local people including furniture, light machinery such as diggers, bicycles, even aid money to build the training centre. During one of his lengthy stays away from Popondetta, villagers broke into his house and used his telephone. They racked up bills amounting to 7000 kina (at that time about A\$6000), and the phone line was disconnected when Nishimura declined to settle the bill.

It had almost become too unpleasant and dangerous to live in the village. At one point, Nishimura hired an English pilot, Bob Dalrymple, the husband of Ms Miyake, to fly a helicopter into the village, stop long enough for Nishimura to rescue a few things from his house and then fly back to Port Moresby. The raskol gangs may have been patrolling the streets of the capital, but Nishimura felt that it couldn't have been any worse than the situation in Popondetta.

In desperation, Nishimura tried one last gambit to win over the locals. On the plot of land next to his house, in place of the abandoned school, he decided to construct another large workshop, a building where he could train the young men in Popondetta to become mechanics. Here, they would learn how an engine worked and how to rebuild a disassembled engine. The building he erected with the help of locals had a high roof and was more than twenty metres long and eight metres wide, the dimensions of a warehouse or small hangar.

For Nishimura, it was another sign of his goodwill, an illustration that he wanted to help the Papuans – as long as there was a measure of cooperation in return. He wanted to contribute to PNG's community life by teaching the local people skills in exchange for their help. It was against his principles to buy bones with money. He wanted to build a relationship based on trust and friendship, rather than profit.

The crisis at Popondetta came at a bad time. Despite the succession of obstacles in his way, Nishimura's passion for his project had not dimmed. He was still determined to head out into the jungle to search for remains, yet now he couldn't walk as far, carry as much or dig as deep, and that meant his success rate was starting to diminish. He had a few loyal friends like Iewago and Eric Torosian, and Miichin Sarigari, but he couldn't lean on them all the time. He was going to have to pace himself, and not take on too much, just manageable projects that would not over-tax him.

What he really needed was a paying job that would help him indirectly with his bone-collecting. And that is how, in 2000, he came to be in the employ of Bernard Narokobi, the Leader of the Opposition and MP for the Wewak region – as Narokobi's adviser, no less. The MP was sympathetic to Nishimura's project, and won over by his peerless work ethic. He figured the Japanese former soldier would make an excellent addition to his team.

Nishimura, who'd become something of an identity himself and built a profile across parts of eastern Papua New Guinea, accepted this dramatic career change for several reasons, all related to his project. He was running low on funds, and wanted a steady income to help finance his campaign. Now he would be paid to travel to inaccessible mountain villages and talk to the villagers. He hoped that the villagers would be more likely to open up to him if he came as a trusted employee of Narokobi. Perhaps they would direct him to Japanese gravesites no one else knew about.

He had not done much digging this far west in New Guinea and Wewak, he felt, might be profitable territory. Between 1943 and 1945, the township was the site of the largest Japanese air base in mainland New Guinea. The base was subjected to repeated bombing by Australian and American planes, most notably a massive attack on 17 August 1943. Nishimura figured that there must be a gravesite, or bones buried somewhere nearby.

His new job meant that, for the first time in twenty years, Nishimura regularly slept in a room with four solid walls and a roof and, joy of joys, airconditioning. He was allowed to stay in one of the rooms in Narokobi's official residence in Waigani, the government district in Port Moresby. The large and comfortable house had four or five guards keeping watch around the clock. Lying back in this unaccustomed luxury, Nishimura felt his troubles at Popondetta were a world away.

In the eighteen months they worked together, Nishimura often accompanied Narokobi on his visits to far-flung villages and townships where they would listen to petitions and grievances from local constituents. Every few months or so, Narokobi and Nishimura were guests at a village feast where chicken or roast pig was served, the latter a special favourite when a big banquet was held. The carcass of a pig was placed on coals in a hole in the ground, then covered with palm leaves. Hot stones and coals were then shovelled on to the palm leaves, cooking the pork in little more than three hours. For Nishimura, who'd survived for two decades on the most bland of diets, these feasts brought alive near-dormant taste buds and were almost more than his digestion could bear.

Nishimura had learnt some of the local Boikin dialect from the East Sepik province, as well as Pidgin English, but given that there are more than 800 native languages and dialects spoken throughout PNG, the most linguistically diverse country in the world, that knowledge got him only so far. He had to rely on Narokobi to translate the detailed conversations.

Villagers did tend to trust him more when Narokobi was around. They told him of four obscure sites containing remains of Japanese soldiers. There were about twenty bodies in Arin, a village in the mountains about twelve kilometres north-west of Wewak, and one hundred in total around the area. The village chief at Arin also told Nishimura that he had in his safekeeping a Japanese flag that had once belonged to a young soldier who had died in his village during the war. The man had fallen ill with malaria and was taken in by the villagers at Arin. But he died there, leaving behind a wonderfully preserved Japanese flag with the signatures of family, friends and classmates, and messages of good luck.

Nishimura asked to see the flag which, despite the odd hole and rip, was in remarkably good condition. On it was written the soldier's name, Tadayoshi Morita, who, Nishimura later discovered, had served with the 3rd Communication Regiment from the 18th Army headquarters. Along with the *senninbari*, or thousand-stitch belt, the autographed *hinomaru yosegaki* (Rising Sun autograph) flag was the most common memento carried into war by Japanese soldiers. The flag, with its messages, was meant to bring good luck and encouragement to young recruits. It was not just a souvenir of home but a reminder to the soldier to do his duty in a way that would bring honour on his family. And it had practical as well as patriotic uses, such as marking positions to keep Japanese units safe from friendly aircraft fire while advancing.

Along the top of the flag was Morita's name, in large calligraphy. The five main characters read: 'Wishing Your Military Luck Lasts a Long Time.' It was signed by friends and neighbours from his home town, who had presented it to him before he set off for war. Nishimura asked if could keep the flag. The chief said if it meant so much to him, yes, of course he could. Nishimura said he would only take the flag on the understanding that he would return it to Morita's family in Japan.

After researching records of the war dead when he was next in Tokyo, Nishimura discovered the identity of the young soldier's regiment and the fact that he hailed from Komatsu City in Ishikawa prefecture, on the west coast of the country. He set about trying to locate Morita's family by contacting various temples in Komatsu City to see if they had the records of a Tadayoshi Morita. Eventually, he found the temple where the Morita family once worshipped.

Poring over the parish register at the temple, Nishimura could find only one remaining relative of Morita: a niece who lived nearby and who was married to a Christian minister. He had brought the *yosegaki* flag with him on his trip, so Nishimura travelled to the temple in Komatsu and handed the flag over to the priests, explaining that Morita had left it behind in New Guinea when he died of malaria, and asking that they pass it on to the soldier's family.

But nothing about Nishimura's work reuniting families with the remains or mementos of their loved ones ever seemed to be straightforward. Because the niece's husband was a Christian, he refused to come to a Shinto temple. So the priests handed over the flag to the representative of the community association, or *chonaikai*, in Komatsu. The association built a memorial for Morita and gave the young soldier a proper memorial service.

And so ended another chapter in Nishimura's crusade. He was sorry he could not locate a son or brother of Morita, and that the reunion of flag with family had been slightly anticlimactic, but the important thing was that Morita had been recognised by his home town for the sacrifice he had made. And his *yosegaki* flag was now where it belonged, framed and behind glass, in the Riasho Temple in Komatsu, where the family register was kept.

THE JAPANESE GOVERNMENT'S PASSIVITY in its post-war dealings with Papua New Guinea was one of the issues Nishimura had hoped that the influential Bernard Narokobi could help him address. He was determined to do something about the indignities visited upon the Japanese souls left behind in Papua New Guinea. He had seen their skulls lined up in neat rows, yellowing with age, put on display in grotesque sideshows, and titillating tourists who found some entertainment in the morbid spectacle.

At Giruwa, for example, two skulls found by local villagers were often on display, alongside smaller bones and rusting ordnance. One of the skulls had distinctive silver teeth and is thought to have belonged to Colonel Shigeaki Yamamoto, who became commander of the 144th Infantry Regiment late in the Kokoda campaign. On 2 January 1943, having earlier refused an order to withdraw from Buna, Colonel Yamamoto emerged from his bunker in front of Australian troops, along with his deputy commander. After making one final speech to the Australians telling them how Japan was going to win the war and praising the Emperor, he is then said to have shouted: 'Now, I will show you how Japanese soldiers end their lives. Shoot me.'

In the eyes of soldiers such as Nishimura, Yamamoto was a true warrior who represented his Emperor with uncommon valour, and upheld the Imperial Army's grand reputation until his last breath. Yet, here was his skull on a bamboo bench, being allowed to adorn a third-rate tourist display. Nishimura felt sickened by the shameful scene.

In the past, he had often unsuccessfully implored politicians from Japan and New Guinea to get together and sort out this deeply unsatisfactory state of affairs.

In 2001, he organised for Narokobi to travel to Japan, ostensibly to inspect a 36-tonne fishing boat that Nishimura had purchased in Kochi on a previous trip, and earmarked for a role in a planned fisheries school in Papua New Guinea. Via the Japanese Embassy in Port Moresby, Nishimura had also lined up a series of Japanese MPs to speak to Narokobi about a concern that to him was more pressing: the issue of Japanese remains. The real purpose of the trip was for Japanese Government officials to formally ask Narokobi, as a representative of the PNG Government, to revoke the PNG law which deemed that the dead soldiers' remains were the property of PNG and, in the hands of some unscrupulous operators, being used as a tourism asset.

Over three days, Nishimura and Narokobi met the Deputy Minister of Foreign Affairs, the Speaker of the Lower House, and various other officials and MPs, including the Governor of Kochi. But not one of the Japanese raised the issue with Narokobi, each of them dancing around the subject. Nishimura was stunned by their reticence. He understood that there was a time to be diplomatic, but when there was such a serious principle at stake, surely there was a time to be forthright and outspoken, too.

Perhaps they felt that there was no value in getting the government of Papua New Guinea offside. There were tuna to be caught in PNG waters, after all, and the appetite in Japan for the fish's red flesh was never sated. And then there was the controversial issue of whaling: no point in upsetting a key South Pacific nation and jeopardising a vote at the International Whaling Commission over the relatively unimportant matter of brittle, sixty-year-old human bones.

So Nishimura flew back to Papua New Guinea with Narokobi, without the agreement he'd been seeking. He couldn't remember feeling quite so dejected. It was a despondency matched only by the black depression he had suffered when he was unable to find any of his friends' remains at Efogi.

In a way, the official visit to Japan mirrored the mixed fortunes of Nishimura's entire crusade. For every success he enjoyed, there was inevitably a disappointment lurking not far behind. He kept being frustrated by people and circumstances outside his control. It was true that his original aim of reuniting soldiers' bones with their families back in Japan had not been as successful as he'd hoped. But he'd fulfilled his part of the bargain by finding almost 300 bodies; he'd just been thwarted by bureaucrats. When he thought of the way the Japanese Government had disposed of the bones he found, without ever making an effort to identify them, he could barely contain his anger.

But Nishimura never once thought he was wasting his time. He kept telling himself that he could do no more; he was trying as hard as humanly possible to find his friends, and make good his promise to them. Unless there was a major setback, he was determined to see the project through to the bitter end.

Then, in the 2002 general election, Narokobi lost his parliamentary seat to Kimson Kare, and Nishimura's career as a public servant abruptly came to an end. Now, he would have to find another way to get outside help to continue his campaign. And the options, even he had to concede, were running out.

CHAPTER 21

Return

ONE JULY DAY, NISHIMURA woke up feeling out of sorts, with a strange soreness in his joints. His body was convulsed with heaving fits of coughing. He'd hardly ever been ill in Papua New Guinea, despite the taxing nature of his work and the punishing tropical climate. Yet suddenly, all the exertions of the past twenty-five years seemed to rise up almost overnight and overwhelm him. For the first time, he truly felt his age. It was 2005 and he was five months shy of his eighty-sixth birthday.

He was staying in Port Moresby, and sleeping in a regular bed. He climbed out, and stiffly walked around. Shoulders hunched, he tried to get his breakfast ready, hacking away with a deep and persistent cough. He felt bad, but not so bad that he needed to see a doctor. He'd got to know his body pretty well by now and figured he knew how to heal himself. Besides, doctors cost too much.

He blamed his illness on one of his Japanese friends, Masatomo Sato, who was in Papua New Guinea on business, and insisted on smoking his infernal cigarettes all the time. Nishimura had arranged for Sato to meet key members of the government, including Michael Somare, who was once again Prime Minister. And this is how Nishimura had been repaid for his work as the key facilitator: with a filthy cough.

Later in the day, Nishimura began running a high temperature, but he had some errands to do so he set off shakily down the street. Within minutes he fainted, falling to the footpath in a crumpled heap. Now there was no question of not seeking medical help. Sato, who was accompanying him, called the Japanese Embassy and his friend Ms Miyake came out to see him with a doctor. After the medic administered first aid, he sent Nishimura to a hospital in Port Moresby where he remained for a week, as his illness quickly developed into full-blown pneumonia.

Nishimura had survived battles that wiped out all the rest of his platoon. He had somehow lived after being shot by a machine-gun. He'd grown strong again after disease and acute starvation reduced his bodyweight by more than half. He'd been to sea on ships that sank. He'd been run over by a tractor in a rice-paddy. He'd been hospitalised with half a dozen bouts of malaria but pulled through. He'd lived in one of the most dangerous countries in the world for almost twenty-six years. And now, irony of ironies, he was almost finished off by a cough.

Initially, he protested about being sent to hospital, saying he had no money. Ms Miyake told him not to worry and that she would pay the bill, which eventually amounted to 500 kina (A$210). This rankled with Nishimura. He didn't like other people footing the bill for his problems. He promised Miyake he would pay her back. And then he was wheeled into Casualty.

In the delirium brought on by the pneumonia, what occupied

Nishimura's thoughts most was the security of his bone collection in Popondetta. As soon as his fever subsided, Nishimura called Miichin Sarigari, his friend and house-sitter in Popondetta, and instructed him to hide the thirty or forty bones still stored under the shrine in different places around the township. He had worked hard to recover these remains and didn't want them falling into the wrong hands, or ending up as part of some freak-show exhibit for tourists.

After lying in a hospital bed for a week, Nishimura began to feel stronger and the doctors decided he was ready to go home. But he'd had time to do some thinking in hospital and he realised that home no longer meant Popondetta or Efogi or Port Moresby or a tent on the Kokoda Track, but Tokyo. His old home town. He was too sick and frail to do any more digging for the moment. He'd go back to Japan, get strong again, take stock, do more research on the battlefields, then return to New Guinea.

That was the plan, anyway, if his health improved and everything fell into place – and he kept trying to convince himself it would. Deep down, though, Nishimura knew it was probably hopelessly optimistic. He knew if he went back to Japan this time, he would probably never return.

Ms Miyake noticed that he seemed to have grown very old all of a sudden. Even when he recovered a little, he had a high temperature, couldn't eat, and was very weak. Because he was still very unsteady on his feet, the hospital provided him with a wheelchair. She remembered him telling her: This is the last time I come here.

So, on 13 August 2005, with Sato at his side, Nishimura boarded an AirNiugini flight for the very last time, sitting in a wheelchair, with an oxygen mask covering his face.

Naturally, there was one last hitch. As Ms Miyake waved Nishimura through Customs, and watched an airline stewardess pushing his chair towards the plane, a Customs official, who was still looking at his computer screen, called her over. Scratching his head, he asked her how Nishimura had been able to reside in Papua New Guinea when his name appeared on an immigration blacklist. The blacklist was right there, on the screen in front of him, he said.

Ms Miyake had no answer. She imagined that Nishimura, after a trip back to PNG, perhaps on one of his boats, had not filled in the correct paperwork after berthing, and therefore had been living in the country without realising his status was illegal. Or perhaps a politician with whom he had crossed swords had used his influence to have the old man declared persona non grata. When he heard about it later, Nishimura suspected he was on the blacklist because the government had discovered he had removed Japanese bones from Papua New Guinea without permission, in contravention of the agreement he had made with Stephen Tago. In any case, the government of Papua New Guinea – which had been involved in a series of run-ins with Nishimura over the past quarter-century – was evidently pleased to let him go, as they did not haul the sick old soldier off the plane.

Back in Japan, it was the middle of the summer school holidays. His daughter Sachiko had no idea of the drama unfolding in Port Moresby. No one from the hospital had thought to tell her that her father was seriously ill and heading back to Tokyo. For some reason it had slipped Sato's mind to keep her abreast of developments, as well. When Sato and Nishimura arrived back in Japan the following day there was no one at the airport to meet them. By then, Nishimura was so exhausted, he could barely move. The two men decided to stay in a hotel in Ueno, a district in Tokyo, rather than risk another train ride to his daughter's home in Saitama.

The following day, with Nishimura only barely mobile, they

finally stumbled into Saitama where, luckily, they found Sachiko at home. When she saw the state her father was in, she rushed him to the nearby Nakada hospital in Kazo City. It was the same hospital he was admitted to after being run over by the tractor in 1979: he had to see the irony in the fact that his 26-year odyssey in Papua New Guinea was book-ended by visits to the Emergency department at Nakada Byouin.

The hospital staff immediately isolated Nishimura, because they feared he might have contracted avian flu. Sachiko and the doctors wondered how it was that he was allowed to leave the care of a Port Moresby hospital, and to board an international flight, in this debilitated condition. He was also suffering from terrible anaemia and needed two blood transfusions to stabilise his system. For a week, his condition hovered between serious and critical.

It took weeks before he felt his strength returning, but he was never again robust. He could feel the slow, inexorable deterioration of his body and knew he was up against the toughest foe he'd faced yet: old age.

When he was well enough, he moved in with Sachiko in Kazo City, Saitama. After twenty-six years apart, she would be able to look after him and, at last, partake in some sort of normal family life. Sachiko had been living in the house since the tumultuous family split in 1979. It was a pleasant, if slightly ramshackle, double-storey home in an unprepossessing, anonymous suburb.

A few of his neighbours, including the two old women who came in to clean the house once a week, knew of his time in the army and his expedition back to New Guinea. But otherwise he walked around the streets as an anonymous old man, with a past as unremarkable as all the other pensioners who shuffled past him on the pavement. Some people even mistook the slightly dishevelled old war survivor for a no-good vagrant.

They called him a beggar. They couldn't understand why he wore old clothes, drove an old car, and didn't eat fancy meals.

Although he enjoyed being reunited with Sachiko, this was an unhappy period of adjustment for Nishimura. He was not interested in being lauded for his work, but he missed his former life. And he wanted the war dead, his comrades, to be given their just recognition. The more time he spent back in Japan, the more he found it astonishing, and not a little insulting, that the Japanese community had effectively turned their backs on those who sacrificed their lives for the country, not just in Papua New Guinea but elsewhere throughout the Pacific.

He sometimes felt as if he were living in a vacuum, or as if the terrible experiences of the war years had never taken place. Then, quite unexpectedly, the release of an American film about the war suddenly gave Nishimura a connection with Japanese society at large.

FEW JAPANESE BELOW THE age of fifty knew much of the terrible detail of Japan's war in the Pacific. Not many would have heard of the remote Japanese island of Iwo Jima, where early in 1945 a battle raged for thirty-five days between American and Japanese troops. The battle was the first assault on Japanese home soil, and the defenders fought valiantly, sustaining huge casualties. At the end, there were 20,703 Japanese dead and 6825 on the Allied side.

In 2006, Clint Eastwood's feature film, *Letters from Iwo Jima*, was released in Japan. Its plot was framed by the discovery of a cache of letters hidden in 1945 and exhumed sixty years later. They symbolised the burial and retrieval of the past, one of the film's subjects, which touched a deep nerve with Nishimura.

The film won wide praise in Japan for its sensitive, even sympathetic, portrayal of the Japanese soldiers, many of whom were left buried on the island or in its eighteen-kilometre labyrinth of tunnels. Although the movie was made by an American director, it provoked much comment about the need for Japanese people to remember their own history.

Before they started making the film, none of the Japanese cast knew anything about Iwo Jima, a fact the American director said he found shocking: 'You lost 21,000 people and then you just ignored them. That would never happen in America,' said Eastwood. Even Ken Watanabe, the star who played General Tadamichi Kuribayashi, said he was embarrassed to admit he knew nothing about the general and his struggle to hold the island, when he was first approached to take the role. It was difficult to say why he and many other Japanese did not know about it, he said: Perhaps it has something to do with the lack of a good education.

How could such ignorance grow up to obscure Japanese history? Nishimura thought that it was partly because of the terms of the Japanese surrender, which forbade Japanese disparagement of the Allies. He said it would be impossible for Japan to make such a film, portraying as it did such an even-handed, almost sympathetic, view of Japanese soldiers: If we did, America would complain bitterly, he said. It was a film that could only be made by the victors.

After Japan's defeat, the Allied occupation government made education reform one of its primary goals to cut out militarist teachings and 'democratise' Japan. The education system was rebuilt on the American model. But while Nishimura had been away, a growing tide of nationalism had recently brought about a revision of the way modern history was taught. New history textbooks promoted by a group known as Tsukuru-Kai portrayed Japan as the victim in World War II, the war itself as a conflict started by the Americans, and deleted any mention of comfort women, those women forced into prostitution and sexual slavery during World War II by the Japanese Army. The majority were from Korea and China. Leading politicians such as Shinzo Abe and Shintaro Ishihara were said to be fans of the Tsukuru-Kai textbooks, which sought to restore a measure of national pride after years of apologising and hand-wringing over the war. Sales of the book, initially, were brisk, but after an outcry from many Asian countries, especially Korea and China, fewer and fewer teachers used it in the classroom.

Nishimura, who considered himself a nationalist, had some sympathy with such sentiments, despite his own loathing of war. But for him the discussion of Japanese attitudes to the war all came back to one thing, the forgotten dead.

As he sat in his house in Saitama, reflecting on all the things that he had seen and done over the years, the one subject that could be guaranteed to move Nishimura to tears was his fellow soldiers' abandonment by their government. While the government of Papua New Guinea, and Australian tourism operators, might be complicit in the continuation of the bone shows at Buna and Gona, it was his own government's failure to intercede on behalf of its own war dead that upset Nishimura most.

To add to the insult, he had recently heard reports that trading in skeletons had become a lucrative trade on Papua New Guinea's northern beaches. Villagers in Sanananda, Buna, Waju and surrounding areas were reportedly selling remains – not just of Japanese soldiers, but of Australians and Americans as well – to foreigners entering the country on tourist visas. Locals were being offered as much as A\$23,000 for a complete human skeleton, the sort of money that villagers in New Guinea found difficult to refuse.

One local newspaper suggested the 'skeletal scavengers' were doing a roaring trade and the government was having a hard time reining it in. It quoted one local boy in the village of Mangufo who, with a friend, dug up fifty-three Japanese part-skeletons between 1997 and 1998 and sold them to an American businessman attached to a petroleum exploration company. They fetched about 100 kina (A$42) each.

Nishimura shuddered each time he heard reports about such desecration.

CHAPTER 22

Imanishi

ONE OF THE FEW bright spots of Nishimura's return to Japan, in an otherwise cheerless homecoming, was his long-lived friendship with Sadashige Imanishi, the only remaining veteran of New Guinea who knew him well, and with whom he could talk comfortably.

At the time of Nishimura's return, Imanishi was aged ninety. His hair, though greying, was still luxuriant, and his skin was clear. He wore no glasses, which made it all the easier to see the twinkle in his eye.

He could easily have passed for a man twenty years younger, yet Imanishi had seen more action in the war than just about any other of his comrades. A staff sergeant in the 2nd Company of the 1st Battalion of the 144th Regiment, Imanishi started his war in January 1936 and fought for most of the following decade, serving in China, Taiwan, Hong Kong, Rabaul and New Guinea.

Like Nishimura, he was the only man in his unit to survive. And he also had a rare insight into Nishimura's life's work, since he was a member of a Ministry of Health delegation that visited Popondetta in 1969. His group had stayed in the village for almost four weeks while they retrieved the remains of Japanese soldiers. In all, three hundred bones were recovered and cremated, then interred at Chidorigafuchi.

In August 1937, Imanishi was part of the Japanese landing in Shanghai. He said later that it was like the Normandy landing, and reminded him of a scene out of the film *Saving Private Ryan*. He fought for another three years in China, and was then promoted to staff sergeant. He also happened to be in southern China when the war ended eight years later.

Comrades around him were killed in droves, but when the conflagration died down, there was Imanishi standing alone and unmarked on the battlefield. The chances of him surviving nearly a decade of this ferocious combat, when mortality rates among the Japanese were more than eighty per cent in some battles, was minute.

When Nishimura arrived back in Japan in 2005, he and Imanishi were part of the rapidly dwindling band of 144th Regiment veterans, the pair still sharing an almost mystical ability to survive. The roll of Japanese soldiers and sailors who fought in New Guinea and were still alive might now total ten or a dozen, no more. They met at various Kochi–New Guinea Association functions through the year, when Nishimura would climb into his old car and carefully negotiate the thirteen-hour drive down to Shikoku.

The two were friends, but their shared experience of war was their common bond, rather than mutual work interests or pastimes. While Imanishi, who became Mayor of nearby Motoyama City after the war, was dapper in his long-sleeved Nike golf shirt and neat pants, Nishimura was happy to get about in a slightly more dishevelled outfit of scruffy checked shirt and trousers that appeared not to have seen an iron for a while.

Mention Nishimura's name to Imanishi and he would smile slightly and shake his head, as if being asked about a renegade younger brother. As a senior member of the Kochi–New Guinea Association, Imanishi had had to discipline Nishimura for the way he continually thumbed his nose at authority, and to distance himself from some of his colleague's crackpot schemes.

But, for all that, Nishimura was still a 144th veteran, and was owed some loyalty by the older man. Imanishi said he was probably the only one to talk to Nishimura all the way through his years in Papua New Guinea, because other veterans hadn't liked what he was doing and had stopped dealing with him.

Before Nishimura's first expedition to New Guinea by boat, for example, Imanishi said he and another 144th veteran went to Kochi port to wave Nishimura off in his 83-tonne vessel. They could see the unkempt state the boat was in and were worried about its seaworthiness, but they knew it would be useless to try and talk Nishimura out of going. So they waved him off from the dock, convinced he'd sink somewhere in the Pacific and never be seen again. Of course Nishimura bobbed up back in Kochi several years later, the same furrowed brow and intense look of determination creasing his face.

Nishimura had often done things that were against the 144th Association's rules, so he was kicked out. Imanishi said: He did things his own way. You must understand that Nishimura was not like your average Japanese person. He was not interested in conforming. We don't tolerate unique people very well in Japan.

For Imanishi, personally, it was not a matter of whether he liked or disliked Nishimura. Nishimura was what he was, someone very different and unpredictable. You could only laugh at some of the things he did.

Imanishi remembered two Nishimura moments that stood out for him: the time his friend sailed to Papua New Guinea without ever having skippered a boat before, and when he built the memorial to Japanese soldiers at Efogi without any authorisation.

It was Nishimura's decision in 1989 to build that stone monument, without the permission of the Kochi–New Guinea Association or any other body, which riled many of his comrades. It was thought he was a law unto himself and it was decided that his membership be suspended. That was the start of Nishimura's testy relationship with the association that was to last another eighteen years. When he could, Nishimura would still attend the Shinto ceremony at the 144th's annual reunion in Kochi City as a private individual, but rarely would he be involved in any of the socialising afterwards.

Nishimura's solo bone-collecting crusade, also planned and conducted without authorisation from his regiment, his government or the PNG government, brought a smile and an exasperated sigh from Imanishi. All bone collection had been done through the official channels – the governments of Japan and Papua New Guinea, and the veterans associations – until Nishimura arrived. He decided to do everything by himself. He didn't care if he was breaking the law or the rules; he just went there and started collecting the bones, Imanishi said.

Imanishi's wife, Toshino, had died in 1993, and occasionally, as Imanishi was leading his quiet life in Motoyama, the peaceful surface of his day would be ruffled by an unexpected visit from Nishimura, back in Japan briefly on a flying visit about some fanciful idea or other. Imanishi remembered how Nishimura had been one of the first people in Japan to use car satellite navigation equipment, long before the public became familiar with global positioning systems, and this helped him negotiate his way from Tokyo to Imanishi's home overlooking the Yoshino River, about fifty minutes' drive from Kochi City.

Once, Imanishi noticed the familiar dark blue Honda coming up his driveway. It was Nishimura and he had come to pick Imanishi's brains about a plan he had. Over a cup of green tea, he said to Imanishi, who had been a farmer after the war: Teach me how to do rice farming. He wanted to teach the locals in Papua New Guinea how to grow their own rice, a crop he thought had great prospects in all that rain. So Imanishi gave him a crash course in the finer points of paddy-field agronomy, and Nishimura thanked him and went on his way.

Some time after that, Nishimura returned with another farming question on his mind. What about cattle farming, he asked? I'd like to know more about that. He had a plan to help the Papuans build a big cattle farm. They talked about farming for a while; as it grew late, Imanishi asked him to stay the night in a comfortable bed inside the house, but Nishimura declined. He slept in the back of his car, instead. That was what he wanted to do.

On another occasion, Nishimura came to visit Imanishi out of the blue, but this time he travelled by train. In a rare moment of extravagance, Nishimura agreed with his friend's suggestion that they stay together at a local *ryokan*, or traditional Japanese inn. The next morning, as Imanishi drove Nishimura to the train station, they were involved in a car accident with a young couple from Osaka. Imanishi was injured and needed treatment; Nishimura got a small rip in his jacket.

After the insurance formalities were sorted out, Imanishi thought nothing more of the incident. But he learnt that Nishimura had later driven all the way to Osaka – maybe a seven-hour trip in the car from Tokyo – and visited the insurance company to tell them he wanted to be compensated for his torn jacket. Initially the insurer said no, that he did not have a case for a claim. But Nishimura persisted. These were bureaucrats he was dealing with, after all, and therefore little more than a red rag to a bull. Eventually, Nishimura was given 40,000 yen (A$440), just to get rid of him. Imanishi couldn't believe he would go to all that trouble; it was only a small tear. But that was Nishimura.

Like Nishimura, Imanishi was still haunted by the fact that he had been spared death when everyone else in his unit was cut down. I don't know whether I was very clever or very lucky, he said. I don't know the answer to that. It's a question I've often asked myself: how could I survive this horror? What saved me, when all my friends have been killed and I don't have a scratch on me?

While Nishimura was evacuated from Giruwa on 12 January 1943, Imanishi's unit had to stay a further eight days before receiving orders to leave. On 19 January, General Yamagata, the commander of Imanishi's brigade, evacuated from the Giruwa position without orders. Before he left, he gave six other commanders a letter saying they had to be opened at a certain time the following day. The letter ordered Imanishi and the others to retreat at 10 pm on 20 January. His position was the last one to be evacuated. Imanishi didn't feel sadness at leaving, just concern for those being left behind: That's what I was worried about, he said.

In the study of his Motoyama home, Imanishi kept a photo album related to the Regiment. A faded black-and-white shot, taken in 1941, showed the command unit of his 2nd Company just before they headed off to war. Imanishi sat in the front row, two down from his great friend, Nakahashi, whose luck ran out after escaping New Guinea. Of the nineteen men in the photograph, sixteen died in the war, one was badly wounded and never recovered, and two survived, Imanishi and a Lieutenant Doi.

Another photograph taken in 1997 showed the Festival of the Regimental Banner in Kochi. From one of the flag poles hung the tattiest, most miserable-looking banner imaginable, not so much a flag, as the remnants of a frayed hemline. It came from Imanishi and Nishimura's 144th Regiment, and is as potent a symbol of the destruction of the great 144th as you could find.

The regimental banner was always given by the Emperor, so it had to be protected at all costs, even at the cost of life. Imanishi said: Our banner was completely destroyed because of the hard fighting; all it had left was the hem around the edge. The cloth in the middle was shot out. This was the most important thing in our regiment. If it seemed that everyone in the regiment was going to die, then the banner had to be burned so it would never fall into enemy hands.

The banner had survived, but now it was only a matter of time before the last of the soldiers sworn to protect it drew their final breaths. So while Nishimura might have been unpredictable and eccentric, Imanishi was looking forward to catching up with his combustible comrade at the Kochi–New Guinea Association reunion in October.

Chapter 23

Reunion

On a hot, windy day in October 2006, Nishimura and the rickety remnants of Japan's 144th Infantry Regiment hobbled towards a large white marquee in the forecourt of the Kochi Shinto Shrine. They had turned out for the regiment's annual reunion, attended not only by the handful of veterans still surviving, but by wives, daughters, sons, brothers and sisters of the thousands who died. The previous year there had been fifteen members of the 144th present; today there were just three – Nishimura, Imanishi, and Imanishi's friend, Doi. A planned group photograph, like the one that graced the 2005 anniversary program, had to be cancelled through lack of numbers. The president of the association, Mr Yamasaki, had died two weeks previously. At this rate of attrition, the 2007 reunion would be fortunate if a single member of the South Seas Detachment was able to attend.

A huge banner proclaiming the 144th Regiment Kochi–New Guinea Association was hung at the entrance to the shrine. Red rosettes were given to visitors to wear. Up the stairs to the shrine, a Shinto priest showed the curious through a room that served as an unofficial museum to the Japanese campaign in New Guinea. They may as well have renamed it the Kokichi Nishimura museum, so many of the artefacts and memorabilia and scraps brought back from New Guinea and housed there were collected by the indomitable former grenadier of the 5th Company. There were also the ashes of his fallen friends from Ippongi, his memoir of the conflict, entitled *Battle of Efogi*, and all the documents he had concealed under his shirt. There was also a box with rusting belt buckles, buttons, knives and watches – anything metallic that had set off the sensor on his landmine detector. There were his photograph albums chronicling his 26-year mission in New Guinea, and Morimoto's lunch box, reunited with his family first, then put on display here. Nishimura's army sword – the one that had killed the Australian soldier in hand-to-hand fighting, although never crassly identified as such – was also displayed in a glass case, along with a couple of daggers.

Nishimura arrived at the shrine in his dark blue station wagon: he had driven from Tokyo the day before. He was wearing a dark suit and what looked like a cowboy's shoestring tie done up with an opal-blue brooch, an odd affectation for someone who had never cared what other people thought of his appearance. He'd slept the previous night in the back of the car, as was his custom. In the front passenger seat, an egg container served as his *bento* lunch box; green tea and a packet of biscuits completed the rations that could have kept him going for a week, if necessary.

Nishimura had repaired a GPS box and somehow taped it down to his dashboard. A pair of rabbit-ear aerials attached to his roof-rack completed the navigation system. This was how he negotiated the Japanese countryside on his trips to Osaka insurance companies, Kochi reunions and Hiroshima relatives of the war dead.

He greeted his friend Imanishi, who was resplendent in a grey suit and grey tie, with a purple band on his left arm. But Imanishi looked worried. The drastic reduction in numbers this year did not bode well for future Kochi–New Guinea Association gatherings. Nishimura, however, did not concern himself with such matters.

Almost 5000 men from Kochi City and surrounding towns had died in New Guinea and New Britain, the vast majority of them under thirty, and their names are all listed at the shrine. The service was attended by 200 or so family members, and was a simple, elegant affair, despite the wind that flapped unpleasantly at the sides of the marquee and made the Shinto priests almost inaudible. The national anthem was sung, then a prayer to the war dead was recited by the elder of two Shinto priests. Offerings of food to the divine spirits – rice, fish, sake, bananas, mandarins, biscuits, green peppers and cabbage – had been laid out on the altar, so that the spirits had the strength to protect those still alive.

Then two old men stood up, walked to the front of the gathering and, unaccompanied, sang a military song that had many in the audience dabbing at their eyes with handkerchiefs if they were not already sobbing through the service. This song, which embodied the soldiers' and sailors' cult of death, revealed deeply ingrained notions of duty and sacrifice. The translation went something like:

I see the clouds very far away,
Through the clouds, I can make out the faces of my wife and children,

231

They are holding flags and saying: 'Fight well for your
country'.
We are on the carrier ship, saying goodbye to the mother-
land and praise the nation,
Now is the time to end my life,
So I am writing my death note by the tiny light of the
moon.

The ceremony proceeded according to the usual protocols.
Those dozen or so senior members of the association still living,
not all from the 144th Regiment, sat in a VIP section. One by
one, they rose and honoured the spirits of the war dead with a
simple yet moving ritual.

First, they bowed to their peers, then they turned to bow to
the main group of mourners, before bowing to each of the
Shinto priests. Accepting a sprig from a priest, each veteran
raised the cutting as an offering, stepped forward, rotated it
180 degrees and placed it stem-first on the altar. Then he bowed
twice, clapped twice to awaken the spirits and, backing away,
bowed twice more before resuming his seat. It was an intricately
choreographed performance, but not one old man missed a beat.

Nishimura sat on the end seat of the fourth row under the
main marquee, leaning on his walking stick and listening
intently to proceedings. Without warning, when the service
was nearly finished, he got up and hobbled around the back
of the tent towards his car. Those who saw him leave assumed
he had gone to collect something he'd forgotten, but he never
reappeared. After the service, his car was gone. Imanishi
shrugged his shoulders and shook his head when asked if he
knew where his friend was.

Later, Nishimura explained that he left the service because he
had heard what he had come to hear. The prayers for the dead
were all that mattered to him, so he left after the Shinto priests

had finished the ceremony. The others in the association really didn't mean anything to him, except for Imanishi. Nishimura still harboured resentment towards the association for not sanctioning his mission to Papua New Guinea, then banning him from the organisation for various infractions such as building the memorial at Efogi without permission. His non-conformism had jarred with his fellow veterans, and many of them had frozen him out. The relationship with these men, Imanishi excepted, seemed fractured beyond repair. For Nishimura, at least, there was no going back.

THE KOCHI SHRINE WAS also the repository of most of the folders of lists and records that had once lined Nishimura's bookshelves at home in Saitama. They had labels such as 'Battle Record of the 5th Company'; '144th Regiment Battle Records by Name, Date, Place and Unit'; 'List of Dead Men, 144th Regiment'; 'List of Dead Men by Their Origins and Date'; 'Name List of 15th Independent Engineer Regiment and 41st Infantry Regiment'; 'List of Dead Men, South Seas Detachment'. And so on. Painstakingly written in longhand, they had taken Nishimura years to compile.

Kuroda, the clerk from the 5th Company who kept meticulous records about the fate of all who served in the unit and secretly made an extra copy for Nishimura, had helped Nishimura complete this work. He was one of the few from the 5th Company who had survived. After the war, he eventually became principal of a junior high school in Uwajima, Ehime prefecture. Nishimura tracked him down there in the late 1950s and they met many times, becoming good friends. After Kuroda died, Nishimura sent the only surviving copy of his war record to his son, who lived in Chiba prefecture.

Of the 365 men who died in Nishimura's 5th Company of the

144th Infantry Regiment, about half perished in New Guinea, and half in Burma. Occasionally their remains were identified and brought home, but that was rare. Sometimes, before the young soldiers set off to war, locks of hair and even fingernail clippings were sent back to their homes in case their remains were never found. It was these skerricks of a past life, which might also have included part of the soldiers' uniform, a lunch box or a recovered *yosegaki* flag, that were entombed by families and became the focus of their prayers and grieving.

In the sixty-two years since the fighting stopped, Nishimura estimated he had visited the graves of 335 of these 365 men, more than ninety per cent, although he can't be sure of the exact figure. When he came to honour a fallen comrade, Nishimura would sprinkle water over the grave – a common Japanese practice – prepare some food and water for the spirits, light some incense and then bow his head in prayer.

But there were still thirty former comrades that Nishimura couldn't track down. He could find neither their relatives nor their graves. So he sent a letter to the Yasukuni Shinto Shrine in Tokyo asking for information about them. A reply came back saying the shrine was unable to help because such information would breach privacy laws. But the letter said a search of their records revealed that details had been kept on twenty-four of the thirty soldiers Nishimura had enquired about. There was no record of the other six, however.

This concerned him. It meant that there might be Japanese war widows, with children and grandchildren, who were not receiving their due entitlements, specifically a war pension but also official recognition that their husband or father had made the ultimate sacrifice for his country. These six members of the 5th Company had died in the service of Japan, but no record apparently existed of when, where and how they died. Officially, they were non-people.

Nishimura was now eighty-seven, but that didn't mean he couldn't take on a new mission. He vowed to travel to Shikoku as soon as possible to unravel this mystery, and continue his quest to visit all 365 graves. The most convenient time would be when he came back for the 2007 Kochi–New Guinea Association reunion. So in September 2007, he once again packed supplies and bedding in his car and made the thirteen-hour drive to Shikoku. He was determined to visit veterans associations and municipal offices in Kochi, to try to get to the bottom of this problem. The only information he had to help him was the names of the dead men.

After asking around, Nishimura discovered that one of the thirty missing soldiers, Kikube Tokuhisa, might have been buried on Heshima Island, a tiny outpost off the west coast of Shikoku, on a stretch of water between the Inland Sea and the Pacific Ocean. Tokuhisa was a lance corporal with the 144th Regiment, who died in Burma on 12 June 1945. Nishimura couldn't remember his face, but he was one of the reinforcements for the 5th Company who reported for duty late in the war. These reinforcements were generally much older soldiers, often well into their thirties with families back in Japan.

Nishimura tracked down Tokuhisa's family before he set out, told them who he was and said he wanted to offer a prayer at their father's grave. But they wanted nothing to do with his visit. This was an attitude he frequently encountered: modern Japanese families wanting to be rid of any reminder of their role, however distant, in the war. Perhaps the family were also slightly shaken by the circumstances surrounding the request: an 87-year-old former soldier ringing up out of the blue and wanting to visit the grave of their father who'd been dead for sixty-two years. Nishimura was unperturbed, and resolved to visit Tokuhisa's final resting place without their permission.

At last count, only a few hundred people lived on Heshima

Island, mostly fishermen and their families. The only means of transport to the island was a small passenger ferry, so Nishimura couldn't take his car, which doubled, of course, as his preferred accommodation. Reluctantly, he rented a room in a fisherman's hut. And it was from here that he conducted his search.

Fortunately for Nishimura, a journalist from the *Ehime Shimbun* newspaper had somehow got wind of his visit and, fascinated by the story, asked if he could accompany Nishimura. The young man proved an excellent ally, for Nishimura was now partly crippled after a heavy fall from his bicycle twelve months earlier, and found it difficult to walk any distance over Heshima's hilly terrain.

Nishimura and the journalist found Tokuhisa's grave in a small temple on the island, with scenic views over the ocean. The head monk, who had received advance notice of the visit, was waiting for them, and showed them the tomb. Nishimura felt a sense of quiet exhilaration when he saw the tombstone. He then observed his prayer ritual in honouring Tokuhisa's spirit. Later, the monk posted Nishimura a copy of the *Ehime Shimbun* article about his search.

Nishimura was received kindly by the people of Ehime and Tokushima prefectures, but it was a very different story in his home town of Kochi, where he received virtually no help at all. He had four men on his list whose records he had unsuccessfully searched for before in Kochi City, and now he wanted to try again. They were Seijiro Yamanaka, a sergeant who died at Giruwa on 16 December 1942 after being shot in the chest; Matsuyuki Yamamoto, a reinforcement with the 5th Company, who died in Burma towards the end of the war; Kenji Ike, a first-class private killed at Hill 551, a vital strongpoint in Burma, on 4 April 1945; and Toyokichi Yokogawa, a lance corporal who was killed at Giruwa on 20 January 1943. He was one of the wounded men left behind after the Japanese evacuation who continued to fight to the death.

Recent council mergers in Kochi impeded Nishimura's research: no one seemed to know where the soldiers' records had been relocated. Even the War Bereaved Association was unsure about how to locate the missing graves of the 5th Company men. Nishimura went to the police and asked them if they could help. No, they said, and pointed him towards the Kochi Municipal Authority. The Municipal Authority also refused Nishimura's request for assistance in finding more information about the soldiers, saying it was a privacy issue.

As if that wasn't bad enough, Nishimura was fined for parking illegally in Kochi while asking local people where to find an address. He tried to explain to the traffic wardens what he was doing in Kochi, but they would have none of his excuses. It is nothing to do with us, they said. Infuriated, Nishimura drove off, silently wishing he was well away from the inept petty bureaucracy and back in New Guinea, sleeping under the stars.

In the more remote parts of Kochi prefecture, however, Nishimura had more luck. In Shimanto City, he found a grave belonging to Takeo Wada, a lance corporal who died near Taungoo in Burma on 14 June 1945; in Aki City, he found the grave of Tetsunosuke Kitamori, a first-class private who perished at Giruwa on 5 January 1943. Again, he laid out offerings of rice and tea, before praying for the dead men's spirits.

His discoveries brought him great cheer. Now he felt reinvigorated. After leaving Kochi, he drove north-east to Tokushima prefecture where he had more names on his list to find. A priest at the Gokoku Shinto Shrine in Tokushima, who had helped Nishimura look for graves on previous trips, introduced him to a man by the name of Katsuyuki Sano, whom the priest thought would be a useful ally.

Sano, a man in his fifties, was an important local figure who knew the region back to front. He organised the prefecture's annual 400-year-old dance festival, and taught the dancing troupe in the Gokoku Shrine. When he heard Nishimura explain his mission, he offered to help. For the next three days, Nishimura was driven around Tokushima by Sano and together they located another eleven graves, success beyond Nishimura's wildest hopes.

Most of the men had died in Burma in 1944 and 1945. Nishimura thought he must have met all of them at one time or another, but the three he remembered best were Yoshiaki Kondo, a lance corporal; Hisao Kita, who died in a British mortar attack on Hill 551 in Burma; and Masao Sagawa, who died of malaria at the Army Hospital in Burma. Those three had joined Nishimura's re-formed platoon in Rabaul in 1943, after his original unit was wiped out in New Guinea.

The visit to Shikoku lasted more than a fortnight, after which Nishimura attended the Kochi–New Guinea Association reunion in Kochi, before driving back to Tokyo via the time-honoured route of the Chugoku Expressway. It had been a road trip that spanned thousands of kilometres, three nights in a fisherman's hut on the beach, dozens of conversations with municipal officials and war veterans associations, and cost him a parking fine. But, crucially, it had revealed the grave sites of fourteen men from the 5th Company.

Now there were just sixteen names remaining on his list of 365 to find, including the six 'non-persons' about whom next to nothing was known. But, as Nishimura's eighty-eighth birthday approached, the old soldier wasn't sure he had another trip as arduous as this one left in him.

CHAPTER 24

Sachiko

NISHIMURA COULD RECALL BEING asked once by his daughter to return home from Papua New Guinea, but only once in twenty-six years. After he'd been away a while, his daughter said to him: Give up. You can't find all the bones, so why don't you give up? You've been doing it long enough. You don't have any more to prove to anyone.

But Nishimura said no.

Her father had told her little about his war experiences. Nishimura wanted it that way: I never told her about the war, he said, she didn't need to know about that. She couldn't possibly hope to understand. It's not something that you can tell your family easily.

Sachiko, who knew so little of her father's past in New Guinea, soon realised she would be wasting her time to keep asking him to leave it behind. So instead, she got on with her own life in Kazo City, and went to her job at the local primary school each day, waiting for the time that her father either chose, or was forced, to come home. And that time arrived without warning in August 2005.

She had grown old waiting for him. Now she was a dignified woman in her sixties. Her prominent cheekbones betrayed her family bloodline, as did her quiet, steely resolve. Nishimura's daughter was a chip off the old block, if a more demure one.

When she considered her father's life, Sachiko saw his mission almost as a sickness, for which there was no cure. A part of his genetic make-up, which simply could not be altered. It was his destiny, or it was fate, that he went to war and made a promise to his comrades to come back. And he couldn't help but keep a promise, his nature wouldn't allow him not to do it, she felt.

But when she talked about the night her family split asunder, her pain was only thinly disguised: Her father felt he had a duty to go, she said, and she had no reason to stop him. That's what he wanted to do, and she understood his reasons completely.

Sachiko realised that very few people would go to the same lengths as her father to keep such an old promise. She also understood that any normal family would oppose such a project being proposed by their husband and father. It was only natural. The absences from home would be unbearably long; the cost untenable. So, she didn't judge her mother or brothers too harshly about that.

But that was all she was willing to say about her mother, Yukiko, and brothers, Makoto and Osamu. Any other questions about her family – whether she missed them and might one day like to be reunited with them – were met with a polite but firm rebuff: I don't want to talk about that, she would say.

SACHIKO ENJOYED HAVING HER father home for the first extended stay since 1980. She continued to work as a contract teacher three or four days a week, because she was not yet at the age when she would be entitled to a government pension. But now that her father had returned home she was also responsible for his care: she prepared his breakfast, lunch and dinner every day, and drove him to his regular hospital and physiotherapy appointments, as he grew more infirm by the month.

It was a continuation of the help she had given him while he was in Papua New Guinea. Even though he had been committed to PNG for so long, Nishimura managed to return to Japan every few years – buying boats, asking Imanishi about the finer points of rice growing, organising meetings with Japanese MPs – and Sachiko never went more than three years without seeing him. But there was rarely time for long, relaxed chats. The human tornado would breeze in, career around the place involving everyone in his projects, then blow out again, leaving chores, and often chaos, in his wake.

He had often requested Sachiko to do jobs and run errands for him in Japan, all related to his bone-digging project. She became a kind of secretary for her father, as well, filing away his war records and helping him research various projects.

And their family house in Saitama became an unofficial boarding house for Papuans who came to visit, or study in, Japan. Nishimura's friend, Miichin Sarigari, stayed for three months at one stage. He came to Japan to learn to become a car mechanic, so he could work in the garage which Nishimura had set up for Eric Torosian in Popondetta. Each day, Sarigari visited the car workshop near Nishimura's home to learn the trade from a couple of senior mechanics, hands-on tuition that was arranged by Nishimura.

For all the impediments and hurdles Nishimura had experienced in Papua New Guinea – from language barriers and bureaucratic meddling to the crime in Popondetta – Sachiko felt that he had done an extraordinary job of carrying out his mission. She knew he had experienced a lot of frustration, and that he wanted to do much more but couldn't, she said. Even now, he wanted to continue his work in Papua New Guinea but was physically unable to. It was to his credit, she thought, that he always somehow found supporters, in addition to the many friends he made with local PNG people, and overcame many obstacles to achieve his objectives. She felt his dead friends from the army were somehow helping him to keep his promises.

Sachiko did not necessarily regard her father as a great patriot. Nor did she feel that the government of Japan should have done more to assist his project. His mission was self-chosen.

But she shared her father's anger when it came to the government's inaction over the repatriation of Japanese soldiers' remains, particularly those that had been exploited in bone displays. The Japanese Government should and could have done a lot more to help her father when he was working very hard to retract the PNG law which designated those soldiers' remains as a PNG tourism asset, she said. It seemed to her that the Japanese Government was not really interested in the issue.

Sachiko visited Papua New Guinea just once during her father's pilgrimage – for four weeks in July 1981. She went to Popondetta, Buna, Giruwa and nearby battlefields, just to get a feel for the project he was about to take on. In her luggage, she carried reams of paper, and boxes of crayons and pencils, to give to local schools.

It was during this trip that Sachiko met Kikue Miyake, who was also a Japanese primary school teacher on holidays and who had a special fascination for PNG. Ms Miyake would later work for the Japanese Embassy in Port Moresby and became one of her father's most valuable allies. But Sachiko said there were many arguments, and times when Ms Miyake couldn't bear to deal with her father anymore, before they developed a good understanding of each other.

Ms Miyake was the last person to see Nishimura in New Guinea, having paid his hospital bill of 500 kina, taken him to the airport and waved goodbye as he disappeared through Customs for the last time. Nishimura, ashamed that his friend had to foot the bill, promised her he would make good the debt. And that he did some months later, giving a Tokyo friend, Hajime Marutani, whom he knew to be travelling to PNG, the money to repay Ms Miyake – 19,000 yen, or A$210. And, of course, a message conveying his deepest gratitude. This was his duty; not to carry it out would have been unthinkable.

Asked to nominate her father's greatest qualities, Sachiko would say that he was loyal, a man of principle, a man of strong conviction, someone who kept his promises, was not at all interested in money, and could not tolerate corruption or crookedness.

On the other hand, she said, he could be stubborn, short-tempered and easily misunderstood. Some Japanese families he approached with a war relic he'd found in New Guinea, for example, were suspicious of his motives, thinking Nishimura was trying to make money out of the offer.

Nishimura remained estranged from his younger brother, Toyoichi, after their fight sixty years earlier over Toyoichi's off-hand treatment of their mother. The feud was never resolved, Toyoichi clearly sharing his brother's obstinant, proud and uncompromising nature. Even well into old age, Toyoichi and Kokichi could never make their peace with each other.

His elder sister, Ayako, was dead, but Sachiko was pleased

that Nishimura had re-established regular contact with his younger sister, Mitsuko, now in her eighties and living in Suita City outside Osaka. In fact, Nishimura had visited her on the way home from his epic tour of Shikoku in 2007, since the expressway from Shikoku to Tokyo took him right through Osaka prefecture.

The only cloud now on the horizon was Nishimura's health. The lasting physical legacy of his war, apart from an arthritic shoulder, was the damnable malaria that knocked him flat two or three times a year. There weren't many medical staff at Nakada Hospital who knew much about this tropical disease; they didn't see a lot of it in the suburbs of Tokyo. So when he felt it coming on, he headed to the infectious disease laboratory at the University of Tokyo for treatment.

But the truth was Nishimura has been laid low by this old enemy so many times, he knew exactly what to do to combat the chills, fever, sweating and anaemia it brought on: keep the body cool, and rest as much as possible. He had become so familiar with the parasitical disease, its symptoms and all its sneaky characteristics, that he could tell which strain he was suffering: the falciparum malaria that almost killed him in Rabaul, the Burmese malaria that he first caught on the walk to Prome railway station, or a mystery third strain that had different symptoms still.

Ordinary malaria fever was the one that visited most regularly. Once stricken, Nishimura knew that every day for about a week, he would suffer a high fever that lasts for an hour or so. Tertian malaria was the second strain. High fever and febrile paroxysms occurred every forty-eight hours or so, again for about a week.

Last, but by no means least, there was the strain he believed was falciparum malaria, the most dangerous form of malaria. It really knocked him around, but, thankfully, visited him less frequently. It was marked by continuous high fever for a week or so, and most patients usually became delirious on the third or fourth day. If left unchecked after a week, it could kill. It required hospitalisation, and an intravenous drip feeding antibiotics into the body to treat the infected red blood cells. Some survivors were left with brain damage. Nishimura remembered being put in a cage in one field hospital during the war, after he became violent on the fifth day of a falciparum attack.

Sachiko was concerned about the toll each of these attacks were taking on her father's small, wiry body, and how his immune system would respond to the next invasion.

Nishimura had last been laid low by the disease early in 2007 and she feared if he suffered a serious attack again, with continuous high fever, that would finally spell the end for a man whose special brand of dogged resolve had kept death at bay for nearly seven decades since the war.

Last sighting

LOOKING AT NISHIMURA, I have to agree that Sachiko's fears about her father's health might have some foundation. There is no getting away from it: the light has dimmed in his eyes. It is now early in 2007 and, he has been home for more than eighteen months. Life cooped up in Tokyo's suburbs is not agreeing with him. He has cheated death on maybe ten occasions before, certainly more times than anyone has a right to, but the fight appears to be dying inexorably inside him. He's accepted his fate with a kind of stoic resignation, although he wants to get two or three more projects finished before he admits defeat and goes off to join his old friends, the divine spirits, in the afterlife.

His sense of impending doom will only be underscored when, on 30 June, he receives the news that his great friend, Sadashige Imanishi, has died at home in Motoyama, aged ninety-two. A heat wave, the likes of which Kochi prefecture has not experienced in decades, scorches the region for a week, claiming one of Japan's most remarkable and resilient soldiers among its victims.

Imanishi has put up with Nishimura's maddening eccentricities, mule-like stubbornness and rigid inflexibility, traits that all but the most loyal and patient friend would have had difficulty dealing with. And while most in the Kochi–New Guinea Association had given up on Nishimura as a bad joke, Imanishi has stayed true to him all the way through his travails, however sorely his patience was tested by the younger man.

Six months or so before he dies, Imanishi has sized up Nishimura and his place in Japanese society perfectly. We don't deal with unique people very well in Japan, he sighs. His observation could be Nishimura's epitaph.

With Imanishi gone, the numbers at the Kochi–New Guinea Association reunion in October will start to look thin indeed. There is every chance that Nishimura will be the only living, breathing veteran left to attend the ceremony from the 13,500 or so troops who fought under the banner of the Nankai Shitai in New Guinea. Which, in a way, would be entirely fitting.

In the meantime, though, the jobs are piling up and Nishimura has much to do. He has started preparing for his death, he says: I know I won't live much longer, so I want to make everything easy for my daughter after I've gone. I'm setting up life for her as best I can.

First, with some help, he pulls down a small building on the front of his block in Kazo City, and clears the rubble. Now he's left with the perfect area for six car-parking spaces. Sachiko can charge 5000 yen (A$55) per month for each of them, so she should receive 30,000 yen (A$330) a month. He wants his daughter to be financially secure.

Next, he plans to dig a vegetable patch and plant a small

grove of mandarin trees in the garden, small contributions towards the sustenance of his daughter. The mandarin flower has a beautiful smell, in addition to its delicious fruit, he says.

Soon to turn eighty-eight, Nishimura has begun to use a wheelchair when he is feeling poorly, or is ill with malaria. But it is a last resort. He knows that if he sits still for too long, he'll seize up altogether. He stopped riding a bicycle last year when he fell over and hit his shoulder hard on the road. But his army training meant no bones were broken; he was just stiff and sore. Now he has bought a tricycle which he rides around the neighbourhood every day, even to rehabilitation when Sachiko cannot take him. He also likes to walk for thirty minutes or an hour whenever he can.

He is visiting a physiotherapist six times a week for rehabilitation exercises on his legs, and has already had intensive work done on his hands and neck which helped loosen them up and reduce the pain.

The manifestations of old age annoy him intensely. He hates having to wear his dentures. He'd prefer to go gummy, and leave his false teeth in a glass. This means eating a fairly limited diet. Limited and puréed. Porridge for breakfast, and meals that look like baby food for the rest of the day: vegetable potage, rice porridge, chopped noodles, sashimi, tofu and milk. In keeping with his long-held views about food, Nishimura eats only small quantities of whatever Sachiko serves him. She cooks all three meals for him and when she is going out to work, she prepares his lunch before leaving home. His stomach is still strong, he says, even if his hands have become weak.

There are times when the pain and stiffness in his right shoulder make driving almost impossible. To get around the problem, he has rigged up a knob on his steering wheel and taped it securely into place, so it looks like a forklift steering wheel. No matter if his contraption has not been cleared with the driving authorities in Tokyo. With his right hand he is able to rotate the wheel with minimal stress on the shoulder, even sometimes with his elbow resting out the window.

He's also developed a neat trick for when he pulls up outside his house and needs to reverse into his garage. With his palm on the forklift knob, Nishimura can look around and get his bearings, then rocket the car into reverse, sliding it into the garage with barely a metre to spare on either side.

At the end of the garage is a shed full of the greatest array of tools and equipment you could ever see outside a DIY store. There are drills and drill bits, power tools, screwdrivers, saws, hammers, welding equipment, gas cylinders, work benches and vices. Nishimura sometimes potters around in there, dreaming up new contraptions, although the arthritis in his hands makes all but the simplest task difficult.

One job he was able to finish before his hands let him down was to build a sizeable perspex hut on the top of his flat roof. Made from the lightweight steel rods he manufactured at the Nishimura Machinery Research Institute, with clear perspex sheeting on all the walls and roof, the two rooms receive sunshine all day. The old engineer did not bother getting planning permission first. He didn't have time for such trivialities. Besides, it would be hard to break the habit of a lifetime now.

The hut is used to dry clothes in winter; it is also useful for other tasks, such as drying chillies in the afternoon sun. From the homemade hothouse, Nishimura has rigged up a duct and fan that blows warmer air down to his bedroom to keep him from freezing up in winter.

But really, the building functions as his sanctuary away from modern life in Japan.

Here he lies at night on a couch and sheepskin rug, looking up at the stars and dreaming about New Guinea. If he concentrates hard enough, he is transported back to his hut in Efogi, or can almost imagine that he is camping out on the Kokoda Track. The shell of a Japanese anti-aircraft gun, now used to hold flowers, reminds him of his old haunts. Downstairs, Mr Nakasone's salutation card is propped on the mantelpiece. Despite his old age and infirmity, the overgrown battlefields remain an obsession. They are all he thinks about, the only things that fill his head. Every action he takes now is performed with New Guinea in mind; both for the friends he left behind and the local people.

One of the last tasks he wants to complete concerns a matter of honour: returning a gift to its rightful owner in New Guinea. The Popondetta businessman who asked him in 1995 to procure a boat from Japan, an escapade which nearly resulted in him being blown out of the water by the US Navy near Guam, had given Nishimura a small island he owned as payment for his boat and troubles. The businessman was a freight forwarder by the name of Samuel, and Nishimura had become good friends with him in the final years of his mission in Papua New Guinea.

An egg-shaped haven, Madang Island measures about 160 metres by 120 metres and sits just offshore from Madang. It is a breathtaking piece of real estate which features a pretty little church built by the Germans before the war and was once used as a Lutheran Mission.

Yet Nishimura, at his age, has little use for islands, even ones as pretty as Madang. He has decided to give it to Samuel's teenage daughter, to whom he had been something of a father figure in New Guinea. He could probably sell the land for a small fortune if he wanted to, but Nishimura figures the best thing a Japanese can do sixty or so years after his country invaded New Guinea is ensure the island is left, undamaged and undeveloped, in local hands.

Like the two holdouts, Yokoi and Onoda, who returned to Japan after more than twenty-five years in hiding and felt they had landed in a foreign country, Nishimura has no fondness for contemporary Japan. The country has abandoned its ideals, as well as its citizen soldiers. Traits that once made the nation great have been eroded away, he feels, as surely as if they'd been left in a vat of American soft drink.

There was not a single thing he missed about Japan in the long years he was away. During the war, there was no food and the enemy was firing upon him, but he felt free in New Guinea for the twenty-six years he lived there. He only returned to Tokyo to live when his health failed him. He says: If I hadn't got sick, I would still be in Popondetta or Port Moresby, even after I turned ninety.

Lying on the couch one night, he tries to calculate how much of his own money he had spent during his long project: in flying to and from New Guinea perhaps forty times, building his huts in Popondetta and Efogi, keeping himself clothed and fed, buying fuel for his machinery and boats and, of course, maintaining his landmine detector. All told, he estimates it was probably more than 400 million yen (A$4.5 million), when you include the money he spent on roads and bridges and boats.

He would spend it all again in a trice, if he had to.

At home, Nishimura still pores over his documents, articles and photograph albums relating to the war. Occasionally, he receives visitors who have heard about his life's work and want to ask him questions about the war, or about some relative who has never returned from Kokoda. One day, he was reading a magazine when he came across a story about a war widow who said she had always wanted to know how her husband died in Papua New Guinea. Nishimura immediately got in touch with the magazine editor and said he might have some news for the woman.

Her son happened to live near Saitama, so he visited Nishimura to hear the story. The man's father wasn't in the same unit as Nishimura but he fought close by; Nishimura could tell that from his records, which listed the soldier's name and pinpointed a date and place where he died. Nishimura ascertained the unit he belonged to was positioned about one hundred metres from his own at Giruwa, so he could explain the environment and the situation. He still seems to find joy in contributing this way, Sachiko says.

Sometimes when Sachiko has gone to her part-time job and Nishimura is by himself, he watches television. That is his only real contact with what is happening in the outside world. He has stopped reading newspapers because they carry only bad news – murder and crime. Twice a week, two local women come to clean his house and talk to him. He also has friends in Kazo City who occasionally stop by for a cup of green tea.

He knows it is too late to return to Papua New Guinea: he doesn't want to be a burden on anybody there. In the final act of his bone-recovery campaign, he instructed his friend, Miichin Sarigari, to dig up the thirty or so bones that he had hidden around the township at Nishimura's request when the old soldier returned to Japan. Sarigari handed them over to an embassy official in Port Moresby.

They were brought back to Japan and interred at Chidoriga-fuchi along with the rest of his collection. That meant his campaign, like the boxes of bones brought back from New Guinea, had been neatly packaged up and put in a final resting place. He felt a peace of mind. It brought the curtain down on his extraordinary project which had lasted a quarter of a century.

Now, when he looks back and takes stock of his life, the setbacks and hardships have all been worthwhile. Yes, he has paid a price: the loss of his wife and sons, the loss of the engineering company that he had built into one of Tokyo's most respected, the loss of all his worldly possessions, the sheer discomfort of living in a hut and tent in a third-world country for almost a third of his life, not to mention being cut off from his homeland and all its familiar pleasures. But, for Nishimura, the sacrifice has been small. He can't understand people who continue to ask him: What possessed you to do all this?

You might see it as a big sacrifice to lose your family, but what sort of sacrifice is it against that made by the soldiers who died in New Guinea? Compared to them, I live in heaven. Those soldiers were in hell, and they died in hell. I was very lucky, one of the very lucky ones. After the war, I could eat fresh food, go anywhere, I was free. Comparing my situation to theirs, digging up bones for twenty-six years was quite a small thing, a small sacrifice. I owed them that, at the very least.

He didn't achieve everything he set out to do. But, given that he arrived in Popondetta at a stage in life when most men are ready to accept their first pension cheque and concession bus pass, Nishimura reckons he made a pretty decent fist of it. Which, by his own standards, is really saying something.

I couldn't complete my mission but I did what I could. I did as much as humanly possible. I knew I could never find everyone; that would be impossible. So I made a plan for each place I visited as to how many bones I wanted to collect, and I usually reached that goal. I did my best.

STILL, HE HAS SET himself one last challenge. That will put a full stop, possibly even an exclamation mark, on a campaign that has called on almost superhuman reserves of determination and sheer bloody-mindedness.

One of the war artefacts Nishimura had shipped over to Japan before he left New Guinea was the propeller from a B-24 warplane, a heavy lump of cast-iron covered in scratches and small gouges. The B-24 was the most common, durable and successful American plane involved in the war, and this one was shot down by Japanese anti-aircraft fire near Giruwa, and crashed in a field nearby.

The owner of the field where the plane wreckage lay had admired the gleaming stainless-steel sink he had seen in the galley of one of the boats Nishimura brought back to Papua New Guinea. That would look good in my kitchen, he thought. So he approached Nishimura and proposed a swap: my B-24 propeller for your kitchen sink. That sounded like a good deal, said Nishimura, so they shook hands. And that is how the giant lump of iron came to be propped up in Nishimura's shed in Tokyo.

Nishimura has decided to pull down the front gate to his house and build a new one, with the American propeller as its main feature. He does not think it inconsistent that he rails against the government of Papua New Guinea for allowing Japanese skulls to be put on display but is planning to do something much the same with the propeller of an American plane that crashed in the war, presumably killing all the airmen aboard. He is happy to leave that argument to the bureaucrats.

As my interpreter and I drive away from his home, towards the Kazo City train station, after visiting the old man for the last time, Nishimura can be seen in his shed, rubbing his chin with one hand, a look of determination creasing his face as he tries to work out a way to fit the enormous B-24 propeller into a design for his new gate. He wants this chunk of enemy warplane to be the new symbol of his home. In his mind, at least, it will signify a thumbing of his nose at the enemy one last time; one heroic, if futile, final gesture.

The great war survivor, unvanquished and defiant to the last.

APPENDIX: THE LIST OF BRIGADE HILL DEAD

The definitive document that Kokichi Nishimura compiled, recording the fate of his forty-one colleagues who were killed, or mortally wounded, at Ippongi, Papua New Guinea, on 8 September 1942.

Name	Rank*	Birthplace	Time	Cause of death
Second attack				
Yoshiharu Inoue	L/Corporal	Tosa City, Kochi	7.20 am	Bullet wound in left chest
Harukazu Oka	L/Corporal	Ochi-machi, Takaoka Gun, Kochi	7.30 am	Grenade wound to head
Third attack				
Tsuneharu Yamazaki	Private	Nangoku City, Kochi	8.10 am	Bullet wound to head
Tsuruki Okada	Private	Ochi-machi, Takaoka Gun, Kochi	8.20 am	Bullet wound to head
Shigekazu Sakaguchi	L/Corporal	Tosashimizu City, Kochi	8.20 am	Bullet wound to abdomen
Shiro Hamada	L/Corporal	Kamiura-cho, Ochi Gun, Kochi	8.20 am	Shrapnel wound to front head
Masuru Ogasawara	L/Corporal	Nagaoka Gun, Kochi	8.30 am	Grenade wound to chest
Masami Kataoko	L/Corporal	Suzaki City, Kochi	8.30 am	Bullet wound to abdomen
Saku Yamazaki	Private	Kahoku-cho, Kami Gun, Kochi	8.30 am	Shrapnel wound to right chest

Zenzaburo Ushimado	L/Corporal	Tano-machi, Aki-Gun, Kochi	8.35 am	Bullet wound to right shoulder, back
Kaoru Okamura	Private	Yoshida-cho, Kita-Uwa, Ehime	8.40 am	Bullet wound to lower back
Teiji Yamazaki	L/Corporal	Noichi-machi, Kami Gun, Kochi	8.40 am	Shrapnel wound to front head
Akira Matsumoto	L/Corporal	Mima-machi, Kita-Uwa Gun, Ehime	8.40 am	Bullet wound to left chest
Toyonaru Masaoka	Private	Nakamura City, Kochi	8.40 am	Bullet wound to abdomen
Yoshiyuki Matsuoka	Private	Tosa City, Kochi	8.40 am	Shrapnel wound to right chest
Saichi Tanabe	Private	Ohkata-machi, Hata Gun, Kochi	8.45 am	Bullet wound to lumbar area
Susumu Ogawa	Private	Sukumo City, Kochi	8.50 am	Shrapnel wound to right chest
Kazuma Hirano	Private	Nakamura City, Kochi	8.50 am	Shrapnel wound to right chest
Tsurue Sugimoto	L/Corporal	Ino-machi, Agawa Gun, Kochi	8.50 am	Bullet wound to left chest
Shinichi Yoshioka	L/Corporal	Nakamura City, Kochi	9.00 am	Grenade wound to lower back

Name	Rank*	Birthplace	Time	Cause of death
Masamichi Kurokawa	L/Corporal	Agawa-mura, Agawa Gun, Kochi	9.00 am	Grenade wound to lower back
Kazuaki Obata	L/Corporal	Taiso-machi, Hata Gun, Kochi	9.00 am	Grenade wound to head
Kura Hamada**	L/Corporal	Kochi City, Kochi	9.10 am	Grenade wound to lumbar area
Kazuaki Ike	Sergeant	Tosa City, Kochi	10.05 am	Bullet wound to right chest
Hitomi Tanaka	Sergeant	Noichi-machi, Kami Gun, Kochi	10.20 am	Bullet wound to head
Fukuma Nishimori	L/Corporal	Ochi-machi, Takaoka Gun, Kochi	10.45 am	Shrapnel wound to front of head
Yukihiko Sannomiya	L/Corporal	Tosa City, Kochi	10.50 am	Bullet wound to lumbar area
Fourth attack				
Tatemi Fujiwara	L/Corporal	Agawa-mura, Agawa Gun, Kochi	2.25 pm	Bullet wound to left chest

Wataru Takahashi	Private	Sukumo City, Kochi	2.30 pm	Grenade wound to right chest
Keikichi Miyazoe	Sergeant	Sukumo City, Kochi	2.45 pm	Shrapnel wound in right chest
Masanobu Nishigawa	Private	Ino-machi, Agawa Gun, Kochi	3.00 pm	Shrapnel wound in left shoulder
Akihiko Yokoya	Private	Tosa City, Kochi	3.20 pm	Shrapnel wound to left shoulder
Hidemi Yano	Private	Tosa City, Kochi	3.30 pm	Bullet wound in chest
Kiyomichi Inoue	Lieutenant	Tosa City, Kochi	3.40 pm	Bullet wounds to torso, arm, head

Fifth attack

Kiyomitsu Nakano	Private	Nakayamo-cho, Iyo Gun, Ehime	4.20 pm	Bullet wound to lower back
Ushizo Ogawa	Private	Sukumo City, Kochi	4.30 pm	Bullet wound to head
Mitsuo Itahara	Private	Tosa City, Kochi	4.50 pm	Bullet wound to waist

Wounded***

| Toshimasu Okayama | Private | Nakamura City, Kochi | | Shrapnel wound to right chest |

Name	Rank*	Birthplace	Time	Cause of death
Yoshimi Kubo	Private	Iyo Gun, Ehime		Shot in hip, left shoulder blade
Hisami Iyota	Private	Sukumo City, Kochi		Bullet wound to right chest
Masao Nakahira	L/Corporal	Nakamura City, Kochi		Bullet wound to head
Kokichi Nishimura	L/Corporal	Kochi City, Kochi		Bullet wounds to right shoulder

*All soldiers were promoted one rank after death. Posthumous ranks listed.

**Kura may be a nickname.

***Only Nishimura survived the fifth attack; the remaining wounded died within days.

Notes

Chapter 2: Childhood
Page

13 . . . to visit each of the temples: As pilgrims still do today.

Chapter 4: New Guinea
Page

36 One soldier from the advance party assumed: This was Sadashige Imanishi, from the 1st Battalion, who later became an important friend of Nishimura, and who is the subject of Chapter 22. Imanishi was one of 2000 troops in the advance party who streamed ashore at Gona and Basabua on the Papuan coast on 21 July 1942. In addition to his standard pack, Imanishi carried a bag of rice weighing more than twenty kilograms, 180 bullets, two grenades, a steel helmet and a toothbrush.

Chapter 5: Brigade Hill
Page

61 'Gazing out from the summit': From a diary written by company clerk Nakahashi, of the 55th Mountain Artillery, later published as the *War History of the Force* which was sent to the South Seas (Nankai Shitai), 1941–44. Translated by Lt FC Jorgensen.

Chapter 6: Retreat
Page

69 My grandpa, Paheki, told me: From a newspaper article published in 2006, shedding new light on this key episode in Nishimura's wartime experience. On the thirty-first anniversary of Papua New Guinea's independence from Australia, the article in *The Nation* newspaper, headlined 'Friendships fostered during war', focused on Hojava, his grandparents and their wartime story.

71 At the Japanese field hospital at Giruwa: From an interview with Sadashige Imanishi by the author.

Chapter 7: White pork, black pork
Page

78 'The slight browning of the flesh': From the bestselling book by Piers Paul Read, *Alive*.

78 'After boiling the shellfish': Sadashige Imanishi. Interview with author.

80 He was an officer of the 2/6th: Allan 'Kanga' Moore. Interview with author.

Chapter 8: Home
Page

91 Its astonishingly high mortality rate: Mortality rates taken from *The War Story of the South Seas Force*, as listed in Captain Nakahashi's personal memoir [see bibliography].

Chapter 10: Holdouts
Page

109 Out there in the vast war zone: The figure of 1.16 million amounted to 48 per cent of Japanese who died overseas during the war – a remarkably high figure. By contrast, it has been estimated that only seventeen per cent of the 506,000 US soldiers who died overseas during WWII and the Korean and Vietnam wars, remained listed as missing in action.

Chapter 12: Touchdown

Page

132 Tago was not used to being addressed in such a disrespect-ful way: Nishimura later developed a friendship with Tago that was totally at odds with their first meeting. The MP's village was only a short distance from Popondetta, and Nishimura would occasionally visit him there and share a meal, cross-legged, on the floor of his hut.

Chapter 17: Ashes

Page

175 'I promised my father that I'll come back': From an article in *Mainichi Shimbun* newspaper, 12 August 2005, headlined 'Six decades after WWII, Japan searches for 1 million missing' [see bibliography].

175 'The skeletons appearing from the soil': As above.

Chapter 18: Relics

Page

182 ... in a 1997 Japanese television documentary: From *Forest of Mourning Souls* (NHK, Japan Broadcasting Corporation, 1997).

189 'When I saw the barrel of the gun': From company clerk Nakahashi's journal.

Chapter 20: Government man

Page

208 ... he is then said to have shouted: This translation appears in Paul Ham's book, *Kokoda*, page 478.

Chapter 21: Return

Page

218 One local newspaper suggested: From an article in PNG's *Post Courier* on 6 October 2007 entitled 'WWII skeletons dug up, sold in Papua New Guinea'.

Epilogue: Last sighting

Page

248 There is every chance that Nishimura will be: In fact, Nishimura and a former warrant officer from the 144th Regiment headquarters, Yuki Shimada, eighty-eight, were the only two living representatives to attend the Kochi–New Guinea Association reunion when it was held in October 2007.

Like Nishimura, Shimada had somehow survived the battle of Giruwa in 1942, and the subsequent evacuation. He had stayed with a friend, Private Nobukuki Ono, and helped him through the long march to the Kumusi River – which they reached on 28 January 1943.

But Nishimura feared Shimada, who was not present at the previous year's reunion, was on his last legs. He strained to hear what his fellow-soldier was saying. Shimada's voice was so weak, Nishimura understood little of what he said. Only through his son's help could Shimada grasp the sprig of sacred Shinto tree and, according to custom, place it on the altar of the Shinto shrine. Nishimura thought the 2008 reunion would be lucky to see the two of them together again.

On his way home from the reunion, Nishimura visited Imanishi's grave in Motoyama, placing near the tomb candles, rice and other offerings for his spirit. It was an emotional moment, for now there was no one left for Nishimura to talk to about the war. His closest friend from among the 13,500 troops who left Kochi with the Nankai Shitai was gone as well.

BIBLIOGRAPHY

Interviews:

John Akhurst
Dr Steven Bullard (email)
Associate Professor Chris Griffiths
Noel Hall
Brian Honner (telephone)
Kikue Miyake (email)
Allan Moore
Kokichi Nishimura
Sachiko Nishimura
Sadashige Imanishi
Hiromu Fujiwara

Diaries, journals, company records:
'144th Infantry Regiment Record of Battle: Campaign record of the 5th Company (Parts 1, 2 & 3)', compiled by Kokichi Nishimura (1 October 1986, Compilation Committee of the 144th Infantry Regiment Record of Battle, Kochi City, Japan).
'Battle of Efogi', Kokichi Nishimura (Personal account, 29 November 1996).

'War History of the Nankai Shitai, 1941–1944', Company Clerk Nakahashi, 55th Mountain Artillery (translated by Lt FC Jorgensen). Given to Alf Salmon, of the Australian 39th Battalion, at a reunion meeting with 144th Regiment veterans in Tokyo on 26 August 1972.

Books:

Brune, Peter, *We Band of Brothers: A biography of Ralph Honner*, Allen & Unwin, 2000.

FitzSimons, Peter, *Kokoda*, Hodder Headline Australia, 2004.

Ham, Paul, *Kokoda*, HarperCollins, 2004.

James, Bill, *Field Guide to Kokoda Track*, Kokoda Press, 2006.

Lindbergh, Charles, *The Wartime Journals of Charles A. Lindbergh*, Harcourt Brace, 1970.

Lindsay, Patrick, *The Spirit of Kokoda*, Hardie Grant, 2002.

Read, Piers Paul, *Alive: The story of the Andes survivors*, Pan Books, 1974.

Tamayama, Kazuo and Nunneley, John, *Tales of Japanese Soldiers*, Cassell, 2000.

Articles and reports:

'Friendships fostered during war', Clifford Faiparik, *The National*, Papua New Guinea, 28 September 2006.

'Hunt for war dead a race against time', Akemi Nakamura, *Japan Times*, 1 November 2006.

'Koizumi visits tomb for unknown soldiers', *People's Daily Online*, 30 May 2006.

'Minutes of the Upper House Health, Welfare and Labour Committee Meeting', 151st Diet Session, Tokyo, 27 March 2001.

'Old foes meet with peace', Alison Stewart, *Sun Herald*, 26 July 1981.

'Recovery of Australian Service Personnel missing in action from World War II', *Australian Defence Force Health*, Vol. 1, April 2000.

Reunion program, Kochi–New Guinea Association, Kochi City, 15 October 2006.

'Should old acquaintance be forgot', Alan Dower, *Herald*, Melbourne, 27 August 1972.

'Simply a matter of honour', Peter Alford, *The Australian*, 19 August 2005.

'Six decades after WWII, Japan searches for 1 million missing', *Mainichi News*, 12 August 2005.

'The man who abandoned Japan', Kako Senda, *Chuo Korun* magazine, Japan, December 1996.

'World War II: Sixtieth Anniversary series: Kokoda and New Guinea', *The Australian*, 19 August 2005.

'WWII skeletons dug up, sold in Papua New Guinea', *Post Courier*, Port Morseby, 6 October 2007.

Documentaries:

Kokoda Front Line!, Damien Parer, 1944.

Forest of Mourning Souls, NHK, Japan Broadcasting Corporation, 45 minutes, 1997.

ACKNOWLEDGEMENTS

I AM INDEBTED TO dozens of people for their help in the writing of this book, not the least of whom is Kokichi Nishimura, the bone man himself. Despite being served up all manner of weird and wonderful questions, some of which he found uncomfortable, he was invariably cooperative and patient. Hopefully, the book will give some recognition to his work – not that that was ever his motivation – and to those soldiers left behind in foreign fields.

Special thanks, too, to the two people who enthusiastically took on the task of translating and interpreting my questions for Nishimura, and his answers – Hajime Marutani in Tokyo, a better interpreter you couldn't hope to find, and Sayuri Thomson in Melbourne, who was equally valuable and for whom no question was ever too tough.

Tom Gilliatt at Pan Macmillan deserves praise for seeing the potential in the book long before anyone else and having an unshakeable faith in the project. Malcolm Knox's invaluable feedback and Sybil Nolan's brilliant editing were crucial in transforming a rough first draft into, eventually, a readable book.

Many other people helped bring the book to fruition and, in no particular order, I want to acknowledge their efforts:

271

Mr Susumu Kiyosawa at the Japanese Embassy in Port Moresby, who was instrumental in helping me to get in touch with Nishimura; Ms Kikue Miyake in New Guinea; Mr Tetsuji Miyagawa at the Japan Broadcasting Corporation; Warwick Johnson and Hiroshi Maeda at Optimal Japan Fund Management in Sydney; Dr Steven Bullard at the Australian War Memorial in Canberra; Mr Hiromu Fujiwara at the Chidorigafuchi National Cemetery; the organisers of the 144th Regiment's Kochi–New Guinea Association in Kochi; Professor Chris Griffiths at the Department of Forensic Medicine at the University of New South Wales; and, finally, Mr Sadashige Imanishi, an engaging and gentle man who died in Japan not long after I interviewed him.

Australian troops from the 39th Battalion were unfailingly helpful in discussing the New Guinea campaign, especially Allan Moore, of Mt Eliza; Noel Hall, of Hawthorn; and John Akhurst, of Black Rock, and in giving an insight into the harrowing nature of the fighting, and their enemy.

Thanks also to the seventeen blokes from Group Five of the Executive Excellence Kokoda walk – you know who you are – without whose support in April 2006 I would never have made it to Efogi, and Nishimura's monument, in the first place.

Of all the reference material I used, Paul Ham's remarkable book *Kokoda* was the one I found most helpful, and his extraordinary scholarship in this field should be acknowledged. Books by Peter FitzSimons, Bill James, Patrick Lindsay and Peter Brune were also crucial in helping me build something more than a working knowledge of the New Guinea war.

Finally, I want to thank my wonderful wife, Paula, for her forbearance and good humour while I skived off on this indulgent journey. And also our children, Thomas and Gretel, who will hopefully only ever know peace in their lifetime.